This book may be kept

~~FOURTEEN D~~

Sherwood Anderson:

Centennial Studies

Sherwood Anderson:
Centennial Studies

edited by

Hilbert H. Campbell
and
Charles E. Modlin

Whitston Publishing Company
Troy, New York
1976

For Eleanor

PREFACE

The idea for a book honoring Sherwood Anderson on his Centenary in 1976 originated two years ago in a combination of factors. We both had long admired Anderson's writing and wished to see as much as possible done to mark his Centenary. This relish for Anderson had been sharpened for us by residence for several years in Southwest Virginia, the area where Anderson spent most of the last fifteen years of his life. A few years ago we had the good fortune to meet Mrs. Eleanor Anderson, with whom we later spent many enjoyable days at her homes in Marion, Troutdale, and New York, discussing at length her husband's life, work, and acquaintances. We had also been working for some time on compiling a catalog of the surviving books from Anderson's personal library. At this juncture, in 1974, we approached Dr. Lawrence Thompson, publisher of *American Notes and Queries*, with the idea of devoting one or more issues of *AN&Q* to Anderson during 1976. Both Dr. Thompson and the editor of *AN&Q*, Dr. John Cutler, were enthusiastic about the idea. Through Dr. Thompson, furthermore, we were put in touch with Mr. Stephen Goode of Whitston Publishing Company; and plans were made not only for a September, 1976, special issue of *AN&Q* but also for a volume to be published late in 1976, supplemental to *AN&Q*, to honor Anderson's Centenary.

The catalog of Anderson's library seemed to us to provide a substantial nucleus for such a volume; and, with the approval and assistance of Mrs. Anderson, we made plans to include some other source materials, among them an interview with Mrs. Anderson and a number of Anderson's previously unpublished letters. Amy Wood Nyholm and Diana Haskell, the past and present curators of the Anderson papers at the Newberry Library, both agreed to contribute information about the Newberry collection. We also made plans to include a group of scholarly interpretations of Anderson's career and work. We early rejected, however, the idea of bringing together previously published essays and determined instead to seek material which had neither been published previously nor was being published simultaneously elsewhere. The response to our advertisement for material was far greater than expected and reminded us forcefully of the substantial and growing interest in Anderson among late twentieth-century students of American literature. Although we attempted from the beginning to select essays for inclusion on the basis of quality rather than uniformity of approach or subject matter, six of the eleven essays eventually selected for publication explore Anderson's relationships with other artists, including George Borrow, Edgar Lee Masters, Henry Adams, Alfred Stieglitz, Louis Bromfield, and J. J. Lankes. Two other essays chosen make solid contributions to Anderson bibliography. Of the three remaining essays, one deals informatively with Clyde, Ohio, the milieu of Anderson's formative years; a second explores Anderson's use of the pastoral; and the other ranges over Anderson's novels, suggesting an explanation for his characteristically ambiguous endings. Several of these essays go beyond the use of published sources to draw extensively on unpublished material.

We hope that this book may not only call attention to the Centenary, but may also make some small contribution toward increased understanding and appreciation of Sherwood Anderson's place in American letters. The project could not have been completed without the unfailing kindness, generosity, and cooperation of Eleanor Anderson or without the hard work and patience of Patricia Campbell, who typed much of the manuscript. To both of them we make grateful acknowledgment.

Hilbert H. Campbell
Charles E. Modlin
Virginia Polytechnic Institute and State University

ACKNOWLEDGMENTS

We acknowledge indebtedness to the following persons, publishers, and libraries who have granted permission to use in this book unpublished or copyrighted material:

To Eleanor Anderson and her agent, Harold Ober Associates, for permission to quote from several of Anderson's books; and to Mrs. Anderson for permission to use unpublished Anderson letters and other materials.

To Matthew J. Bruccoli and NCR Microcard Editions for permission to quote from *Fitzgerald/Hemingway Annual,* 1969.

To Harper and Row, Publishers, Inc. for permission to quote from Louis Bromfield's *The Farm.*

To Houghton Mifflin Company for permission to quote from *The Education of Henry Adams.*

To J. B. Lankes for permission to quote from the letters of J. J. Lankes.

To Ellen Coyne Masters for permission to quote from Edgar Lee Masters' *Across Spoon River.*

To the Newberry Library for permission to quote from sources in the Sherwood Anderson Papers at the Newberry Library.

To the Southern Historical Collection, University of North Carolina Library, Chapel Hill, for permission to use selected letters of Sherwood Anderson from the Burton Emmett Papers.

To Georgia O'Keeffe for permission to quote from the letters of Alfred Stieglitz.

To Prentice-Hall, Inc. for permission to quote from Alfred Stieglitz's "How I Came to Photograph Clouds," as it appears in *Photographers on Photography: A Critical Anthology,* ed. Nathan Lyons, 1966.

To Princeton University Library for permission to use a letter from Sherwood Anderson to James Boyd.

To Walter B. Rideout and The Viking Press Inc. for permission to quote from the preface to the Compass edition of *A Story Teller's Story* (1969).

To the Humanities Research Center, The University of Texas at Austin, for permission to use letters from Sherwood Anderson to J. J. Lankes.

To the Alfred Stieglitz Archive, Collection of American Literature, The Beinecke Rare Book and Manuscript Library, Yale University, and to Georgia O'Keeffe, for permission to use a letter from Sherwood Anderson to Alfred Stieglitz.

To Harold Ober Associates Incorporated for permission to use selections from Sherwood Anderson's "I Want to Know Why," published in *The Triumph of the Egg* copyright 1921 by B. W. Huebsch, Inc., renewed in 1948 by Eleanor Copenhaver Anderson.

CONTENTS

SOURCE MATERIALS

EDITORS' NOTE

Sherwood Anderson wrote that he was "one of the few letter writers left in the world," a claim well supported by the voluminous correspondence he carried on throughout his lifetime. Although some 5,000 of these letters have been deposited in libraries — notably the outstanding collection at the Newberry in Chicago — only a fraction of them have been available in published form.

The fifty-four letters printed here have been selected for their importance in revealing some of Anderson's attitudes, activities and relationships during the twenty years (1920-1940) that they span. Four groups of letters reflect his close friendships with Jerome and Lucile Blum, Burton and Mary Emmett, Laura Copenhaver, and J. J. Lankes. The Emmett and Lankes letters are particularly useful in augmenting the Jones and Rideout collection, *Letters of Sherwood Anderson*, which contains but three letters to the Emmetts and two to Lankes. A fifth group of miscellaneous correspondence represents Anderson in his various roles as author, farmer, and public citizen.

To produce a clear and readable text, we have made a few silent corrections of spelling and essential punctuation. Alternate readings in cases of probable slips of the pen are indicated in brackets. Dates and places omitted from the original headings are supplied in brackets when they can be ascertained. In the main, however, we have tried to keep editorial tampering to a minimum in order to preserve Anderson's own distinctive style. We have left unchanged, for example, his sometimes erratic capitalization and his unconventional or omitted punctuation of salutations, closings, and abbreviations. Footnotes have been kept to the minimum consistent with clarity.

For their assistance in preparing these letters for publication, we wish to thank Eleanor Anderson, Diana Haskell of the Newberry Library staff, and Walter B. Rideout of the University of Wisconsin.

TO JEROME AND LUCILE BLUM [1]

Chicago
September 20 [1920]

Dear Jerry & Lucile —

Tennessee & I just got back into town. Found your fine letter. It was the only thing cheerful about coming back here. I'll not stay long. Am going on a still hunt for some kind of hole in the country where I can work and where Tennessee can come a part of each week. We're both beginning right now to make plans for the Alabama thing with you two. Let's all four check that up as something we'll do. I know you'll both get a story and a damn big one out of the nigger. He's somebody nobody knows a hell of a lot about yet.

I wrote off to Huebsch and told him to send you Winesburg at once. The only copy I have here is pretty messy. The new book should be along in a few weeks. Do you want it sent out there? How long will you stay?

I read O'Brien's book White Shadows[2] and it gave me a sense of where you are and the life you are living. God wouldn't I like to be there with you two. [3]

Tennessee is pretty well. It's too damn bad she has to go to work teaching because she married me who won't settle down and support a woman as a respectable man should. Lucile she has done some heads of Americans that are great. I get to talking to her about some imaginary character — say Mrs Windpeter Winters. We talk about her several days and then she takes some clay and there she is — very realistic vivid things.

I'm glad you're painting, Lucile. One of the most joyous things that has happened to me is finding out that one can paint — without the schools. At least one can feel about for line, color and form. I did four things up north and as soon as I'm out of this nasty city bedlam I'll get at it again. The trouble with me now is that I have in hand a novel that fascinates me.

Well whatever happens have no illusions (caused by being far away) about living here. The dreary political jungle you're in. There is noise, death and weariness of soul.

God bless the wind that has carried you two out of it — for the time anyway.

Sherwood.

2

Dear Jerry & Lucile —

I don't know whether or not a letter will travel down to you before you cut out for America. Today I'm out in the country — just over a hell of a cold but now working again. It [is] pretty warm and the ground is soggy. You know the greyness here all winter. I'm going to New York in Feb — about the lst then come back here for the spring. April and May should be lovely here. I don't want to miss that and I'm hoping you two will be along by that time.

I keep wondering how much in earnest you two are about wanting to go south next year — to Alabam. I'm full of it.

Was looking Tennessee over the other evening. She won't stand much more of the grind of teaching in Chicago — will just about blow out. She's promised she'll quit next year — bust up her whole scheme.

What I want to see her do is to go down into the southwest Sep lst and stay in a dry climate until about this time. That would give me a little chance to scratch gravel thro the fall and earn a little money. Then my notion is that the four of us with one or two others, if we get just the right ones, cut out for Mobile.

We could live there — it's a sleepy old town or cut out for one of the beaches. The negroes are wonderful on the docks there and we would cut up country on the river boats.

God knows I'm full of notions, work to be done, things to be laid hold of.

One thing strikes me all the time — the profound shallow smartness and weariness of intellectual and artistic life all over America now. It's absurd. One would think all beauty had been dug up and labeled — all the land of mystery explored.

It [is] an aftermath of the war I dare say. No doubt the damn war was fought because of spiritual weariness.

I'm getting a book of tales in shape now. When it's off my hands I want to cut back into the novel that is waiting — half finished.

I only go into town once a week now and then stay out here but I want companionship. There is a painter here — Felix Russman — a good painter I suppose and a nice fellow but he paints too many moonlights.[4]

If these fellows who paint to sell — (perhaps they have to — having kids and all that) didn't have to be taken as artists it would be all right. They always insist on art more than anyone else. Sometimes you want to say 'go have a bon fire man' and then you've got to think

'Now don't go upsetting this man's little circle of life.' It cramps talk,

3

makes companionship impossible. I like a little healthy slamming back and forth — blows taken and received now and then.

I've been getting a good deal of spreadeagle talk — notices etc on my new book but don't fancy it sells much. My books never do.

Once in a while I get scared. Have rather set my heart on the southern thing with you two and then I say to myself 'O, hell, I'll bet they won't do it.' You happen to be the pair most essential to the happiness of the venture.

Sherwood —

Tennessee isn't here. I guess you know she loves you both.

Chicago
April 2 [1921]

Dear Jerry & Lucile.

When this gets into your hands I presume Tennessee and I will be either in New York or at sea — bound for Paris. We sail May 14 — on the Rochambeau from New York. Here is the story. Paul Rosenfeld had an unexpected windfall and invited me for a 2 months trip to Paris and London. It seemed to me a great chance as I want at least one look at the two old towns. Also Winesburg is being translated into French and there is some chance I may get hooked up for English publication.

The point is that I don't want this to interfere with our getting up something real for next year. I want the 4 of us to try living and working together.

We should be back in New York about Aug 20 and if you are there I'll find you. In the meantime you can write me Paris c/o Jacques Copeau — 21 Rue Du Vieux Columbier — and tell me where I'll find you when we get back.

For a time Tennessee planned not to go but later changed her mind.

Have had a good and a bad year. I got things into shape where I thought I would have pretty near uninterrupted work time and then I got filled with poison from infected antrums and there have been weeks when I was dead on my feet & from the hair down.

Damn it I was full of bully work — a host of real short stories to write, a novel to finish, a play to write.

I got some of the stories finished and have made up my new book — a

4

book of tales to be called Unlighted Lamps[5] to be published in Oct. It's tales, poems and reproductions of some fine heads Tennessee has made.

God damn this climate. I've a notion that is what has checked me.

I'm crazy to see what you two have been doing and to see you and have a talk and make plans.

Well you'll want to loaf and see some people — only don't get sewed up for next year until we have our conflab.

Heaps O Love

Sherwood.

New Orleans
January 13, 1922

Dear Jerry and Lucile —

I got down here yesterday, having stopped in Kentucky where I did a little advertising work. It turned out all O.K. but I'm getting to be such an ass that it's hard to do. You have to sit up solemnly and discuss schemes for selling something with some man and all the time have to sit on yourself to keep from saying "O hell, let's cut this out. I don't give a whoop whether you sell it or not."

After I had spent the day at that I met a Kentucky man I knew and he asked me to take a motor ride with him back in the hills. It was a fine moonlight night and we moved a lot of moonshine whiskey from one barn to another — about 35 miles away. There must be a regular underground system as when they used to run slaves off to the north. Suppose we might have landed in jail. I don't know.

As for New Orleans, I can't tell whether it would hit Jerry or not. I think the old town — that is to say the French and Creole quarter — is charming. It's very much like being in one of the old smaller French towns. I have a room with a fireplace, about the size of the one on the second floor of your house where you sit, and am very comfortable. My landlady, a handsome youg Creole, is to bring in my breakfast and I aim to go right to work, writing in the morning and loafing about here in the afternoons.

I'm afraid to say Jerry would like it down here but he knows how glad I would be to see him and to have him to loaf around with — afternoons. Plenty of niggers but you maybe get them better when the warmer days come. I don't know. Things look pretty good to me now.

With Love

Sherwood.

Jerry — Let me know what you decide.

Dear Lucile —

Just got back to Chicago after a great time in New Orleans. I wrote the book I had on my chest when I left New York — now I'll have to settle down and give it another going over. Think I've got something. Can't be too sure yet.

New Orleans was a delightful experience. I wrote something about it for the March number of a little magazine called Double Dealer.[6] You'll find it at the Nash or Pagan book shop — I think. Would send it myself if I had it.

Anyway New Orleans got me hard, the place, people and everything. Some day I'll tell you more about it. New York and Chicago are like tense closed fists. New Orleans is an open handed place.

Tennessee has to give up her place here April lst as they are tearing the building she lives in down. She is going out with me to the little place I have at Palos Park. That is only an hour out of Chicago. Write me 10th Floor Brooks Bldg — Chicago until April 1st. After that Palos Park.

The point is that when you come out here both of us would like to see as much of you as we can. Will Jerry come. The place at Palos is tiny but if you could spend some days out there we'd manage to skirmish up a room in the neighborhood. After April 15th it should be fine in the country. — And I've got a fliver.

The thing I started in New Orleans may go to 3 or 4 volumes — can't tell — but it is told in episodes and the 1st episode is a complete thing in itself. It's a great theme — if I'm able to really handle it.

Well I know how you feel about spring — the blood begins to dance when the sap starts up the trees.

The New Testament thing is experimental.[7] What I suppose I'm after is a new intensity of prose handling.

Gee I hope you come out and old Jerry too.

Sherwood.

[on board ship]
Monday morning [November 6, 1922]

Dear Jerry and Lucile —

The boat — the Momus — passed Cape Hatteras and got into the gulf
stream yesterday afternoon.

I'm lucky. First my roommate, an old sport of 65, turned out to be a
veteran race track gambler and horseman. He had three pals aboard, all also
running horse men so we formed a little group and have had great times
talking horse. One of the horsemen is like Jerry. He gives point to his story
by acting it out. Yesterday he was describing a neck & neck finish and began
prancing along the deck to show me just how a foxy rider can throw a horse
off stride right under the nose of a judge. He pranced along giving me just
the jock's movements as an old fat woman came around the corner. Bang
went the race horse man into her ample belly.

"O, I beg your pardon," said the fat lady, sitting on the deck.

"O, that['s] all right," answered the story teller, going right on with his
story.

I'm in luck. The 1st officer is an ambitious young writer and he spotted
me. So he gave me the use of his cabin and I sit up here, fine and dandy, at a
big desk on the upper deck where passengers are not allowed to come. It's
so hot that this morning I am working in my shirt sleeves with all doors and
windows open.

Will stay about a week in New Orleans and then come back. Bernardine
has her divorce and she and Otto[8] are going to be married soon.

I think it would be great fun if we could all come out for a weekend —
bringing our own grub. Would that be too much of a mess.

No place to put off mail before New Orleans.

Heaps of love to you both.

New Orleans
November 13 [1922]

Dear Jerry —

There are other things I want to do first but some day I would like to
come and live down here for a year or two. You and Lucile may want to do
that later — also. The nigger thing comes back strong. It wants staying with
though. I've seen some things here again that are illuminating but I will talk
to you about them rather than write.

7

I shall not stay long — will leave here by the end of the week — I think. The trip down set me up and I am working but I am not too happy. For one thing I want Elizabeth[9] with me. I'm most completely in love with her and she gives me something I miss horrible when I'm away.

I'm working on a most subtile story, full of shades and lights.

The people here I played about with last year do not interest me much now. They are all messed up, as people seem to be everywhere pretty much and there is damned little going toward anything but a greater messiness.

I thank God for you and Lucile, that you are my friends.

There is one man here who knows something, has subtilty. The rest — it's better to go walk on the docks with the negroes.

Some day, perhaps, after two or three years, when things have cleared, when we are both working well, we might come down here and live — say seven months at a time. Oct 1st to May 1st. The thing would be to live & work in town but to have a Ford and go out into the smaller nigger towns. It isn't so much that we write of the nigger, paint the nigger but that we get their abandonment to feeling, their rhythmic sense of life, skies, the river here. Everything at moments seems in them, and they in it all. Do I make myself clear?

Love to you both

Sherwood.

[Berkeley, California]
[Late April, 1924]

Dear Jerry & Lucile.

Elizabeth and I were married about three weeks ago[10] and Elizabeth wrote to Lucile at Paris.

But the other evening we were at a big dinner in San Francisco and Frederick O'Brien was there. He told me you were back in this country and he thought you were at Mt Kisco.

What about you both. What are you up to. Had really a hell of a year in one way but a pretty good year in another. Got a book done I think is pretty good, in spots anyway, and did a lot of solid reading. There have always been a lot of men I have wanted to know more about, what they really thought and felt and how they said it.

There was my chance — a pretty complete library right at hand.

We got us an old second hand car that hung together pretty well and every afternoon ran out into the desert or up into the mountains. It hung together anyway until we didn't want it any more.

Tried to tell in that book what one story teller was up to anyway.

Then I got into a novel but didn't like it much. Kept going on it anyway. Didn't know until the last minute which way T[ennessee] was going to jump — talk of her "right" etc — which God knows she may have been all right about.

It got cleared up and I threw that novel away next day. Now I'm working on a Lincoln. Have been wanting to do that for a long long time.

We were married at a little California town and spent a week later, dodging reporters by living right under their noses under another name at a San Francisco hotel. Went to see all the sights. Had a grand time.

Then I got down to work. The Pralls have a lovely place in the Berkeley hills and there is a little house for me with a big desk and a fire. Have the run of the University library which is good as I am still reading like a hound.

As it turns out I have a violent case not only on Elizabeth but on her whole family — gentle kind wise people — no fake about them. They have two of the most lovely houses I've ever been in set close together in a garden.

Don't find anyone much yet in San Francisco and am hungry as a dog for some painting and the sight of a few real artists.

We may possibly take a boat from here, go through the canal and to Europe. My oldest boy [11] is getting out of high school this spring and I'd like to give him a look around. It depends largely on how much money comes in.

Did a little painting this year but out of a dozen or more tries got only one little thing that sticks. You can love two mistresses I fancy. The worst of it is I keep imagining there was quite a lot of good work shown in New York this year. I wonder if that's true.

Well I'm working again now and I hope you both are. Do write.

With Love.

Sherwood

TO BURTON AND MARY EMMETT [12]

[Troutdale]
July 4, 1926

My Dear Emmett.

I am answering your note at once — to thank you for your so-flattering letter and the check— also under the circumstances flattering.

I shall want a little time to find something I think you'll be interested in to send.[13]

As I was for years an advertising solicitor and copy man I know the hurried conditions under which you must write. Some day, when I see you, I shall be able to tell you many amusing tales of little subterfuges practised to gain time for other writing. All my first novels and stories were written under such circumstances. I remember, in particular the tale "I'm a Fool," written at the copy desk one morning while I was presumed to be writing copy for a gas engine company.

The money you have sent, my dear Emmett, shall go into stone and logs for my house.[14] When it is built you will run up here some summer day and see it.

As regards the ultra moderns — my own point is that method must never become more important than matter. It is, after all, the story teller's job to tell the story.

I think these periods of breaking new ground however vastly important. What, for example, have I not stolen from Joyce?

Stein is something special. She isn't a story teller — perhaps not an artist. She has given me a lot. An artist in phrase making, word combinations, something like that. She is a sort of tool maker.

That's a lot.

I've done something of that myself, but most of it is buried away, among manuscripts, in my shop.

You may be sure I shall come to see you when I am in New York.

In a few days, or at most a week or 10 days I will find something, just suitable to send you.

Sincerely

Sherwood Anderson.

[Troutdale]
[September 6, 1926]

10

My Dear Burton Emmett.

I think that the only reason I sometimes wish I had money — that is to say enough of it never to have to think about it any more — is that — when the arts are concerned — the bringing in of the money question always brings something else.

I really hope I do not believe in any immature nonsense about Freedom and all that.

Sometimes, in my own mind I put it this way — that the possession of money brings power and that power is corruption in itself.

However for an artist to gain a reputation brings the same thing.

His damn little reputation must be preserved.

You see it is rather rankling that I took your $200. I would so much rather have given the things.

It may be that all a man can give another is friendship — respect.

You have made me feel that for you.

A confusion of thoughts in my mind about the whole matter. The prices did seem silly — a confusion.

Young Sprague seemed to me rather crude. Benchley in Christmas "Life" did a take off on me that was a masterpiece.[15]   Get it out of your files and read it. Hemingway did a whole book — "The Torrents of Spring" — to accomplish the same purpose and did not pull it off.

The house is slow business — but I think will be rather lovely at last. It is being built mostly by ex moonshiners — logs and stone.

Good lines though.

Was in New York a day — 2 weeks ago — to see a sick brother.[16] Had to come right back. When I am there again will look you up — you may be sure of that.

Sherwood Anderson

Ripshin
[May 8, 1927]

Dear Man —

After all writing is not your sole function — as it is mine. I know how such an office as yours eats your time and energy.

For myself, I love writing letters. Sometimes I think I am one of the few letter writers left in the world.

As for New York — Paris — my odd winter. You see man I've got a

11

little fame. Nothing could be worse. It is likely to make a man lose his simplicity. Why couldn't it have come to some fellow who wanted it — say Jim Tully.[17] He's got a thick neck.

Now I'm back in the country. Here people know nothing of writing. Simple men, with natural impulses.

I shall write a book about them, brief sketches — their hungers, impulses etc. Not now. I'll write it along, playfully.

The trouble with New York, Paris, for such as me is that I'm too susceptible. Joyce — Stein — talk in cafés.

Writing, writing, writing.

Art.

Everyone wanting to do something new — find a new road.

Waldo Frank-ing.

Here I get back to nature — can pray a little. I walk past fields being plowed, see dust floating in the air — boys playing baseball.

Reality never did come out of the centers. New reality breaks up out of the ground — in odd places, like corn growing where horses have been fed.

I saw such a stalk of corn — growing at the edge of a wood last year — such a grand ear. I saved it for seed — thinking it should have the right to propagate its kind.

What made me so ashamed of the letter to you — (it was a relief anyway) — was thinking afterward of men like Dostoyevsky.

What they went through.

Me with my full belly — 5 suits of clothes, a stone house.

It would be fun if you could motor down — with your wife, later in the summer.

Many thanks for your good letter.

[Ripshin]
[June 28, 1927 postmark]

Dear Burton Emmett

It is as a matter of fact the substance from which a long and absorbing book could be made. It would take a man to handle it though. Fyodor Dostoyevsky might have been able to do it.

There is something fascinating. Just a newspaper clipping that suddenly creates a world of lives for you.[18]

The mother — the brother and sister in court. I'll keep the clipping.

I haven't written you because I am deep in a novel. It has started and stopped a dozen times. If you want mss — here are piles of it.

All false starts.

And yet perhaps something building up. The people becoming every day a little more real.

I struggle to get them in relation to each other and to the world about them.

When it goes I am happy. When it falls to pieces, because the structure isn't sound, I have days of being miserable.

You would think, wouldn't you, that a man who has written so much would be more sure of himself.

With me each new book is a new world. I have to feel my way painfully into it. I remain, I'm afraid, a dreadful amateur.

I am hoping you and your wife may drive down here, perhaps in the late summer. Sometimes I wonder if it is wise.

I have got through our correspondence a sense of you both. In an odd way I have made you both friends of mine.

Suppose you did not like me — at close range.

However I am hoping you will dare try it.

Some day when I am not so absorbed I will write in answer to your former letter. I think of you often enough.

Sincerely

Sherwood Anderson.

[Ripshin]
[October 1927]

Dear Burton Emmett . . .

I went over to Marion yesterday but the attorney I was to see in regard to the letter wasn't at home and would not be there until the first of next week. As I felt there was no special hurry I decided to wait for his return rather than see another man.

It is arranged that next week I am to be at the office of the paper every day, getting the hang of things.

Yesterday was a golden day. I am sorry you cannot see this country now. The leaves are falling fast. Yesterday a scurry of golden leaves in the mountain road as I drove along. All the hills on each side the road spread with a gorgeous carpet of color. Man I often wish there was no such thing as

13

money in the world. Ever since I left I have been a little ashamed that, when I saw you for the first time, I had to speak to you of money. And how nice you were. O, I want it all to come out right — I mean that I shall soon be able to pay you out.

I dug a little into the pile of manuscript. The Dark Laughter I have got ready and will send on. I remember that when the novel was about finished I was dissatisfied with the ending. There was an afternoon in New Orleans, a grey murky day. I got Elizabeth and we walked for two or three hours. I had been thinking and thinking of the ending. It wouldn't come off. How discouraged I was. Mrs Emmett should be glad she is not married to a novelist. What fellows we are. Such absurd despair. I remember walking through the streets declaring to Elizabeth that the whole book I had just done was a complete failure. I felt like crying.

Afterward however I did write another and more satisfactory ending to the novel. Both endings are enclosed in the manuscript. There are other manuscripts here that will need to be put a little in order. I will send them along later.

I am sending, for your amusement, copies of the two papers. You see what they are. By the way there are two books on my poor self this fall — one published by Robert McBride and the other, called The Phenomenon of Sherwood Anderson by a man named Fagin and published by The Rossi-Bryn Company of 625 Saint Paul Street, Baltimore, Md. The latter is the more sympathetic book. The other book, written by a man named Chase, is not very sympathetic.[19]

I keep asking myself the question, why is everything I write a subject of controversy? Sometimes I have a mad passion for an entirely obscure life. I want just to keep still, go quietly and unnoticed through life. Well, I don't succeed in doing it very well. Elizabeth and I had a long talk about it yesterday morning. Thank God she has some sense. She is going to break in at the paper with me. She will probably do more to make it go well than I will. When I write something that arouses antagonism I suffer horribly. I mean such things as the article in the New Republic.[20] What matters is not the truth or falsehood of such a thing.

However there is in all such things hatred, a desire to kill. I presume every man and woman is like a plant. There is the desire to grow and grow.

But how are any of us to say whether we are really plants or only weeds that must be cut out. People so often, I am quite sure, feeling that of my writing. Someone is reading something I wrote. I may have been too frank. The reader is hurt, grows angry. Such a controversy about me since the beginning.

As Elizabeth points out it has two sides. She for example spoke of you two. The very thing that antagonized another perhaps brought you two to me. She accuses me of being too greedy, of wanting the love of the whole world. It may be true.

At any rate as I told you I am happy having something definitely ahead to do.

No more today. I must remember you are a busy man. I shall take you many times as a friend to whom I will write when the mood comes. Do not feel you have to answer.

I thought the little cartoon might amuse you. I am putting in also a snapshot of the house we built, altogether with local unskilled labor.

Sherwood Anderson.

[Ripshin]
Sunday [October 16, 1927]

My Dear Emmett . .

By all means keep the clipping. With me such things have a way of simply getting lost or thrown away. I guess you can see how disastrous it would be for me to take them seriously. My own problem lies in quite another direction. Just at present Elizabeth's brother, David Prall from the University of California, is here for a two weeks visit. Yesterday he and I took a long walk in the woods. I was trying to explain to him. When a man is young what he thinks he wants above everything is what is called recognition. It comes. In America nothing is done very temperately. There is too much. What is fine about it is also offset by what is ugly. Of course, dear Emmett, I realize it may all be very temporary — a thing you do not quite believe. While it lasts however it throws a man into a new position. One achieves that strange thing called power. Do you remember what Henry Adams said — (you must by all means read Henry Adams — The Education of Henry Adams) — " a friend in power is a friend lost."[21]

The responsibility of being a public man, a public character. I much doubt if a man can be that and be an artist. However one has to accept what life offers.

My own fight to save myself from the feeling of power of importance. Time will of course take care of it but to a man of fifty time is of importance too. One can't wait too long.

What I mean of course is that time will put me more nearly in the position of utter obscurity than you, dear friendly man, can realize. Life marches fast. Think for a moment of the men who have for a minute filled the eyes of the big world or of the more narrow and intellectual world. "Where are the snows of yesteryear," sang Villon. It was a true song.

In the meantime a man lives and faces the present. For the last few days, to amuse myself I have been reading a book on the Jesuits. There was a long chapter on "The Retreat." As I told you I think I have been in retreat too much, too much occupied with self. That is why I look forward to the necessary activities of the paper. There is something dreadful in too much contemplation of self. That is one reason why I am so glad to have all of these things that concern me personally or the work I may have done in the past go to you. There is much here to send. I shall slowly get it together and send it along as I have the chance to look it over.

As for the foreign books I have some I can send and can send you names of the publishers of the others. The German edition [of] The Story Teller I do not happen to have seen. I am writing the German publishers to send me several copies of the book. When they come I shall send yours. For the Russian, Spanish, and other editions I will simply look up the names of the publishers. Some of them I have never seen.

Glorious days here. The nights a[re] cool with frost but we have not yet started our furnace. Wood is very cheap so we keep an open fire going. Tomorrow, that is to say Monday, I begin going over to the paper, getting myself used to it. I dare say I will find that lawyer in in a few days now. I am trying to be as business-like as I can and go over everything as well as I can before making the actual purchase.

About coming down. You can leave New York — over the Pennsylvania — at about 3:40 P M and be in Marion at seven twenty or thereabouts the next morning. Unfortunately the getting back is a bit more difficult. You have to leave Marion at 1 P M and go by day train to a place called East Radford where you get the sleeper to New York. The thing to do is to so arrange it that you can have at least two or three days here.

And dear man do not feel that you must answer my letters. I am a scribbler. I feel you as a friend. I am likely to write you at any time. A scribbler will you see scribble.

As Ever

Sherwood A

There are as you see two addresses. At Grant we get parcel post to our door but it is a day later than Troutdale. Telegrams must be addressed to Troutdale. After November 1st the quickest address will be simply Marion Va.

Marion
[October 28, 1927]

My Dear Emmett —

I can't send the corrected agreement today because I left the only copy I have of the one I did send over at Troutdale. We haven't moved over here yet. I am to take charge on Monday. Certainly there is nice feeling about it here in Marion and I should make it go. I will have the new agreement drawn on Monday — giving you of course full assurance of complete ownership.

I can't well make a list of manuscripts and send because I haven't gone through them all to see just what I have got.

Anyway you are so generous with me that I'm going to see that you get all I've got. I will of course send the notes along with the new agreement.

You know dear man that while I suppose I can't give you legal assurance you are going to get your money back. Both Elizabeth and I feel that as an absolute obligation.

The letter sent to Grant hadn't got there when I left last evening to come over here. Our mountain mails are uncertain you see. Lordy I wish you and Mrs Emmett could come down.

As Ever — Sherwood.

P. S. I wired about the money because I do not like to get off to a bad start in Marion by not having it here as promised — that is to say by the 1st.

[Ripshin]
[October 30, 1927]

Dear Emmett —

I am writing this on Sunday, over at the farm. Mail to Grant is very uncertain and I did not get your long letter — written after seeing Mr Young — until yesterday morning at Marion. Both letters were there. I immediately wired you — having in mind that, if there was to be any delay in the closing up of the deal at Marion I should in fairness to the people there, let them know at once.

Your prompt wire answer of course reassured me on that point.

I am putting in the two notes — a sensible way of handling the financial obligation. A lawyer tells me that, if not paid at maturity, such notes automatically begin to pay interest.

My plan — as far as I can carry it out — is to turn all of the profits of the business at Marion right back into paying it out. I hope my incidental outside writing may support me while I am doing this.

Of course — dear Emmett — why not say — dear Burton — a kind of shyness keeps me from doing so readily as yet — you and I both know that my obligation in such a matter is rather, well, extra legal.

There are two or three big boxes of manuscript here. How much of it will be worth while to you I can't tell. My notion of rather digging down into it is that there may be stuff in it I can use —

And then I may find stuff I did not know I had.

I rather dream of having you down here sometime and going through some of it with you. We will continue to come back over here for week ends all winter.

However you had better send all mail to Marion.

As regards contemporary stuff — if it does not seem to you too absurd to be bothered with it I would like to send it right along as written.

Usually I make a quick draft — in pencil — then later work from this on a typewriter. My notion is that the first quick draft is what you are interested in.

So many things to talk to you about.

I wonder incidentally if there is anything specially I can do to keep my small papers in the minds of agency men. I am afraid they are too small for you busy men to remember often.

Sincerely

Sherwood Anderson

Marion
October 30, 1927

Dear Sir.

I am writing you this letter to acknowledge my obligation to you for the five thousand dollars ($5000.00) you have loaned me without interest and that is to be used as part payment for the newpaper property I am acquiring at Marion Virginia.

To cover this obligation I am enclosing two notes, each for twenty-five hundred dollars ($2500.00) and maturing four and five years from date.[22]

In addition to these notes and to cover, as nearly as it can be covered, my obligation to you, I hereby agree to send you, from time to time as I can go through them and straighten them out, the original manuscripts of all my published works yet in my possession and also such unpublished manuscripts as have not been destroyed.

All of these manuscripts are to become your property and I hereby waive all rights in them for myself and heirs. I shall continue to send you such manuscript, of works yet to be written, as long as you and I live.

In addition to this I shall also help you in any reasonable way I can in the collection of items of interest to you from other and contemporary writers.

I wish this letter to be a complete acknowledge[ment] of my obligation to you.

Sincerely

Sherwood Anderson

Witness J. R. Collins

Marion

[November 2, 1927]

Dear Burton —

Here I am at my editorial desk. We got out our first newspaper yesterday. It was fun. I think I had better send you a copy of the first issue of both papers. At any rate the town seems pleased with it.

I brought over the manuscript of Tar — which — as it is a bulky package I will send by express.

As I suspected — the moment I had something else to do I began wanting to write. Well, after a few weeks, when Elizabeth and I get our hands in — I will have more time.

As to the notes. Dear dear man. I already know your spirit. It is so much better to have the notes in your hands. You have already fulfilled every understanding of our talk. I do want you to feel all right about everything.

Sincerely

Sherwood

Will write you more fully after the rush of our first days.

Marion
[November 5, 1927]

Dear Burton Emmett.

I think the papers were a bit delayed but Elizabeth says she has now sent you all copies. There was a big demand for the first issue which we could not meet — not expecting it. However Elizabeth saved it for you.

If you look at the paper you will see that I have begun a weekly personal column. This I am copyrighting. A thought has occurred to me. There is such a wide spread interest in this venture here, not only on the part of people in general but on the part of my fellow editors all over the country that I believe this weekly column could be syndicated. It would be such a nice way to supplement the income from the paper. Surely all sorts of rather dull things are syndicated and I believe there is a widespread interest in small town life.

What I am liking about this job is the way things just flow in here. At present I get so many new impressions that I can't keep up with them. To date the outside subscriptions without any pressure from us as yet keep coming at the rate of from five to ten dollars a day. I shall be very much interested in how the little flyer at advertising comes out. Anyway I believe that we are going to be able to show results for our advertisers. The local advertisers are already feeling the increased interest. One advertiser told me the other day that every advertising put in the papers brought people flocking into his store. I don't believe you agency men need hesitate to recommend the papers to any general advertiser.

Some day, when you are not too busy and if you have any ideas about syndicating the column let me know.

With my best to you both. Please do not miss the funeral things in the paper. Some of them are rather rich. These people love to talk about their dead.

As Always

Sherwood Anderson

Dear Burton . . At my request Elizabeth — my business man here — made out the subscription bill for the two papers but she says and rightly that it is absurd for you to pay a subscription. God knows you have done enough to help launch this venture.

We have been here long enough to know what one problem is going to be . . The man we bought from had just put on a big subscription campaign and had got in a good deal of money. He has built up the papers but this year we will not get in much from local subscriptions. They all take it and they are are all paid up.

The local subscription price is $1.50 a year. For outside subscriptions we get $2.00 on the News. That is the one we are building up. You see nearly everything we print in the News is lifted and put also into the Democrat — except the political stuff. The two papers do not duplicate in circulation and of course this saves composition. What we will have to work for is all the foreign advertising we can get and the problem of subscription money may well be taken care of by these outside subscriptions. They are coming in now, several a day from all over the United States.

Elizabeth thinks this might well be built up to quite an extent. I am enclosing a small advertisement. Would you mind having one of the boys in the office find out what this would cost, run one time in The Mercury, three times in the Sunday Book supplement of the New York Times and three times in New Republic. If it doesn't cost much I think we will try the venture of putting it in. Whoever looks it up might wire us.

If it pays of course we could try it in other book and literary supplements.

I am running in the paper a column each week I call "What Say." Already I have had an inquiry or two about syndicating this. I will begin to copyright it after this week. That might work out into a good thing too.

As it happens we have got publicity on this venture from one end of the country to the other.

The people here like the paper. For example we tried a small newsstand sale and the papers were snapped up. Last week when the paper went into the post-office crowds were waiting for it. They even phone in to tell us how much they like it. I think Elizabeth will be able to hold yours truly down when I get too strong. I am making her my Morals Editor.

Lord it's fun anyway.

We didn't get over to the farm this week end — the weather too bad.

As far as I can see the work here doesn't take the edge off me. It just puts it on.

If you do feel you must subscribe take just the News. No use taking them both.

Lordy I could get help cheap here. I think every young writer in the U S A is writing in for a job and offering to work for practically nothing — a lot of old city newspaper men too. I have had two or three offers to buy a half interest at what we paid.

As Always.

Sherwood

[Lenoir, North Carolina]
[late June 1933]

Dear Bert

I will put the $500.00 in the bank. I have a curious nature as regards money. The extra $500.00 will make me nigger rich. When I get below $500.00 I am inclined to worry and think of money —

Of course I may spend it. Who knows better than you or Mary how precarious is the theater. I do not forgive myself that you and Mary did not see the play. As a matter of fact, when I saw you, the play was not yet a play. In the conference had with the Guild they said . . . it is not a play yet. It is grand stuff — fine character drawing but not a play.[23]

I am going to write you a long letter. I am on my way down south to get Elenore and bring her home. I am going to make her marry me.[24] It is early morning. You won't mind a long letter —

First of all as regards what you now think of as your rather harsh letter to me and mine to you. My dear man — any one who ever saw you walk across a room, heard your laugh — would know that you might as well have gone the road I've gone as the one you did go. I think you are often confused as I am. When I speak as I do often about money — growing harsh often, bitter often — even flippant — the whole thing is never personal. So much of life dear Bert is a kind of queer unaccountable accident. You happened to meet the Chesterfield man and he to like and trust you. There is a kind of iron honesty and fineness in you that all who come close recognize. A keen woman like Elenore sees your fine worth at once.

But what I am trying to say Bert is that accident rules our lives too.

The accident also that I have talent — as the throat of a singer has a certain form. How are you to account for that. As in business you see many men as fine as either of us surely struggling to the end in the ruck so also in the arts. In the arts how many men finer than I will ever be go on to the end, putting in all they have and getting no where —

So we accept all this.

There is something else. As an artist I am often called by the critics a naive man. Never believe it Bert. I am complex — often calculating — sophisticated. There is a little black devil in me, perched always back in a little cave in my head. What drives me Bert I don't know. This I do know — that the only thing that saves me from being a plain son-of-a-bitch is that I am, as much as any man that ever lived — an artist.

What does all this mean. It means that always, every minute, day and night, I am after something — some abstract pure beauty. Why? God knows why. It may all come to nothing. Everything I have done or may do may be forgotten in two generations.

It doesn't matter. There is the devil in me that drives me on. Often I grow cruel, intolerant, brutal.

You have to think too dear man of what I have gone through . . . the long struggle in business . . . later some of my finest things called ugly and even nasty —

The need always of a little money, freedom to go on working, trying to create.

Having to stop often, put all aside everything to get a little money.

And all of this leading often to intolerance. God damn money I've cried. It is what has made me a revolutionist.

You see dear man I belong to a race of kings too. This talent I have and know I have is something a little outside me. It is something I serve as a religionist serves his god.

So times of brutality, flippancy. You sat on a boat, feeling humiliated that you had written me a certain letter about money and at the same time, I sat at home feeling humiliated and mean that I had written you rather harshly—

Thus both of us hurt.

At the same time, deep in us, a respect and love for each other. It's life Bert — so cruel, unaccountable, absorbing, often beautiful. You see it dear man. Let's forget it. At least dear man I have this in me. There is a kind of persistency. I don't ever change my mind about a real friend . . . and I will suffer really if I have to think that I have in any way hurt the inner fine thing in you.

I am making a play of the play. I had to eliminate Barton[25] — throw him out of the picture. He didn't have the stuff. But I have found out one thing — I can write plays and I will make a play here that will find a solid place in dramatic literature. I know that.

23

Bert the $500 this summer will ease my mind, free me for concentrated work. Again you have done me a fine thing.

Please please forgive any occasional outcropping of flippancy in me and know that I love and respect you. Get well man.

My love to Mary,

Sherwood

Elenore would want her love sent.

Of course I'll not mention the Seabury. I do not know him but have heard of him as one of the best. I think it a grand idea. All of us so often need help in getting at this queer tangle.

O man, man, know that you have the love of many.

[Washington]
[October 5, 1933]

Burt & Mary —

I must write you a note from here. I came down with Elenore, to an AF of L meeting, to watch, look & listen but have got in up to my neck.

It's rather swell. All of the stiff, cold formality of government seems to be gone. Everyone is working. No one seems high hat — no one cock sure.

They really are trying. Last night Henry Wallace[26] came over and wanted me to go to work, a kind of public relations writer — and some big new workers educational scheme wants Elenore.

I had a long talk with Wallace. I'd really like to get in and help but wouldn't want to tie myself here in Washington.

We are trying to work out some scheme. Jesus, I wish I were rich. I'd like to attach myself to Wallace or some other of these fellows as a kind of ambassador to other writers, & also as a kind of scout to keep going and looking at the country for them.

I swear to God they really are in earnest and I'd love to do it as a volunteer. I can't tell you how much I really like some of these people — as I like you two I guess — feeling really in many of them a corking willingness to work like hell, take risks, a real feeling that there will have to be a new deal. They aren't, apparently, saying 1/2 they think.

And there is with it all a kind of swell laughing thing.

This in haste.

24

Love

Sherwood

New York
March 23, 1934

Dear Burt and Mary:

I have been slack about writing. I just got back the day before yesterday from a long trip in the South and while I was gone was so constantly on the move that I did not even write Eleanor anything but post cards. I went all through the upper South through the Tennessee Valley Authority project, went to Muscle Shoals, then to New Orleans and through the lower South. I was to do eight articles for "Today" and have done six of them. I am working now on the other two.

In the meantime, after being with me for a while, Eleanor came back here. She is well again and I am again upstairs at work in the studio on the second floor. Everything seems to be all right here, although I never come into the house without a queer feeling that I shall find you two here.

I am in a hopeless jam with the play, the whole thing being my own fault. I made the bitter mistake of trying to collaborate with a pretty second-rate man who was of no help to me and now he is trying to hold me up. I simply had to withdraw the play and am now waiting, hoping he will come to his senses.

It seems to me that all my work this winter has been more or less scattered, but there is so much of that quality in life now that perhaps it is inevitable. I am thinking of a project. For some reason I do not find myself very deeply interested in writing novels just now. There is something I have wanted to do since I was a boy and I half think now that if I can get the money together so that I can afford it I shall begin the attempt next Fall. I want to write a big history of the Civil War with all its implications. I have been reading and preparing for it for years and believe if ever I am to do it I should get at it. If I attempt it, I believe I will go to Washington next winter and work in the Library of Congress down there.

It is still bitter cold here but we are beginning to think of Spring and Summer, and that brings the thoughts of you two back here again. It will certainly be grand to see you.

With love to you both.

Sherwood

25

Dear Mary —

It is a cold day, with a drizzle of rain. I have read the last of your book — the proof I mean.[27] It is a real pleasure to dedicate it to you and, Mary dear, my doing so does not in any way commit you to helping me. I want you to know that.

It is for our friendship and the many many kindnesses you have done.

I can't help feeling sorry you did not see the new Winesburg. It is really so lovely.

Paul R[28] is here — really dear such a curious, interesting and sometimes quite ridiculous man. He works at a novel in the upper tent but, I am sure, is more critic and essayist than novelist, or story teller. We play croquet and he is terribly upset when beaten.

He has never married, a confirmed bachelor and a brilliant talker.

Mother C seems quite well but E is upset. She has hardening of the arteries and high blood pressure and that is dangerous. I don't know what will happen to her husband if anything happens to her.

There was a mixup in that order to Burpee for the delphinium seed and it never came. Had the money order traced and it had been cashed. Placed another order and had John make me a bed down near my cabin, where I could watch and water. Hope to get a variety of plants.

That bee balm — we went up the mountain in the fog to get, just such a day as this has been gorgeous — the rich soil you made developing masses of big blossoms. I'll save seed.

The novel is quite different from the version you read — much more pure story telling. You know I rewrote it entirely this winter in Tucson.

What would you like to do after January. We could go to Mexico or the Phillipines.

I'm afraid, Mary, from all I hear that Roosevelt may be defeated. What I am afraid of is that both Landon and Knox are tools of Hearst. If elected it may mean a new policy of rigid suppression of all liberalism — that sort of thing is running through the world.

The idea of the strong man etc. to run affairs — something perhaps between Germany and Italy. It will be hard here to build up the idea, as in Germany and Italy — of a superior race, to rule, as we are such a mixture.

I can't quite understand the bitter hatred of Roosevelt as business men are all doing well. It's fear of a more liberal future I guess.

Anyway, what has happened in Italy & Germany, perhaps also in Russia, is the end of all real art. It can't flourish in hatred Mary.

We want you back Mary. Lots of love

TO LAURA COPENHAVER[29]

Dear Friend —

I am writing you from the observation car of the train on which I have come east with Elenore. She is writing a lot of business letters at a desk in a corner — letters concerned with her work in San Francisco I presume. She has put off writing for two days because of the strange and magnificent country we have come through . . . and, of course, because she has had such good company. I told her I would write you.

We will get to St Paul & see Katharine & Henry[30] at 10:45 tonight, Tuesday.

I really did a lot of work in S. F. — a great deal on the novel and most of a new book.

It has been a curious time. I think perhaps I have had what the communists love to call "a leftward shift," again. There seems to me now a possibility of taking the communistic doctrine — much as you take Lutheranism. You say "I chose to believe." I see the strength of that. Why should I now not say "I chose to believe Communism is the way."

If you take it this way why should you not feel a new strength in yourself, something to check life by? I have always wanted, and I'm sure have needed, a religion somewhat more definite than the poet and dreamer's romanticism about the importance of his own life.

—   —   —

But you would much rather hear of your daughter. I am more in love with her than ever but do realize, what I am sure all you others who love her feel, that she will probably be a fool to marry me.

Although I saw little of her in S. F. (it seemed little any way) we had grand times and met charming and interesting people.

She is modest about it all but I'm sure she did a good job out there. My own friends who saw her loved her. She was very tired when she left there but the long days on the train — plenty of sleep etc — have rested her. She looks grand today.

She can only stay at Stillwater a day or two & then must go on to New York. I'll probably follow her, almost at once, going however to Marion. I have a lot of work to do yet.

Much Love,

S. A.

[New York]
Tuesday [August 2, 1932]

Dear Friend —

I saw Elenore last night and she told me Mazy[31] had gone home. I shall be sorry if they do not use Ripshin. It was stupid of me not to think of that long ago.

Went to a communist demonstration last night and there were 30,000 reds out. Took Elenore. She is working like a Turk these days & tells me her San Francisco report is gradually getting into shape.

I am being urged to go as a delegate from America to the World's Conference against war at Amsterdam Aug 28th and am half ready to do it. Romaine Rolland, Shaw, Einstein, Barbusse, Gorki and others.

Liverights tell me they will be giving me full proofs of Beyond Desire on Wednesday evening or Thursday morning and I will immediately send one set of proofs to you. Elenore is arranging things so that she can give me Sunday but before I return proofs I would very much like to have your criticisms. May I suggest that, if Mary[32] is willing, you have her up for an evening or two. Perhaps you could both run through the book.

I know it is a lot to ask but Elenore says it is all right and that you will enjoy doing it — I hope she is right.

Mimi & her man[33] are coming down today, to spend the evening & go back tomorrow. I'll take them to a restaurant, perhaps to the one to which I took you & Elenore — Cafe Royal on 2nd Avenue. You can eat outdoors, on the side walk over there these summer nights.

I think your honorable daughter is pointing her work in the hopes of getting home by the 12th or 13th.

It is interesting being in the city now although terrible too. Here you may lift the lid a bit and see the terror of the depression in a way that has never touched Marion. My very best to Mr Copenhaver & Miss May.[34]

As Always

Sherwood Anderson

New York
[August 16, 1932]

Dear Friend —

I am in this hotel[35] in NY and no one but Elenore knows where I am.

28

I intend to give the day to the book and not appear in public until tomorrow at noon. Our friend Mr Eaton missed his train but I had Charlie Wassum and some friend of Annabelle's.[36] Nothing was said about fountain pens. I will see Elenore at noon. I'll hold this note to see if there is any definite word of her coming.

The real purpose of the note is to tell you again how very grateful I am to you and my gratitude covers more than the work you did on this novel.[37]

Your house has been a refuge for me. It has been the thing that made Marion possible and livable to me. I could not have stayed on there but for your house.

It is perhaps too bad about Elenore — that I had to fall in love with her — but I attribute that to her charm. I'm not all to blame.

The thing you must all know is this — that when I found you all I was a licked man. The warm friendship — even affection — I have got from you has brought life back. I work again — perhaps better than I ever did.

It is what I have got in your house that has made this possible and if it is not important to others it is terribly important to me.

The same to Mr Copenhaver and to Miss May.

Sherwood

Elenore thinks she may be home on Friday.

[Kansas City]
[January 1933]

Dear Friend —

I hope you miss my coming in to quarrel with you about communism, God, the church etc. I brought the grey coverlet — the checkerboard one [diagram drawn in here] I had in the car and you'd be surprised how nice it makes my room. I've gone back to my diet of 2 big grapefruits a day — and I keep figs and dates in the room. Then I got an electric coffee pot for $1 and can make coffee, when I jump out of bed in the morning — in five minutes. I like the good black kind with chicory.

I won't be seeing much of Elenore — a luncheon now and then and an hour's walk — (I have to see she goes to bed early as she works so hard) but it has come to mean everything to me to be near her, hear her voice on the phone before I go to bed etc. I don't quarrel and argue with her as I do most people I love but we are far from agreeing on everything. I think

I am more emotional than she is (perhaps) and she more level headed. I've an idea I shall always be courting her.

You have often lectured me about not feeling guilty about life and my own connection with it but, my dear woman — it's rather like you and Mr Copenhaver having ideas about drunkenness — neither of you ever having been drunk.

I've been so damnably stabbed. Well I know I brought it on — or rather my nature brought it on me — but that doesn't help.

But anyway I do get back, more and more, my self-respect — (Elenore having helped me more than anyone else ever did) and as I do I am quite sure I make it easier for her.

I've thought a good deal about you and of the points wherein I disagree with you fundamentally. The will — for one.

The next is a certain determined thing I've noticed in you — that your daughters shall — in a certain subtle way — keep free from their men — whereas I believe the real freedom comes, not in that way — I mean a keeping something back — but rather it comes to men and women — really, I believe, by giving all — absolutely.

I've an idea a certain self-respect comes from that — the best sort.

I tell you frankly that, having as I believe a year or two's living ahead — for both of us (it wouldn't be so rich but it would do), I'm not so strong for Elenore's going on as she has in the past. It's no good. After all the work of the YW — like most such organizations — does in some queer way, I believe, now'days lose its flare. When a world is cracking up this mending broken chairs for fat women to sit on isn't so hot. Really I'd give anything now to take her away — to the sea and pine forests. She has had people, a world of people, for years and later — if she wished — could return to them.

I tell you I love her more than I ever dreamed I could love and it's all terribly important to me. Really that's why I'm here — to watch a bit and if I see her getting ragged I'm likely to get ugly if she doesn't come away from it.

I still like my crazy room — in this crazy hotel — and think I'll work. I've been trying to shake the play — and the play feeling — out of me so I can feel like the novel again — so I've spent two days just writing letters — worlds of them.

I do miss seeing you. Ask Mary about any more of the Lawrence books. Elenore says Mazy has the Carswell Life[38] and that she will write to have it sent on to you.

I rather thought I would be able to get back into novel form when I quit dreaming out acts of plays at night. I haven't stopped yet.

Elenore looks all right.

It would be nice if you wrote me here but, if you do, address S (not Sherwood) Anderson, Hotel Puritan, Room 609.

30

Dear Friend —

It is Sunday and Elenore is down with a cold. These women, trying to help the fight of working women — that they shall not work more than eight hours a day etc — no night work — they themselves working all day and all night. With Elenore as usual it is a case of overwork. She always lies so about it — saying "I don't do anything" etc . . . a bit like her mother in that.

This eternal interviewing people — going to meetings and conferences — always having to handle stupid people. You know it takes it out of her.

So I'm glad I'm here. I know you think it silly but there is something in being near.

I just sent her — by messenger — a dozen cans of tomato juice. Occasionally anyway I can have her out — in the car — away from the tenseness of it for an hour or two.

I've made up my mind she's got to rest, after this siege. You can imagine what it is like. Everywhere now the standard of better hours, pay etc for working women — built up slowly, through years, is breaking down. There is tremendous increase in prostitution. Open prostitution had practically disappeared — at least from the streets of American cities — but now it is again everywhere. I seldom go a block at night here — out on these wind-swept prairies — but that I am solicited.

It's all amazing. Yesterday I took a long walk with a boy — 23 — rather sensitive looking, who had panhandled me on the street. He told me he had walked all night in zero weather — on the night before — having no money for a bed and no work in sight.

Randolph's[39] remedy — to go wash cars at ten cents — thus pulling down the standards of living of all car washers. The sort of thing organizations like Elenore's are trying to fight.

And this 23 year old boy just another Randolph — in his philosopy. I made him walk with me — tired eyes — going without sleep — that curious dirtiness that comes from never taking your clothes off — sleeping in them etc. I wanted to find out if there was any fight in him.

None — alas.

Little or no sense of thousands of others, like himself. He talked sentimentally of being a lone wolf — survival of the fittest — regular "rugged individuality Hoover" stuff.

I dare say ready enough to crush others down to survive.

Will someone please page Jesus Christ.

As for Elenore — you have to bear in mind that such organizations as the one she is with are pretty much compelled to get funds to go on with the fight from the very people benefiting from all this. And God what twaddle to be listened to — you ought to know — your experience with missionary societies — DAR etc.

You may hate me for it but I said to Elenore the other day — speaking of John Cronk's mother[40] — "Say, wasn't she a twaddler too?" . . . meaning — well she was very popular among the wives of the well-to-do apparently. I guess you can't be very popular and say anything approaching very near to truth.

You know very well I don't quarrel with religion. I do quarrel with its always being used to side track reality.

All of which about what — Elenore. I think she ought to rest more, play more. I have that feeling about her. I'm determined she shall — job or no job.

I have a few thousand dollars and am free from personal debts. I've got Ripshin.

I've an idea now of getting a few people over there every summer. I can, I believe, rather hand pick them — cost shared. We'll put out a big garden this spring. Maybe — toward spring Mr Copenhaver would go over some afternoon with Bob[41] and help plan it.

Elenore should really have some kind of work that would give her three or four months each year for rest and play.

I'm deep into the new novel. You may not like it but it's real story telling — half playful and terrible too — a bit — in the writing — in the mood of a Story Teller's Story.

It is play rather than work to write it. I don't even know myself how it is coming out but the people in it are alive.

S.A.

[Photograph of Eleanor Anderson attached]
[Kansas City]
Sunday [January 1933?]

Dear Friend

I think I had better write and report on Elenore as she is so on the go she tells me she doesn't write as often as she should.

The above was taken at a big dance hall — lower middle class — where we went to dance on Friday evening. They had a little booth in a corner where they did 4 of these for 10¢ and I pushed her in. The girls in the place were very pretty — out with their beaus — such girls as clerks in 5&10 cent stores. These big impersonal dance halls (there are two here) are a new development in American city life. There should be more of them. This place is as big as a city block and the roof is of blue cloth with stars showing through. Very theatrical but rather grand. There is something free and easy about the place — a big orchestra, perfect floor. You take your lady — pay your 40 cents and dance as long as you want to. There is another, even bigger one — called "Pla-More" — where you pay $1.00. We were there one night.

It is rather good to be in the city again. E goes often to K C Kansas — across a long bridge & viaduct — over the Missouri River & I often run her back and forth in the car. It saves her a good many steps and waiting on corners for street cars.

Then occasionally I can steal an hour or two in the evening for dancing— a thing we both love and that I'm pretty sure is grand for her.

She is going to be all right. Up to now she has stayed rather in the background in this study out here and I hope she keeps it up. They are likely to get rather crazy about her — I mean the women who run things — and then they would all be for having her to dine, speak etc. It [is] pretty wearing.

Anyway she is pretty well and generally O.K.

As Always,

S.A.

[Washington, D. C.]
[October 1933]

Dear Friend

Washington is very exciting. Both Elenore and I have been offered jobs here. Wallace wanted to take me on and some new workers educational scheme wants Elenore.

I've got a sort of half formed plan I may sell to Wallace and his crowd, to make me a kind of underground ambassador to the backwoods and to the writers. They are trying. There is a really corking spirit. They are not chuckle-headed or high hat. I went off to lunch with 1/2 of Wallace's department and we had gorgeous talk and then Wallace and his wife came to see me & Elenore. His wife is nice & he likes Elenore, as everyone does.

I can't work down here, as it is too exciting.

33

Tell Bob that I said that a surprising number of men here know about him. He's got a real opportunity. Jesus I wish he'd get the community a bit more and a bit less of Bob's individual reactions. I think he's tired hearing me say so. You say it to him.

He went too far for example in praising the Lincolns[42] about the park. It was silly.

Mazy looked grand.

Did Elenore tell you I had joined Nathan, O'Neill, Dreiser, and the others on the Spectator?[43]

I will write more later. Now I'm going to sally forth again.

Love to all

Sherwood

[New Orleans]
Wednesday [March 27, 1935]

Dear Mother . . . It is Wednesday and I presume that E is on the train and bound here. Her letters recently have been very sketchy, I presume necessarily. You must all have been on the jump in New York. I hope the show turned out well. I do not know whether or not you are at home.

I have not said anything to E but am a bit afraid maybe I have got that Amoeba.[44] As soon as she comes I'll have tests. She knows the man here. I do not know whether or not Mr C has gone for the operation or when he will go. You see I do not know much. Well, I'll have E to give me all the news tomorrow.

After talking of it for a month it now turns out that Roger Sergel[45] is to arrive here also on Thursday morning, a few hours after E comes. I'm not so pleased, would like to have what I can get of E for myself alone for a while and besides Roger's wife is coming and E cannot have much time for her. There are too many demands on that woman. You have no idea. All seem to think of her as tireless. It is largely her own fault, or perhaps the fault of her nature. She gives herself so freely and always protests that she is not tired, etc. She will even, if I let her . . . I do try to stop it . . . take on all of my own little literary children. It's really too bad.

I got the novel through the first book and as I have not been quite A-1 have been resting for a few days. I wrote for the play Mother because the man Fagin . . . University of Baltimore . . . who runs a little theater there. . .

34

wanted to try to put on Winesburg and I am trying to steer him off into doing instead the two one act plays. I want to do another one this spring, if I can, and make up an evening of the three plays, calling them Short Stories.

And now appears Guild flirting with the idea of doing Winesburg again. I had a letter from the agent, saying they had been in to see her. They thought the play should be worked over again by a skilled play maker and suggested Sidney Howard and I wrote back, saying I would be glad to have the play gone over by such a first rate theater man as Howard but not by any of the ordinary New York theater carpenters . . .

And that, if any man were to be paid for anything of the sort, it would have to be paid out of Barton's share, I having already sacrificed enough.

Also I did say, quite politely I think, that I wasn't in any great hurry. I have got the feeling that the play will inevitably get to Broadway and even that it will succeed there and so I can wait. I don't want any more butcheries. Do you blame me?

At least Mother the novel is an experiment and that makes it nice for me. I'm not going to hurry it. In reality I need something of this sort back of me, as a kind of wall at my back, a thing to do, to look forward to doing, a job if you please.

And this winter has shown me more than ever that I need E, about and with me. It will have to be worked out. It is a real marriage, at least for me, and her absence leaves me too footloose, up in the air, too much as though a part of me were gone.

It is nice to think that soon I will be turning the nose of the Chevrolet Northward again. Love to all in the house.

Sherwood

[New York]
[November 1936]

Dear Mother

I should be at work, instead of writing to you — a sadist, who keeps telling us she is coming to us & doesn't do it.

O.K. We'll come to her.

Save enclosed for E.

Mary gave a really beautiful dinner party. I'll whip that old lass into some decent shape yet.

I'll tell you all about the dream of Kit, in the movies, when I see you—

a long talk last night, with John Emerson.[46]

Still a kind of stunned feeling about the election, felt everywhere. It's going to be a great & real test for Franklin D.

Lincoln was abused and hated as he has been. At the war's end he had just such power and, in the North, universal acceptance as FDR has now. It sobered and dignified Abe.

It could ruin a man not really big. We'll see.

A possibility [of] an "Era of Good Feeling."

It has happened, a few times, in history.

A lot of love to all

S.A.

[New York]
Thursday [November 1936]

Dear Mother

Eleanor is leading a pretty fast life, working all day and playing all night — (Thank Heavens it won't last long) and I'm afraid hasn't much time to write so, you see, I give you our news.

1st That Libby Holman[47] is really at work on getting Winesburg done in New York — believes almost passionately in the play. She may pull it off.

2nd Scribners had two cablegrams from England yesterday making two offers of advances on an English edition of Kit — one for 70 pounds — one for 120 pounds. Of course, as you can imagine, I took the 120 which, with English tax, agents' commissions etc , will net us something less than $500. The publisher will be Hutchinson.

Mr Charles Studin[48] gave a big cocktail party for us last night, everyone there, a big jam, and Eleanor very lovely. She makes a hit with everyone. We went afterwards, some 10 of us, to dinner at Whit Burnett's[49] house, the whole evening great fun.

It is however hard on poor E, as people stay very late, myself lying in bed.

Love to all.

S.A.

Dear Mother . . .

As you see here we are, quite nicely settled in Mexico City, in a very comfortable, very bourgeois hotel, having a big parlor and bedroom at 10 pesos a day, a peso being about 28 cents, garage free, and it is so very nice that I have a notion we will just stay here, instead of going on to the other place we talked of. The hotel is The Geneve 7A De Londres Mexico City Mexico.

And what a drive down, over the most magnificent highway I have ever seen, at one point 8000 feet, such terrific vistas and it all so strange. You go through stretches as long as 80 or 90 miles with no towns at all, an utterly wild country, and then into tiny little Indian villages, the agriculture as primitive as that of Bible times, often the ground just scratched with a wooden plow hitched to an ox. There are desert wells, with the women in their native costumes gathered about, the water jars on their heads that make you think of Rebecca, and others, pure beasts of burden, carrying great packs on their backs. Also many trains of pack animals, always tiny burros, heavily loaded, with barefooted men and children driving them.

It would be impossible to tell you, in one letter, of the adventures with our amazing Mary,[50] her narrow escapes, fool things done, always with that amazing innocence of hers that makes you forgive everything. Anyway we got her here alive and as chipper as a sparrow. She is rather gorgeous at that.

The city seems beautiful although I have not been out in it, this being our first morning here, but E is already out and taking in the town. It is full of American tourists but we will escape them. At the edge of town the city furnishes, free, to us tourists, a guide, who takes the wheel and escorts you about, to wherever you want to go and stays patiently with you until you are settled. I think we shall be very happy here.

Lots of love to all

S.A.

Dear Mother.

I am ashamed that I have not written. I did write you a long letter, filled with deep gloom, but did not mail it. I got tired of my own gloom, bored with it. It is all, I dare say, due to the fact that I have not got hold of a theme that has really absorbed me, taken me out of myself.

I am still somewhat troubled by the sinus.

That for me. Eleanor seems particularly well and in fine spirits. She has, I'm sure, been writing. We stopped at Hedgerow and all seemed as usual there, with many new faces. Here the Millers[51] are moving out and really seem to want to go. It will be better than it has ever been here as we will not be under Mary's feet and she will not be under mine.

As for work I shall, I presume, just have to wait until I am ripe — go daily to my desk, sit down, perhaps pray. It seems I am only happy when self is a little gone.

Eleanor says you have been in bed. I do hope it is no real illness. Are you still in bed and do [did?] Mr C have a good time at Baltimore?

Mary is going away, for the week-end, to the Eastern Shore, and we will have the house to ourselves.[52] We will see Lewis and Nancy[53] also Paul Rosenfeld tomorrow. It may be Paul will come in to dine with us today. We went to see the preview of a new play "The Death of Danton," staged by Orson Wells. I saw Luise Sillcox[54] and hope to get her busy at clearing up the Winesburg thing.

Hope Aunt May is going strong — as usual.

Love to all.

Sherwood

[New York]
Wednesday morning
[October 1938?]

Dear Mother,

I am sorry to hear that you are still not well. E wonders if the anti-cold medicine we have all been taking has anything to do with it. I got from Mazy a prescription, a special kind of throat spray, that seems to be helping me.

To tell the truth Mother I am in one of my low periods and my own trouble may be more than half psychic. I have been terribly discouraged about my earning power. For example the story "A Chest of Drawers" sold for only $75.00. I have really earned nothing for a long time and find myself, pretty much, living on the generosity of two women, Eleanor and Mary.

It in some curious way hurts my pride, poisons my days. Can I write the sort of glamorous stuff now demanded? I probably couldn't if I tried.

Being in this low state of mind, I have the inclination to become, more and more, the recluse, bury myself in books. Although you are ill Mother you do have the work there that you do. E goes to her office. I go to my desk and write and then, day after day, destroy all I write.

What I need, I know, is an acceptance of defeat, to take it as man's lot, be as cheerful as I can. I get, alas, no satisfaction out of past achievements.

So that is my state. It is pretty bad. The one thing that holds me, makes me want to go on trying is my love of E. She is super fine Mother.

Much love to you and all in the house there.

S.A.

E wanted me to ask if the cloth for the suit given me by Ferdinand ever came.

[Olivet, Michigan]
Wednesday [January, 1939]

Dear Mother:

In relation to the new book of short stories . . . are you sure you are not somewhat prejudiced?[55] I am afraid so.

The check about which John Sullivan[56] inquired has been received, and I have written him to take it off his mind.

My present plan is to leave here on Saturday the 28th, spend the 28th and possibly the 29th driving to Yellow Springs, Ohio, where I am to be, for three days at Antioch, the 31st and February 1 and 2. Then it depends on Eleanor. There is some talk of our meeting in Washington and, if she does not meet me somewhere on the road, I will drive on to New York.

Frankly Mother when you say that we need God the words mean nothing to me.[57] I'm sorry but it has always been so. If however you say that we need constantly something from each other that most of us most of the time seem unable to give that indeed does mean a lot to me. What I am quite sure happens when we grow angry, flare up, is that we too often flare up at someone having nothing to do with the real cause of our anger and about something that is also not at the bottom of it.

There is one thing that I have found here that is, just now, good for me . . . I mean the opportunity for association with men. It has been good. There is always, perhaps always will be, a wall of a sort between men and women. One wants very much the society of women at times. They stir us into a new sharpness at times but then there comes also the need of men. I have had recently rather too little of the latter. It is good to have it for a time.

To be here has also brought up something else. There always is the question of my sticking to Mary. I think perhaps the real fly in that ointment is basically her lack of taste. It is hard to keep up an association with one who has so basically that lack. Sometimes it seems that it would be better to tackle almost anything than to try to go on with it.

Be sure of my love, dear Mother. What I say of women does not apply to two, yourself and Eleanor. And my love to the others.

Sherwood

TO J. J. LANKES[58]

Marion
January 29, 1929

Dear Mr. Lankes: —

I like both the bookplates, but to tell you the brutal truth, if you go on and finish one of them for me, I shall probably frame it and hang it up somewhere but will never put it in a book.

I do not much like the old bookplate idea, although I never saw any work of yours I did not like.

The boys in the shop also fall for it. The linotype operator asked me only the other day if I would give him one of your small things I have had framed.

The trouble with the bookplate idea, to my mind, it is a kind of assertion of the property rights in the book. Heavens knows, property rights are already asserted too much.

Yours truly,

Sherwood Anderson

[Marion]
[September 22, 1930 postmark]

Dear Lankes

I am leaving Marion for a few weeks. Your letter came, celebrating my birthday etc , sending the snap of Burchfield.[59] Well, I like his work, always have. He gets somewhere.

So do you, although they don't buy your stuff.

I don't know any such female. If I did what do you think. Would I turn you loose at her? Every man for his own shooting.

After all I don't have so much sympathy for us. We get kicked about a lot but how would you like to be one of them?

I'm going out to Chicago. I have a little car and I'm restless here. I've been working some but I want to smell the damn horizon. I may stay out there a week or two and then come back here. After that I think I'll go for two or three weeks to N. Y. I'd like to look about down there.

I'll sell my place. It's a country gentleman's place and I'm no good at that.

Keep putting the ball over the plate. What else is there to do.

S A

Marion
[July 11, 1931 postmark]

Dear Lankes

I am not at all surprised by the attitude of the publishers about the woodcut of my mug. They are just that way. My own publisher has long been using one made apparently from a photograph by some commercial artist. It makes me look pretty much like a middleweight prize fighter but I haven't cared much. You know how a man gets to feeling about his mug. He has to shave it every day. "The hell with him," he says after a time.

I have been working pretty steadily but am in a slump just now. You know what that means. A man doesn't give a goddamn for anything much until it passes.

Mrs Copenhaver, of whom I am tremendously fond, my one real friend here, has been dangerously sick for ten days and that has shaken me.

There have been steady rains every day for a week. It's hell not to be doing anything you like.

41

As Always

Sherwood Anderson

Dear Lankes

The picture came and is just what I wanted. It connects you with your work which, as you know I feel, is very beautiful. It will be good to have this much of you in my house.

You know I said once that your work did the thing I think most important. I can't remember how I said it. The idea is that it draws us closer. One of the strange and terrible things about American life is a kind of universal loneliness. It is so hard for us to get at each other. There was a woman came here yesterday. She was doing a thesis, for a degree, on my own work. I sat looking at her and hearing her words and I had [a] queer feeling that she was another no one had ever touched. I don't mean she hadn't been slept with. I didn't ask her about that. As you know I have lived a long time now among these mountain people in their poor little houses but, since I have had several of your things about, the houses have taken on a new significance and through the houses I know better the people in the houses. I am sure that is what you would want your work to mean. It does.

Affectionately

S Anderson

[Yellow Springs, Ohio]
January 30, 1939

Dear Lankes

I am afraid I'll be missing you in New York. I have been doing colleges a little myself, three weeks at a small college at Olivet, Michigan, and now here I am, for some days more at Antioch, at Yellow Springs, Ohio. I guess I know how you feel but damn it there doesn't seem to be any out. Wherever you turn you are stuck. They make you pay so damn much just to keep alive. Great God, there isn't any answer, a man just goes on, fighting for a little open space, a moment to breathe.

I am in a house, here in Antioch, and downstairs they have the radio on. Hitler is talking to the world and I have fled up here because it all makes me ill. I get it in the pit of the stomach, want to vomit.

So how can I write anything with any sense to it, with that voice in the house. They invade us more and more. Christ

Sherwood A

[Marion]
June 4, 1940

Dear Lankes:

I have been thinking about you a lot lately and am ashamed of myself that I have not written. To tell the truth I have been rather ill for the last month and am just pulling out of it. The whole thing may simply have been due to the war and the gloomy outlook for civilization.

I recently came down here to the country from New York and it is certainly good to be here where you can remember that grass grows and that water runs in the streams.

As there is nothing at all that fellows like you and I can do about the whole matter I made up my mind to try and stay away as much as possible from the newspapers and the radio and to try to get some work done. Perhaps it doesn't much matter what becomes of the work if a fellow can get a little absorbed in it and can, at least for a time, take his mind off what is going on in the world.

I agree with you that we are probably going into a new kind of civilization and God only knows what it will be like. It looks ugly enough from where I sit.

Anyway I am going to the farm now and paint the barn. That will be something to do.

I hope you will write me from time to time as I want very much to keep in touch with men like you.

As always

Sherwood Anderson

TO ALFRED STIEGLITZ[60]

New Orleans
April 22, 1925

My dear Stieglitz;

I am mighty glad that you and Paul agree with me in the Huebsch matter. Perhaps I had become rather sentimental about it. I suppose when you are going to do anything it is good morals to do it well. Between ourselves what I felt was that Mr. Huebsch was not a success as a publisher and that I was about the only man who had stuck to him. My leaving cannot help but give him a bad jolt. A fellow hates to kick any kind of man when he is down and this is just about what it comes to. I have to face that fact.

On the other hand, if my work is of any value at all there is no reason why it should not reach a larger public than it does and it will certainly take a load off my shoulders not to be constantly harassed by the effort to make a bare living.

Good things of this kind never come singly and as soon as this deal was closed I got a good advance offer for the serial rights of my "Childhood" book.[61] This I shall plunge into as soon as the novel is off my mind.

The novel will be finished early in May and I am calling it "Dark Laughter." I believe it is the most firmly put together piece of work I have done.

I am mighty sorry that Georgia[62] has to bother with selling her pictures but on the other hand meeting people, talking with them about her work may have its good sides as well as its bad sides. It is something like the lecturing business for me I fancy.

As is quite natural I am already feeling the effect of not being so worried by extraneous things and working better than I have for months, also I am in a good deal better shape physically.

I suspect that you have all your life had so much excess energy that you have always given more out of yourself to others than you can now afford to do. If you can really take life in a quieter way, see fewer people and live more in yourself you will not have such terrific times of going to pieces. I am pretty sure of that.

I hope Paul's book[63] is going to be a go but I am doubtful. His theme is one that only few will understand or care about, however he is writing better than ever before and that is the main thing, isn't it? My love to you both,

Sincerely,

Sherwood

44

TO CHARLES AND MABEL CONNICK[64]

[New Orleans]
[Early March 1926]

My Dear Charles and Mabel.

You must plan to come to Virginia. I fancy the late summer will be the best time for your comfort.

We will get at the house as soon as we get there. An architect friend[65] is making drawings. He makes some and brings them to the house — a patient man. We make changes every time.

Our idea is a story and a half house in front — heavy stone wall. Then two wings going out at the back — perhaps of logs — old ones square cut.

Wish we could consult with you about windows. Perhaps we can. I'll send you a drawing as soon as we get through changing it about.

The magazine came with your article. Wish we could have been over there with you. It must have been fun. Nice spirit in the article.

After my lecturing I was all in — dead. Ferdinand Schevill[66] came from Chicago and we loafed — lying on the levee in the sun — walking about. Last week I suddenly wrote two poems. Perhaps I'm coming back to life again.

I wish you knew Elizabeth and that Elizabeth knew Mabel.

Two weeks ago we had a great shock. I had a younger brother Earl — an unsuccessful painter who disappeared 15 or 18 years ago. He couldn't make a living and was ashamed of living on his brothers. In all these years no word from him.

Then he was picked up on the street in Brooklyn — a stroke. The doctors say he will get well. I am going to take him to the farm. — A silent sensitive man when he was young. My brother Karl found — in his room in Brooklyn — many drawings. He had been working as a baker for five years in that place — living alone — working on his drawing nights.

Elizabeth will be mighty glad to have the drawing.

But gladder — believe me — if she can really get to know you two this summer.

With Love

Sherwood

[Kansas City]
[January 19, 1933 postmark]

Dear Mabel.

I got your letter and it made me happy. The critics were rather second-rate about Beyond Desire I thought, but, in a dim way, I think I understand.

Isn't it just all a part of the decay that is going on? The day of the capitalist — the individual — is gone and making anything new is so hard. We all shirk it so we can do nothing but destroy.

Particularly the men. I have a kind of feeling it isn't so true of you women. I tried to say so in the book — Perhaps Women — but no one paid any attention. After all you women can't be so much concerned with the preservation of a thing that has so dirtied men, made them so cheap.

I think — in America — our dream was so childishly grand and gaudy that the come down is too much for us. I feel it everywhere in men — the drooping mouth, the small vanity.

Recently I have been working with another man — a New York playwright — on a dramatization of Winesburg and we placed the drama there — the attempt of a woman — Elizabeth Willard — of the story "Mother" — to turn her son away from the father's influence — embodying all the cheapness of American individualism.

I think we made a real play and while we were at it — for about a month — I never looked at a newspaper. Then I did look. Again I was amazed at the eternal concentration on the more trivial aspects of everything.

That man's story is America now Mabel and God help us if there isn't more hidden away in you women.

You see I'm on the drift. I got through the play and sent off the book of short stories[67] — a few of them 1st class — so I got into my little car and cut out. I needed people — new scenes etc.

I still alas have that beautiful Ripshin — standing empty and I still dream that you & Charles — or someone — real like you people — will come and take it and spend your summers there — in the hills — so I can have you near.

I can't afford the place myself and anyway don't want it alone.

I could have sold it to a cheap rich man — to take his whores to — but I wouldn't.

You & Charles write me — whenever you can. I always do count on you two. I'll come that way one of these days.

Sherwood —

Permanent address always Marion.

TO ARTHUR H. SMITH[68]

Marion
June 6, 1932

Dear Arthur H. Smith:

I received your letter with the copy of the little book — HISTORY OF WINESBURG, OHIO. It is very interesting to me. As I have stated before on several occasions, and as publicly as possible, I did not know that there was a real Winesburg, Ohio until at least a year after my book was published.

It was no doubt stupid of me. To make quite sure, I went at the time to consult a list of towns of the state, but I must have got hold of a list giving only those towns that are located on railraods. Imagine their arrogance in making such a list as that.

My dear sir, I do not believe you or any of the real citizens of your real town of Winesburg need feel arrogant toward the citizens of my imaginary WINESBURG and surely I, of all men, do not apologize for them. It is true that none of them were very successful in life. They did not become bankers, or stockbrokers, establish any of our great modern industries or rise to the management of great businesses, but were simple, good people who remained in obscurity in their own little village. Life hurt and twisted them. Lusts came to them. On the whole they remained sweet and good. Do not feel offended if I say that I hope that the real people of the real Winesburg are at bottom as decent and have in them as much inner worth.

As a preacher, you, at least, should know what I mean.

In your book you spoke of my book, concerning the people of my WINESBURG as a "burlesque." I forgive you for that word. I put it down to the fact that you are not familiar with the terms of literature. The book is, of course, in no sense a burlesque, but it is an effort to treat the lives of simple ordinary people in an American middle western town with sympathy and understanding. A great many critics have even said there is a tenderness in it. The book has had an interesting career. When first published, it was almost universally condemned — the average American looked upon it, as I dare say most of the citizens of the real Winesburg would look upon it at the first reading. It was called immoral and ugly. Even the word "filthy" was frequently used.

After a few years however this kind of condemnation of the book passed. I even dare say that people began to love the book. It has been translated since then into almost all the European languages. In Russia, the government had it printed and distributed and here in America, in its various editions, hundreds of thousands of people have bought and read it — I believe with sympathy and understanding.

Referring again to the people of the book — the people of my own WINESBURG — they are people I personally would be glad to spend my life with. Certainly, I did not write to make fun of these people or to make them ridiculous or ugly, but instead to show by their example what happens to simple, ordinary people — particularly the unsuccessful ones — what life does to us here in America in our times — and on the whole how decent and real we nevertheless are.

My dear Reverend Arthur H. Smith, I have enjoyed reading your own book about the real Winesburg but if you ever reprint it in another edition I beg of you to strike out the word "burlesque" in describing my own book about the imaginary people in my own imaginary WINESBURG, OHIO. The word is so very inaccurate.

If there is in the real Winesburg a local weekly paper, it would please me to have you send on to it this letter to be printed in Winesburg.

Also let me convey my greetings to the real Winesburgers. I trust they are all good kind god-fearing people. No doubt, they are.

Sincerely,

Sherwood Anderson

TO JAMES BOYD[69]

[Marion]
April 15, 1937

Dear Jim:

The wreck of the winter is forgotten and I am quite cheered up because I have been able to get a little work behind me. I have just been plowing straight through it and not looking back, and heavens knows what it will look like to me when I have to take the look back. However, just plowing is something.

It is too bad about Kate.[70] How late in the summer will you be staying down there?

We have been having a kind of family reunion here at Eleanor's home, her brother, an army doctor, having just returned from two or three years in the Philippines. This will break up on the twenty-second of this month when Eleanor and I are going to Washington and then to New York. We will be in New York at 54 Washington Mews until about the last week of May. I mention all these details because I am still wondering whether or not it is possible to have you with us here. If that can't be worked and you are still there in June we will try to get a week-end with you.

Tom Wolfe, Max Perkins and I had a rather gorgeous evening eating and drinking together in New York. You know how I feel about Max and I also fell hard for Tom. He seems to me pretty fine stuff, nothing slippery, nothing slick — a straight out man.

Tell Kate that Eleanor has a batch of pamphlets, clippings, etc., that she will send her in a few days.

There are many things to talk about. I hope I may see you soon.

Sincerely,

Sherwood Anderson

TO JOHN SULLIVAN[71]

[Ripshin]
September 19, 1939

Dear John:

I am leaving with you an outline of the things it seems to me it will pay us to do about the farm this fall and winter.

Sometime this fall I think it would be a good idea to clean out the hedge along the road. I notice some of the grape vines, young trees, etc. are getting a start again.

I have spoken to you about getting out and planting the young maples in front of the house.

You understand about getting out the apple trees over on the Swan place. As suggested I believe all this wood should be hauled in and piled with the other wood by the shed back of the house as it is cut, brush burned, etc. As you suggested it would also be a good thing to clear up the place where the old sawmill stood. If you could get a chance to talk to young Woods, you might ask him whether or not he wants the cull lumber left there. If he doesn't want it, we could haul it up and store it on the pile beside the green house.

As you suggested it would be a good idea to move the grapevine from the chickenyard and put it in front of the house. Some manure should be put about it and also about the grapevines that aren't doing very well near the pump. If we have enough manure to spare we ought to put some about all the grapevines in the vineyard.

I think we should enrich the island where the raspberries are planted and perhaps get some more plants and try to make a real raspberry patch of it.

There will be some climbing roses sent to you in April of next year. These I want to put around the wall before the house. We are going to try to get some roses that will come later in the year.

If you have any manure to spare I think it would be a big help if we could put some around each of the two grapevines by my cabin. You spoke of putting a grapevine where the rose was that died but I believe instead of doing that I would put there one of the climbing roses that are coming in April.

You understand about ordering new strawberry plants for the strawberry bed and I will send money for this at the proper time. I will leave it to you to order them. Also more carberry [?] roots if needed.

Before I go away I will leave you dynamite to blow out the stumps in the field above the cabin. I think you might also get rid of them in the field above the house.

I notice that some of the stones in the stone terrace in the front of the house are loose, particularly where the gate is near the apple tree where we park the car. I think a little cement will fix this.

There will be some wine left in cases in the cellar. I would like to take this out of the cases and just store the bottles in the cellar at the front of the house where the water does not come in, taking it out of the cases and storing the cases in the green house. I have got two new locks for the doors to this little cellar in the front of the house and will leave these padlocks with you.

I think it would be a good thing at the proper time to cut the suckers off the apple trees as they seem to be getting rather thick.

In the spring I would like to make two zinnia beds on each side of the steps of the two bark houses.

I do not think I will fool any more with delphiniums but will try to have about the same kind of flowers around the croquet ground that we had this year. We have some fine big zinnias and perhaps you can get some seeds from them each and some from the other flowers.

You understand about fixing the chicken yard for next year. I think we might have some of the small colored sun flowers up there as well as other flowers scattered around with the seed you put in.

If the prices are reasonable for green hams, I would like to buy about ten this year and have them cured. I will send you money for them. Many of these things we have talked about, John, and I am only making these notes to clear them out of my mind.

I think when the barn is done the yard should be all cleaned up. Take all the kindling over to your house as we have enough. Any good lumber should be piled over by the green house.

In the spring we will paint the barn. I think I will paint it red with the doors white.

It would be a good thing to get out posts for the fence beyond the barn as we will need to refence that new field along the road.

You understand about the trimming of the grapes. They do need some enriching I think. If the frost doesn't get them we will try spraying next year.

I think, John, if we could get a decent deal I'd like to buy all of that piece Will Privett got from Dan's husband. See if you can dicker with him as though you wanted it yourself.

Keep your ear to the ground for any talk of a store at the corner of Price's.

Keep good health.

Sherwood.

TO CHARLES COX [72]

Marion, Virginia
October 5, 1939

Dear Charles Cox:

Answering your letter about the American Way, the trouble is that what I tried to say at Salem was just that there was no such thing as The American Way. To me it seems just one of those phrases we use and does not mean much of anything. There is a rich man on a vast estate.

Is his way of life the American Way?

There is a criminal in court.

Is his way the American Way?

The Negro, the coal miner, the Georgia Cracker, the successful merchant, the Sunday School Superintendent, the gambler.

These are all Americans.

Whose way is the American Way?

Wouldn't it be better just to think of people as people. I am afraid of such phrases.

Sincerely yours

TO MARGARET BARTLETT[73]

[Los Angeles]
Monday evening
[December 11, 1939]

Dear Monte.

I dare say you are a good deal accused of living too much in a life created in your own mind . . . "in the clouds," they would say. It isn't really in the clouds, you know. It's pretty much just Monte, her reforming of others to fit into a mould she has made. It makes too much a sad wreck of fact and, what is worse, of relationships, dear child.

So you have built this picture of me, in your own mind, perhaps in the mind of your sister. Why? What is the satisfaction to you in that Monte?

Here is the simple fact. In the morning of the day I came out there, you coming to get me, I was at work on a complicated story. Now you will see how earthy I am. I needed to go to the toilet. I didn't. I was too absorbed.

The result a pounding headache all day and all evening. If there was a shaking of the head that was it. Naturally I didn't want to mention it (you drive me to it) and did want to meet your sister again and also her husband. When I got out of the house that night I was so half blind with pain that I could scarcely drive home and later sat up in a chair all night.

You see you do deserve a spanking. There is something you don't seem to understand but you are a grown woman and as you have written me this really nasty letter, implying, as it did, that I felt above your sister and her husband, I guess I'll just give you the spanking.

Don't you, won't you see, my dear, how all such notions destroy all human relationships? Really you make me feel that you think of me as something like a damn movie star.

There was your brotherinlaw I instinctively liked, Gene I liked a lot too. I had hinted to you that I didn't like at all the trick of calling attention to me, as you did in the presence of Don Caples and again, alas, in your sister's house. Didn't you see how I tried and tried to drag the conversation away from self, to something (horses) such a fine mutual interest your brotherinlaw and I had . . .

We were speaking of Kentucky, the Knight farm, a house there, in which La Fayette once slept, something about a special room built . . .

You . . . "We will have to build a special room to our house because Sherwood slept there."

That sort of thing, playing across my nerves, already racked with the pain my dear, when I was so liking the people I was with, feeling them so warm and friendly.

Can't you see how I love to lose myself in people, how it is my life, how I hate that false sort of thing, destroying everything.

That's where the poison is, my dear.

And I can't help wondering if you have said something to the others, I so liked, implying something of what is in your so terrible letter.

There's your spanking my dear. It was coming to you. It may be that, if we could see more of each other, we might get on a basis of real friendship. Do you think you could drop that nonsense?

Sherwood

Am leaving in the early morning. If you will take back the nasty suggestion of your letter and story, write me and say so to the Pioneer Hotel — Tucson, Ariz.

If you still feel I am the impossible ass the letter suggests, forget it.

TO CARROW DE VRIES[74]

New York
January 17, 1940

Dear Carrow De Vries:

I am delighted that you found something in LAVENGRO. There are some more books of his you might enjoy. One called THE BIBLE IN SPAIN, the other THE ROMANY RYE. I think the more you read THE MEMOIRS OF A SPORTSMAN, the more you will get out of it.[75] Definite pictures are made that stay in the mind. The more you think of them, the more complete I think you will find them.

I am not much alarmed by what you speak of as your laziness. We are all lazy. Perhaps, in this matter of writing, we should all be willing to wait until the urge within us is so strong that it cannot be resisted. After many years of work, I have myself found that about two-thirds of all I do has to be thrown away.

However, I do go to my desk and my work every morning. If I can do nothing else, I write letters to my friends. I do it very much as a professional golfer goes to the golf course to practice his shots. But then, you see, I am a professional writer.

I was delighted to hear from you. Give my best regards to Mrs. De Vries.

Sincerely,

Sherwood Anderson

TO JACQUES CHAMBRUN[76]

New York
November 28, 1940

Dear Jacques Chambrun:

A man named Warren Wade of NBC came in to see me one day recently. He is a fat man, rather of the actor type. He had read the review of my latest book in the Sunday Times and had got and read some of my books.

He had got some idea into his head about getting a sponsor and doing a small town stunt on the radio. It seems that most of such small town programs have rather made fun of small town people. He suggested that my stuff was more human and said he would like to work with me on such a program.

Of course, I merely stalled him off. I am afraid that if there were anything in such an idea he would hardly be the type of man I would care to work with.

However Mr. Chambrun, my talk with him did put an idea into my head. As you know most Americans, even in our cities, were born and brought up in American small towns. I was a country editor of a small town weekly newspaper for several years. During that time I did all of the work myself, was editor, reporter, advertising manager, secretary, treasurer, and everything else on the paper. I couldn't afford any reporters so I invented them.

There was an imaginary young mountain boy named Buck Fever in my employ. For several years he conducted a column in my paper. For a long time the people in the town thought there actually was such a boy.

I invented also a lady named Mrs. Homing Pigeon, a rather charming lady, deeply interested in the town and in public affairs. She was a very public spirited lady I assure you.

There were other purely imaginary figures who worked for me when I ran the paper, and I rather do think, Mr. Chambrun, that, as nowadays many Americans look back with rather longing eyes to the small towns, it might be entirely possible to make a very absorbing weekly program of the every day life in an imaginary American small town, the working of local politics, the passing of the seasons, the small town courts, the school, the local uplift movements and the feelings of the people in their every day life in a typical American small town.

I made a book of such happenings out of my own experiences as a small town weekly newspaper editor. The book is called "Hello Towns." The book would, I think, give you an idea of what I mean, a kind of small town editor of the air, as it were.

Now I am not sure that I would want to do such a thing but this man's coming to me did start my mind working on such an idea and I thought I would like you to think about it and to know what you think. It might be worthwhile doing as there is, I am sure, just now a kind of hunger in people to get back nearer to the soil. I am thinking of something that might come from the editor of an imaginary small town newspaper called the Grape Vine News, a sort of weekly story of the soil, towns, and the seasons, telling something of the news of the farms and the towns through the year and feeding this hunger in people. If such a thing turned out to be a real idea it would have to be something sponsored by a really decent sort of sponsor. That is to say, if I were to take it on.

Anyway I thought I would put it up to you.

Sincerely yours,

Sherwood Anderson

NOTES

1 Chicago artist and his wife, close friends of Anderson.

2 Frederick O'Brien, *White Shadows in the South Seas* (1920).

3 The Blums had gone to Tahiti in June 1920.

4 Mentioned in *Story Teller's Story* (1924), pp. 359-60.

[5]Published with the title *The Triumph of the Egg.*

[6]"New Orleans, *The Double Dealer* and the Modern Movement in America," *Double Dealer* 3 (1922), 119-26.

[7]Portions of *A New Testament* were published serially beginning in 1919.

[8]Bernardine Szold Simons, Chicago friend of the Andersons, and Otto Liveright, Anderson's literary agent.

[9]Elizabeth Prall, later Anderson's third wife.

[10]April 5, 1924.

[11]Robert Anderson.

[12]New York advertising man and collector, and his wife.

[13]Emmett wanted Anderson's manuscripts and later collected a large number of them.

[14]His country home, "Ripshin," under construction near Troutdale, Virginia.

[15]Robert Benchley, "A Ghost Story (As Sherwood Anderson Would Write It If He Weren't Prevented)," *Life* 86 (Dec. 3, 1925), 21, 64.

[16]Earl Anderson. See letter to the Connicks, early March 1926.

[17]American author and vagabond.

[18]Emmett had sent Anderson a clipping concerning the court case of a marriage between a brother and sister who had been raised apart.

[19]Cleveland B. Chase, *Sherwood Anderson* (New York: R. M. McBride, 1927).

[20]Lawrence S. Morris, "Sherwood Anderson: Sick of Words," *New Republic* 51 (1927), 277-79, which concludes: "The author of 'Winesburg, Ohio,' is dying before our eyes."

21"Every friend in power is a friend lost," *The Education of Henry Adams* (Boston: Houghton Mifflin, 1918), p. 248.

22Emmett discharged this debt in a note written in March 1932 at the bottom of the letter.

23Anderson was working on the dramatic version of *Winesburg, Ohio* which was first presented June 30, 1934.

24Anderson and Eleanor Copenhaver were married July 6, 1933.

25Arthur Barton, New York playwright, who had been collaborating with Anderson on the *Winesburg* play.

26Wallace was then Secretary of Agriculture.

27*Kit Brandon,* dedicated to Mary Pratt Emmett.

28Paul Rosenfeld, music critic, author, close friend of Anderson.

29Laura Scherer Copenhaver, prominent Marion resident and Lutheran churchwoman, later Anderson's mother-in-law.

30Katharine and Henry Van Meier, sister and brother-in-law of Eleanor Copenhaver, Stillwater, Minnesota.

31Mazie Copenhaver Wilson, youngest daughter of Laura Copenhaver.

32Probably Mary Chryst Anderson, wife of Robert Anderson.

33Anderson's daughter Marion and her husband Russell M. Spear.

34May Scherer, Laura Copenhaver's unmarried sister.

35Hotel Albert.

36Marion residents. Anderson had ridden the train to New York on the previous day.

37*Beyond Desire.*

38Catherine M. Carswell, *Savage Pilgrimage: A Narrative of D. H.*

Lawrence (1932).

39Randolph Copenhaver, Laura Copenhaver's son.

40Katharine Scherer Cronk, sister of Laura Copenhaver and Lutheran Church official.

41Robert Anderson.

42Prominent Marion family.

43Anderson had become an editor of *American Spectator*.

44Amoebic dysentery. Eleanor Anderson had previously contracted the disease.

45Head of Dramatic Publishing Company in Chicago, close friend of Anderson.

46Childhood friend, later actor and playwright, husband of Anita Loos.

47Broadway star of musical comedy, famous for her "torch song" delivery.

48New York attorney, frequent giver of parties for writers, artists, and musicians.

49Short story writer and from 1933 the editor of *Story*.

50Mary Emmett.

51The Ashley Millers, friends of the Emmetts.

52The Andersons were staying in the home of the Emmetts at Washington Mews.

53Lewis Galantière, writer and translator, and his wife Nancy, an artist.

54Executive Secretary of the Authors League of America from 1926 to 1961 and active crusader for the rights of American authors.

55She had written Anderson that his contribution to an anthology of short stories was the best in the book.

⁵⁶Caretaker at Ripshin.

⁵⁷She had written: "We need God in order to have some one who can forgive us — wash us clean."

⁵⁸Virginia woodcut artist.

⁵⁹Realist painter of rural and small-town scenes.

⁶⁰Noted photographer and champion of modern painting.

⁶¹*Tar,* published serially in *Woman's Home Campanion.*

⁶²Georgia O'Keeffe, American painter and wife of Stieglitz.

⁶³Paul Rosenfeld's *Men Seen* (1925).

⁶⁴Stained-glass artist and his wife.

⁶⁵William Spratling.

⁶⁶Professor of History at the University of Chicago, close friend of Anderson.

⁶⁷*Death in the Woods* (1933).

⁶⁸Methodist minister, author of *History of Winesburg, Ohio.* Anderson published this letter in a slightly revised form in the *Smyth County News,* July 7, 1932.

⁶⁹Novelist, whose best-known works were *Drums* and *Marching On.*

⁷⁰Boyd's wife, Katharine.

⁷¹Anderson's caretaker for many years at Ripshin.

⁷²Cox had written to Anderson from Jefferson Senior High School in Roanoke, Virginia. The school magazine was to have an issue on "The American Way," and Cox asked Anderson for his "respected opinion and thoughts on our theme."

[73]Writer from Reno, whose father, a judge, had granted Anderson's divorce from Tennessee Mitchell in 1924.

[74]Michigan author. De Vries quotes part of this letter in his essay "The Essence of Sherwood Anderson," *Artesian* (Winter 1958), 24-8.

[75]The first three books mentioned are by George Borrow; the last is by Ivan Turgenev.

[76]Anderson's New York agent.

SHERWOOD ANDERSON ON *POOR WHITE*

Eleanor Copenhaver

(Editors' note: Eleanor Copenhaver, who was to become Mrs. Sherwood Anderson in 1933, conducted this interview with Anderson late in 1931. It was submitted by her as a class paper to Professor Carter Goodrich of Columbia University on January 16, 1932. The interview is here published with Mrs. Anderson's permission, from a copy in her possession. An earlier draft, now in the Newberry Library, shows suggested changes in Anderson's holograph.)

I took from the list the novel *Poor White.* The author lives in my own Virginia town. I thought I could see him there, during the holidays, and get from him the economic background out of which came his impulse to write the book. I took with me a stenographer and after explaining the object of the inquiry, I asked some questions and have put down the answers.

Q. "Will you tell me a little of the economic background of your childhood and of the changes that must have gone on in your home town to give you the impulse to write *Poor White?*"

A. "The question is interesting. I wrote the novel, *Poor White,* having in mind the town as the hero of the book rather than the people of the town. I do not think this was realized when the book was published. None of the critics mentioned it. It happened that my native town was a good place to study a tremendous change that was going on all through the Middlewestern country when I was a child and a young boy. At that time towns that are now big industrial centers, like Akron, Youngstown, Muncie, and Anderson in Indiana, Lima, Ohio, and many other towns that might be mentioned, were just such villages as the one I lived in. The original village had been on an old turnpike and there was a little old brick inn and remnants of old store buildings. With other boys I used to go there when I was small. The new town had been built almost a mile away on the railroad. The coming of the railroads had already made a new town and a new kind of town life.

"There was left, however, much of the old life. The streets were unpaved, people burned coal oil lamps. I remember when I was a boy eight years old being taken on an excursion of twenty miles to see a town lighted by electricity. I remember the wonder of the people talking on the streets. 'They light a whole town in one second.'

"In the very street in which I lived there were several small workshops. There was the wheelwright, the blacksmith, the carriage maker. My father worked in a harness shop. All harnesses were cut out of hides and made by hand.

"Already shoes were made in factories. The coming of the factory was in the air as I have tried to describe in *Poor White*. If you will take the book, which I see you have in your hand there, and turn to page 128, you will see how I have tried to dramatize the thing I am talking about.

"If you please, let me take the book. Let me read you something. This is on page 130. 'A vast energy seemed to come out of the breast of earth and infect the people. Thousands of the most energetic men of the middle States wore themselves out in forming companies, and when the companies failed, immediately formed others.'

"I do not believe I will continue to try to read from the book. It excites an author after several years to get a book of his own in his hands. I might be tempted to read you the whole book.

"The idea is of a great awakening to the possibilities of machinery. There is a vast energy in the people. It is a new country. You should bear in mind, that the people who came to America and went west over the mountains to the Middlewest were physically, at least, people of great energy.

"They must have been primarily physical. Poets, scholars, and thinkers do not become pioneers.

"These people have brought with them, however, the tradition of their old European life. In *Poor White*, I have devoted pages to trying to describe this old life.

"But I do not want you to think that there was no poetry in the new life.

The whole industrial impulse, when it began, was tinged and colored by a tremendous idealism. I remember as a small boy going to a photographer in our town who read to me through long Sunday afternoons from Bellamy's *Looking Backward.* The book had a great vogue. It expressed for America at that time just about what the dream of communism must express just now for the whole western world.

"Why, I could talk to you on this subject all afternoon. Think of the things implied. The hugeness of the country, the mines, the vast undeveloped richness, oil wells, gas wells, the millions of square miles of fertile prairie. Nature had been depositing wealth for millions of years in this new land and into which these people had suddenly come.

"You must remember this also that the emphasis on industry was inevitable in such a land. The country simply could not have been settled without the railroads. Without the railroads, I do not believe the United States could have remained one country. As soon as the people passed over the mountains, out of the comparatively small and unfertile coast states and got into this broad new empire, transportation became immensely important.

"But I am afraid I am getting away from what you want me to talk about."

Miss Copenhaver: "No, go on. Transportation bears on the subject."

Mr. Anderson: "No, I will return to the town. In *Poor White* I have tried to dramatize the effect of the coming of industry upon a people that have suddenly come out of Europe, out of an old civilization into America. I have tried to show how the growth of industry affected all the life of every citizen of the town, how almost at once it began to kill off old leaders and make new leaders, how and why money became of increased importance, how the new life affected marriage and all of the relationships between all of the people of the town.

"I am sure you do not want me to talk all evening, but I wish you would read the scene where Steve, who is taken as the prototype of the new leader-man in America, is approaching the man he wants to use, the inventor. You see Steve has his dream, too. As I remember it, he walks up and down at night afraid to approach the little telegraph office where the inventor sits.

"You see that inventor is terribly important to him with his new American dream. If he can get his hands on an invention and control it, he can at once exploit it and grow rich in the exploitation. He already dreams of that.

"He does get control of the invention and does exploit it. The first attempt at manufacture fails. This is interesting, too. It shows, I think, how the industrialists have been able to make the people pay for their experiments. They did it later with the bicycle and with the automobile. You will see that everyone in the town of Bidwell, Ohio, was ruined by the failure of the first factory — except Steve, the promoter.

"I think the same thing was later done with railroads. It was done with automobiles. To our own town there came first a bicycle factory and then later an automobile factory. The automobile factory was later absorbed into the organization now known as General Motors. This organization simply bought the plant in my home town to get rid of it. They closed it up. The town never succeeded in becoming a great industrial center as did Akron, for example.

"But that is not the point. The point is that a new life was made. The new man growing up in the town, who went to work in the factories, did not have the same connections with life his father had, his father having learned one of the old trades.

"I have tried to make *Poor White,* as I have explained to you, a dramatic story of this change. Now are there any questions you would like to ask?"

Q. "Then you think, Mr. Anderson, that all of this had something to do with the breaking up of individualism?"

A. "I think I can answer the question from the book itself. Let me find the place. Here it is. Let me read you a little from page 62. 'A new force that was being born into American life and into life everywhere all over the world was feeding on the old dying individualistic life. The new force stirred and aroused the people. It met a need that was universal. It was meant to seal men together, to wipe out national lines, to walk under seas and fly through the air, to change the entire face of the world in which men lived.' "

Q. "Did you mean to imply by the title that class cleavage was implicit in the coming of industry?"

A. "I think so. You have to think of it as against a background of agricultural life. Bear in mind that the men of an earlier day in the Middlewest who were most respected were men like Jefferson. Everything about industry implied something new. It implied group investment of capital, men living on dividends of companies for which they did not work. Instead, their capital worked for them. In the old life, the individual was, it is true, a small capitalist. He owned his own farm or his own little shop, but he also worked in it. He controlled it.

"The coming of industrialism meant a new kind of man in control. Many times an investor never saw the man who controlled his capital.

"For example, a man who controlled the factory erected in the town of Bidwell might be a New York financier who never visited the city.

"And this implies something interesting, too. Somewhere in the book I have talked of this, of the Morgans, Rockefellers, etc., as new gods. These men loomed large in the imaginations of men. They became half-mythical figures.

"You should read some of the periodical literature of about 1900. You will be surprised to find how much the newspapers and magazines of that day were filled with panegyrics of such men. Many times, bear in mind, not inventors, not scientists, not scholars, not thinkers, they were exploiters. At that time these men were held up as the heroes of American life. Think what effect this must have had on the attitude toward life of the young Americans."

Q. "Do you think Americans are less responsive to the suggestion of political control in their affairs than the European peoples? And why?"

A. "You must bear in mind that America was a new country. The American man had cut loose from an old European civilization. He cut loose because he dreamed that in America he would find a new life. Classes were to be wiped out. It was to be a real democracy. No matter what they actually did, all of the early leaders of thought in America talked about democracy. Of course, this influenced the American workman in a way the European never could have been influenced. It made a different man of him with a different kind of dream.

"In *Poor White* I have tried to show this dream in the old harness maker who was himself a laborer, but who invested his savings in the factory. You should read the passage where he goes at night and kneels before the machine. That could never have happened in Europe. You cannot take people and give them such a splendid dream as they had in coming to America and then expect them to be like the less adventurous people who stayed at home in Europe. There is something that I would like to say to you of that small town life. I remember that as a boy in the kind of small town of the Middle-west I have described in *Poor White* what men were always saying to me.

"It happened that my own people were poor. There was in the town a kindly feeling for the boys of my own family. The solid men of the town wanted us to succeed in life. I remember how persistently they said to me over and over: 'Succeed! Make money! Money makes the mare go.'

"Now I do not believe this implies that the Americans are money-minded. If you want money-minded people go to the French peasants or the French lower middle-class man. Look how Americans throw their money away. You do not throw away the thing you love. To the Americans money is the symbol of a dream. It is this dream in the people expressed by industrialism, cutting across the old and often laborious and brutal individualistic life, that I think makes the drama of the novel *Poor White,* and it is for this reason that I said to you in the beginning that the town and not the people of the town should be taken as the hero of the book."

AN INTERVIEW WITH MRS. SHERWOOD ANDERSON

Conducted by Charles E. Modlin and
Hilbert H. Campbell, August 23, 1975,
at Rosemont, Mrs. Anderson's home
in Marion, Virginia.

Q: Mrs. Anderson, we would like to establish for the record some information about your own education and career. Were you born June 15, 1896?

A: Yes, but do you have to put that in?

Q: With your permission, yes.

A: Well, all right.

Q: Where were you educated?

A: I graduated from Westhampton College of the University of Richmond in 1917 with a major in English. I taught high school English in Marion during 1917-1918. I attended Bryn Mawr College from 1918 to 1920. The summer of 1919 I worked as camp director for College Settlement in New York.

Q: Excuse me, did you take any degree at Bryn Mawr?

A: I received a two-year certificate in Social Work — Social Economy it was called then.

Q: Mrs. Anderson, you were for many years a prominent official with the national YWCA. Can you tell us when you were first affiliated with the YWCA?

A: Yes, I went directly to the YWCA from Bryn Mawr; that would have been the fall of 1920.

Q: What position did you hold with the YWCA?

A: From 1920 to 1923, I was assigned to social work in rural communities. From 1923 to 1947 I was with the Industrial Program of the National YWCA, of which I served as head from 1937 to 1947. I later worked in Italy and Germany and did quite a bit of consultant and liaison work for the YWCA with both Federal and State Departments of Labor.

Q: Did you not also attend Columbia University?

A: Yes, I took the M. A. in Political Economy from Columbia in 1933. I wrote a thesis for Professor Carter Goodrich, using material from a YWCA study made in early 1932 of women's working conditions in San Francisco. Four of us conducted the study in, as I recall, March, April, and May of 1932. Such studies were massive, and we carried them out in other cities also, including Kansas City and Chicago.

Q: You obviously continued to work with the YWCA after your marriage to Sherwood Anderson.

A: Oh yes, and for many years after his death. I had taken an eight-month leave when we started the trip to South America in early 1941.

Q: When did you retire from the YWCA?

A: In 1961.

Q: We are sitting in your beautiful old family home, Rosemont. Can you tell us something about your family's residence here?

A: I have a lot of written material on that. Do you want it?

Q: Yes, but perhaps you would comment just briefly.

A: All right. You know that Rosemont is much older than my family's association with it. My maternal grandfather, Reverend John Jacob Scherer, bought it in 1878. The house was built earlier, but my grandfather added to it. My father put on the porch, for which he was accused of ruining the architecture.

Q: When did Rosemont come into the possession of your father, Bascom E. Copenhaver, and your mother, Laura Scherer Copenhaver?

A: That would have been in 1920, when they bought it from the Scherer heirs.

Q: Both your mother and your father were prominent people. Could you comment briefly on their occupations and accomplishments?

A: My father was County Superintendent of Schools in Smyth County for thirty-six years. He started moonlight schools for adults who could not read and write. He served on the State Board of Education and was at one time on the Board at Radford College. He was active in community affairs.

Q: And your mother?

A: My mother was very active in church affairs. She wrote a great many religious pageants for the national Lutheran and other churches. She wrote hymns, including "Heralds of Christ," which is in the hymn books of several denominations. She traveled a great deal to speak at regional and national religious meetings.

Q: And she was a teacher?

A: Yes, she taught English at Marion College for more than thirty years.

Q: What about her writing other than religious works?

A: She wrote a great many things, some of which were published in magazines like *Harper's, Scribner's,* and the *Atlantic Monthly.* She published a book called *An Adventurous Quest.* She also wrote fairy stories for

69

children which were not published.

Q: And the Rosemont Craft Industries, now called Laura Copenhaver Industries, was started by your mother?

A: Yes, but that's too long a story. In the 1920's, when she was publicity agent for the Farm Bureau, she conceived the idea of getting money for poor mountain people through a crafts industry. They could combine their wool, their skill in weaving, and their traditional patterns to make quilts, rugs, etc.

Q: This is a fascinating subject, but we must get back to you. When did you first meet Sherwood Anderson?

A: In 1928, but I can't give you an exact date. I met him in this room where we are sitting. He and my mother were already friends before I met him.

Q: How did your mother meet him?

A: He walked by the house, was impressed with it, and came to call. I think he fell in love first with the house, then with my mother, and then with me.

Q: Had you read Anderson's books before you met him?

A: Yes indeed. I especially liked *A Story Teller's Story.*

Q: Apparently your father was not overjoyed at the idea of your marrying Sherwood. What were his objections?

A: All right, I'll answer that. My father felt that Sherwood was too old and had been married too many times. But that all changed. They became friends. They were never congenial in the way that Sherwood and Mother were, but they admired each other at a distance and became in a sense real friends.

Q: Sherwood sometimes called your mother his editor. What did he mean by this?

A: Well, Sherwood has written a good deal about that. I know that he admired her very much as a critic and as an editor. She was severe with him, and he would listen to her. For — let's say — a twelve-year period, she worked on his writings.

Q: That would be a period beginning as early as 1929?

A: Certainly; it might have been as early as 1928, but I'm not certain.

Q: What type of criticism did she offer him?

A: I'm no critic, and specifics are hard to recall now. But Mother was extremely well-read, and she had no reservations about offering sharp and detailed criticisms. I remember that she would try, in a joking way, to get him to do what the critics said he couldn't do — that is, to write novels with a complete, finished quality, to round out his endings.

Q: Do you feel that she had any substantial impact on the kind and quality of his writing during the period of their association?

A: That is a hard one. Yes, I would say so. He didn't always listen to her, but he always respected her judgment.

Q: Were her criticisms basically artistic rather than moral?

A: Oh yes. She never tried to reform him. Sherwood and Mother were real friends. He would jokingly tell her that she was not a puritan or a good Lutheran, and she would tell him that he was not a good pagan.

Q: The standard line in Anderson criticism is that your influence was important in developing Sherwood's awareness of social problems in the early 1930's. Would you comment on that?

A: Sherwood used to joke about my having made him a radical. Of course I didn't. He was well formed long before he met me. He did travel around a lot with me to mills and industrial conferences, and this put him in touch with a lot of other people.

Q: Did Sherwood ever help you with your reports and articles?

A: Yes, he did; but let's don't create a scandal. He helped me with many reports and articles and sometimes wrote them up himself. I was getting paid sometimes for work he did. For example, one report I published in the YWCA magazine on a famous AFL convention in Florida was written entirely by Sherwood. Maybe this was dishonest, but shouldn't the YWCA be grateful?

Q: During the years you were married to Sherwood, how much of the year did you spend at Ripshin and how much elsewhere?

A: We were typically at Ripshin from May to October, at least insofar as I could get vacations or time off from the YWCA. And I did some of my work at Ripshin. We never stayed at Ripshin in the winter, since the house then had no heating system. In the winters we would be in New York or traveling. We would come back to Marion for Christmas. We made trips to southern Arizona, to the Rio Grande valley, to the West Coast, and to Acapulco — before it was famous.

Q: Did Sherwood get bored after awhile in the country at Ripshin?

A: Never, I think.

Q: Besides writing, what were his pastimes at Ripshin?

A: Well, we delighted in entertaining a few friends at Ripshin — Paul Rosenfeld for example. And we were both very fond of taking walks.

Q: What about farming?

A: Sherwood spent a great deal of energy studying pamphlets from the VPI Extension on ways to improve the land. He tried to enrich the fields, but of course that is rugged, poor land over there. Henry Wallace visited us at Ripshin when he was Secretary of Agriculture. Sherwood asked him how he could improve the land, and Wallace told him he should just let it go. Sherwood kept cows and tried to make different kinds of cheeses. He made wine and cider. He was very proud when he could bring in a bushel or two of peppers, which he sold to local stores. He never attempted tobacco.

Q: Did the farm ever earn any money?

A: No.

Q: Did Sherwood ever buy moonshine?

A: Not that I recall. We didn't drink very much then; for one thing we couldn't afford it. Wait a minute. Sherwood must have brought some moonshine to a dinner party we had here. There is a famous story about that. My innocent father, thinking it was water, served it to General Lee's niece and got her drunk. My poor father didn't know what he had done. That story went all over town.

Q: Was Sherwood Anderson a well-read man?

A: Well, how do you define "well-read"? He was reading constantly, and I think of him as well-read. He did sometimes try deliberately to give the impression of being a small-town lightweight.

Q: What do you remember his reading?

A: Much about his reading has been written down by Sherwood and others. He was constantly reading the Russians — Turgenev, Dostoevsky, Gorky, Chekhov. George Borrow was a favorite writer. He read the King James Version over and over. He repeatedly read Shakespeare's sonnets. He owned and read a great many books on the Civil War. He had great favorites among the Civil War historians; some he couldn't bear. Sometimes he liked to get dull books, just pick up anything to put him to sleep.

Q: Mrs. Anderson, what writers come to mind as those whom your husband admired most or was closest to during the 1930's?

A: He had a very large acquaintance among literary people. I could give you a few names which come to mind, but it would be only a fragmentary list. Dreiser, of course. O'Neill, although there was not a long-standing friendship as with Dreiser. Paul Green. Jim Boyd. Sherwood admired John Cournos very much and thought he was unappreciated. And Gertrude Stein, of course.

Q: Was Sherwood ever annoyed by the large number of would-be writers who sent him manuscripts or requests for advice?

A: No, he was unusually good about that. I think he perhaps spent too much time with such requests. Sometimes manuscripts would come in without even stamps enclosed.

Q: Was Sherwood Anderson ever a communist?

A: I get tired of people asking me whether Sherwood was a communist. To the best of my judgment, he was not. We know that he went to that world conference, which was semi-communist. We know that he and Dreiser joked about being communists.

Q: Were you more or less radical than Sherwood in the 1930's?

A: Goodness! Well, I don't know. We were both very much for those southern trade-unionists. And I guess we knew in a way that Gastonia was communist. But the rest of those strikes weren't communist, weren't communist dominated.

Q: Did you ever consider youself to be a communist?

A: Oh no! Who said so? I was on the Committee for the Spanish Loyalists. You wouldn't regard that as communist, would you?

Q: What do you know about Sherwood Anderson's religious beliefs?

A: That is very difficult; I don't think I can give a clear answer. You could say he was anti-church in a sense. He saw through a lot of insincere ministers.

Q: Did he attend church in Marion?

A: No, except for funerals and weddings. He had friends among the ministers, but he would sit on the courthouse steps when other people were in church.

Q: Was he religious in any sense?

A: Oh, of course. He was deeply religious, I think. But I don't know how to explain it. He disliked hypocrisy, but he was respectful of the good the churches did. He was very respectful of my mother's beliefs.

Sherwood was an ardent student of the Bible, but I guess I'd have to say he was skeptical about most of the churches.

Q: Did he believe in an afterlife?

A: I'd better say I don't know.

Q: Could you briefly mention some recreational activities that Sherwood enjoyed?

A: Certainly. Walking. Gathering mushrooms. Fishing. Not hunting; he wouldn't shoot animals. But he did love to fish. He was passionately fond of driving his automobile. Croquet, of course, which he played over a long period of time. He liked to follow baseball. To the end of his life he enjoyed horse races and went whenever he could.

Q: Which literary figures that you met during the 1930's did you admire?

A: I loved Dreiser.

Q: Why?

A: Goodness, what a question! Why do you admire anybody? Well, although he wasn't attractive, he was so obviously honest. I liked Gertrude Stein very much. She wasn't supposed to like women, but we got along unusually well. Of course, I was careful not to horn in on her talks with Sherwood.

Q: Wasn't it expected that the wife would talk to Alice B. Toklas?

A: That's right. When my sister gave a dinner party in Minnesota for Gertrude, my sister and I were left with Alice.

Q: What about Thomas Wolfe?

A: Well, you already know that story. I liked him, but he was very neurotic when he thought someone was criticizing him. At a party in Washington Mews, I said to him, "Tom, they say you're Jewish." I was jokingly referring to something I had read in a piece in the *New Republic* or the *Nation.* He jumped up and screamed. And a few days later he took it out on Sherwood at the Brevoort Hotel. In front of a large crowd, he screamed at Sherwood that I had a wonderful mother but my father was a Jew.

Q: In what parts of the day would Sherwood do his writing?

A: He very definitely worked in the morning, usually "warming up," as he called it, by writing letters to friends and associates. He rarely worked in the afternoons or at nights.

Q: Did he have his good and bad days as a writer?

A: Certainly. Some days he just couldn't write. He'd say, "The pen wouldn't move."

Q: What did he do on the days that he couldn't write?

A: If he were at Ripshin, he would pick mushrooms, go fishing, visit Andy Funk; or he would read or sit and talk to Mother.

Q: What about the good days?

A: He would work about four hours in the morning. He got up regularly at 7:30, had a light breakfast, and went off to the writing cabin. I would take coffee down to him at about 11:00.

Q: What would you do while he was working?

A: I had a desk in the small cabin near the house and wrote up YWCA reports. I also did a little housekeeping, but we always had two or three mountain girls helping us, so I can't really say I was a household drudge.

Q: Were you able to help Sherwood in any way with his writing?

A: He would sometimes discuss his work or ask me to read it. Sometimes I'd make a few suggestions but not often. Usually I would just check spelling and punctuation.

Q: Wasn't Sherwood interested in writing a history of the Civil War?

A: Absolutely. He discussed it with Gertrude Stein and Lloyd Lewis; they were going to collaborate. When you read some of Sherwood's letters, you might think he was joking, but he always meant to do that. He was especially interested in Lincoln and Grant. And I remember his teasing Mother about "that old Sunday School teacher, General Lee" (I don't know that he ever taught Sunday School).

Q: Could you tell us something about your work of assembling your husband's papers after his death?

A: I had files of them all over the house here in Marion. I read and marked all the letters, but there were so many manuscripts that I couldn't read them all. Jim Boyd said it was dangerous to leave them here, so I sent them to New York and read more of them there on Saturdays. But I let some things slip. I don't know how some things ever got to Chicago.

Q: Would you comment on your experience of managing the literary estate of Sherwood Anderson?

A: It's been a great satisfaction, but I regret that I haven't done it better. I have seen a great many people. I've tried to take care of Sherwood's interests but not to push. I don't feel that I should try to build up Sherwood's reputation among critics. He wouldn't want me to go around boosting him. As for preserving the manuscripts, I think I've done that fairly well.

THE NEWBERRY ANDERSON COLLECTION

The Sherwood Anderson Collection Comes to the
Newberry Library

Amy Wood Nyholm

After a long period of murmured rumors and vague, broken-off words like "perhaps," there was something in the air that said the day was coming close. And finally there was a summons to a luncheon with the Director, Stanley Pargellis, Lloyd Lewis, the distinguished newspaper editor and historian (then also a part-time member of the staff in order to continue his researches) and a small, dark haired, gentle woman with a very appealing look. It was the young widow of Sherwood Anderson, who to me at that time was simply the author of *Winesburg* and *Dark Laughter*. I heard it being promised that I would *always* be there (we thought of always in those days) and that I would make the cataloguing of the Anderson collection my dear and special pride, that pride a professional cataloguer takes in special things. It seemed that the collection had lain for some months elsewhere and nothing had been done for its arrangement, about which the young wife was very anxious. She wanted it to be used, to be a storehouse of learning for young scholars, which Newberry could promise easily, being in the center of many universities and colleges, as well as being in the center of the country.

It finally began to arrive — boxes and cases and packages; and there was an air of excitement in the Newberry, for although some two years before we had begun a Manuscripts unit, in 1947 it was not as yet a really significant project. The coming of the Anderson collection changed all that, for excitement seemed to come with every package. It was not only the material. It was the fact that from the beginning, young men and women began to arrive wanting to use it for a possible Ph.D. topic. One young man, later to evolve into a serious Anderson scholar, said almost hungrily: "This is our meat and bones."

And so began a period of intense learning for me, curator of the collection. In those days, the "strictly chronological" method of arrangement was the accepted thing. I began to arrange the collection and slowly began to realize that this, like everything else in life, was good for some things, under some conditions, at some times. For good as this arrangement is for large, more or less anonymous historical collections, it just doesn't work for literary collections where hundreds of scholars want to use a collection for hundreds of different authors and want their letters without having to paw through the whole collection, even if the library were willing to have this constant and perhaps rough and destructive use of the material.

It was Christmas and my family was arriving. I remember clearly my anguish, trying to keep my mind on these two demanding pulls. And I remember clearly waking Christmas morning with the finest present of all. I had solved it. I would call it *"Out, In* and *Works."* [1] All Anderson's letters would go into a chronological order, thus making a chronological spine, as it were, for the boxes standing on the shelves, and enabling any scholar working on Anderson alone to progress in simple and orderly fashion through the changing events and development of his life. All letters to Anderson would go into an alphabetical order, thus enabling the work of each person who wrote to Anderson to be produced instantly. The third group of boxes was "Works" by Anderson, thus enabling every title, with all its revisions and drafts, to be produced instantly, for each would take its place in alphabetical order.

Presto, we were in business — and a rushing business it was indeed.

My intense period of learning went on. I learned that some people are magnets and some people are catalysts and that Anderson was both. Old friends, new friends, men and women, critics, scholars and readers all turned up. All had stories they longed to tell, all wanted to "remember when," all had somehow had their lives changed by new insights, deeper perceptions, the magic of interaction with a magnetizer and a catalyst.

The work went on for the better part of a year and finally the great day came. With appropriate ceremonies and speakers, the collection was formally opened for public use by accredited scholars, and if there was a flow before, there was a flood after.

My own learning went on and on. I began to see the vital importance of saving letters which can help the present more clearly understand the future in the light of the past. And I understood how vital it is to preserve the various drafts of significant works, so that one day critical editions can be produced. I began to conceive of such a series of edited works for Anderson. Such solid work as this constitutes a high grade Ph.D. dissertation, and I am happy to say that a dozen or so have already been produced by eager and earnest young people who perhaps never again will have such a concentrated amount of time to give. It was a soaring experience both for me and for them. Once again Anderson was acting as catalyst, for between me and these young researchers were established bonds of understanding, love, and respect that nourish the whole of one's life.

I also learned something extremely valuable that not all people in the academic world realize. To say "Oh that topic has been done" is false. I have seen books come out of this, and other collections, that are as different as night and day. I have seen people who dislike a central figure of a collection produce high grade and stimulating work centered on him just as much as those who come in love and adulation. No one thinks alike, feels alike, or has identical values; and any attempt to prove otherwise is academic fascism, an ugly word but a truth. No one who has worked long years with manuscripts can fail to learn that, willingly or not.

It was almost twenty-five years that I worked on and off, as the material drifted in from many sources in the course of our development project; and the collection stands as a monument to what should be done for each of America's significant literary figures. But that will be possible only when there are others as devoted, as dedicated, and as determined as Eleanor Copenhaver Anderson, the gift of whose friendship became as important as the privilege of being the curator of her husband's works for almost twenty-five years.

The Sherwood Anderson Papers at the Newberry Library

Diana Haskell

The private papers of Sherwood Anderson were given to the Newberry Library in the winter of 1947 by his widow, Eleanor Copenhaver Anderson. Already, a notable collection of midwestern literary papers had been assembled at the Library from the inception of its collecting program in 1945, including the correspondence and literary manuscripts of authors Henry Blake Fuller, Joseph Kirkland, Mary Hartwell Catherwood and Henry Kitchell

Webster, and the files of journalists Francis F. Browne, Victor F. Lawson, Edward Price Bell, Hermann Raster and William Rapp. It was fitting that the Anderson Papers also should find a home in Chicago, where Anderson spent his most creative years and became known as a founder of the Chicago school of literature.

Cataloging of the immense collection — undertaken by Amy Wood Nyholm — took a year to complete; however, portions were opened to qualified scholars as early as May 1948. It soon became apparent that Anderson's correspondence, comprising some 5,000 letters written by him and 7,000 letters written to him, would constitute a unique source for studying the American artist in relation to a commercial society. Howard Mumford Jones after his initial survey of the correspondence noted that Anderson's letters "are in many respects the equivalent of a full-blooded book . . . [they] reveal a rich and interesting personality" ("Statement concerning the Sherwood Anderson manuscript collection"; undated report to librarian Stanley Pargellis).

A prolific letter-writer, Anderson once wrote to publisher Roger Sergel that he "[took] letter writing partly as a substitute for drink" (Winter, 1935). The silent rows of manuscript boxes house letters full of sympathy and sound advice to embryonic authors, as well as long candid correspondence with literary notables such as Gertrude Stein, Ernest Hemingway, Theodore Dreiser, Waldo Frank, Floyd Dell and many others. Messages to his family and close friends reveal his concern with the relationship of artist and family, and his personal struggle against conventional middle class life. And when he had no one in particular to write to, Anderson often spilled out his thoughts in unmailed letters to a composite "friend." He even wrote a series of letters to his young wife, Eleanor, to read one a day for a year after his death.

Anderson's literary output was also considerable. There are some 1,100 pieces of original work, including hundreds of short stories, both published and unpublished, novels, fragments, sketches and penciled notes. Manuscripts for most of his published works are here, sometimes in several states of development. There are also several examples of his watercolors, including one painted by him to help finance a trip to Europe which was recently purchased by the Library.

From the time of receipt of the original gift, the Library has made a determined effort to contact all friends, relatives and correspondents who might be willing to contribute their Anderson mementos to the collection. In this fashion, the Sherwood Anderson Papers have grown from 12,941 items in 1949 to 16,926 items presently recorded. Significant pieces are still being added. Recently, a fine letter to Harry Hansen (ca.12.20.22) and a set of letters to Whitney Wells (1923-1924) were purchased.

The Library has also assembled an excellent collection of Anderson's printed works, translations, critical editions, biographies and other related items, and constantly adds to its holdings as titles become available. Two issues of the in-house *Bulletin* have been devoted to Sherwood Anderson: the first (Series 2, no. 2, 1948) celebrated the acquisition of his Papers, and the second (Vol.VI, no. 8, July 1971) commemorated the fiftieth anniversary of the publication of *Winesburg, Ohio* in 1919. At the Library's celebration on June 4, 1969, the Newberry Library Associates announced the completion of their purchase of the manuscript of the novel and formally presented it to the Library, thus adding the most important single item to an evergrowing, vital research collection. It may well be assumed that the Sherwood Anderson manuscript and printed collections will continue to afford research potential for many years to come.

NOTE

[1]For anyone seriously interested in manuscript arrangement, this was finally put into formal style and published as "Modern Manuscripts: A Functional Approach" in *Library Resources and Technical Services*, 14 (Summer 1970), 325-340.

A CATALOG OF SHERWOOD ANDERSON'S LIBRARY

Compiled by
Charles E. Modlin and Hilbert H. Campbell

Introduction

This catalog represents an attempt to list, insofar as information can
now be recovered, the books left by Sherwood Anderson at Ripshin Farm,
Troutdale, Virginia, or at Rosemont, his wife Eleanor's home in Marion,
Virginia, at the time of his death in 1941. Although Anderson continued his
restless wandering during the latter part of his life and never lived in any one
place for very long, he considered Ripshin his home after building a house
there in 1926 and returned to Ripshin to live whenever he could. Among its
many uses for Anderson, Ripshin served as a place to keep his books. After
his marriage to Eleanor Copenhaver in 1933, he also maintained a study at
Rosemont, her family home in Marion; and a few of his books were shelved
there. Although some of his books remain today on the shelves at Ripshin
and Rosemont, a substantial number of them have been moved to other locations by Anderson's children and grandchildren. Fortunately, most of the
books moved to other locations have been kept intact in groups and are
today readily identifiable. A few other scattered volumes which are now
owned outside the family have also been identified and listed. Inevitably,
some books owned by Anderson at the time of his death are no longer
identifiable. Indications are, however, that such books represent only a
small percentage of the total library. Anderson's children made some par-
tial lists of books on the shelves at Ripshin shortly after their father's death

in 1941; and we have used these lists as a basis for adding to this catalog the titles of a few books which certatinly were once on the shelves at Rip-shin but which cannot now be located.

A catalog of Anderson's personal library is valuable for the indication it gives of what he bought, perhaps read, and considered worth keeping. Although the mere presence of a book on his shelves obviously provides no proof that he read it or was influenced by it, the fact that he owned it and thus may have read it can provide clues which, when used along with other kinds of evidence, can be valuable to scholars. There are, of course, other significant sources of information about Anderson's reading, including most notably his own frequent references to his reading in autobiographical works and letters. This catalog is, like others of its kind, one sort of tool for literary scholarship, which must be used with an awareness of its limita-tions and in conjunction with whatever other tools are available.

Anderson's personal library as here represented is relatively small. He was an inveterate reader all his life, but he was never a "collector" of books in any sense of the word. Books to him represented ideas rather than objects; and once he had obtained what he wanted or needed from a book, he seems to have retained little veneration or possessive feeling toward it as an object. His letters are full of his eagerness to share what he had read with his friends; and many books probably passed forever out of his posses-sion because of this impulse. In addition, his always nomadic life, especially up to the time he built the house at Ripshin Farm in 1926, was not condu-cive to the accumulation and retention of a large personal library. Despite his wide early reading, it is unlikely that any large percentage of the many books he owned or read in Clyde, Chicago, Cleveland, Elyria, New York, Reno, New Orleans and other earlier places of residence were retained to be placed on the shelves at Ripshin. Many books with dates or inscriptions earlier than 1926 can be found on the shelves at Ripshin or Rosemont, but many more were undoubtedly left behind somewhere. Furthermore, many of the books Anderson read, both before and after his move to Ripshin, were borrowed from friends or of necessity from libraries in cities or towns where he happened to be travelling at the time.

One looks in vain for many markings or annotations in the books on Anderson's shelves; for he rarely marked his books, even those that we know he habitually read and re-read. He did sign his name in the front of many of his books, but this seems to have been by chance rather than any indication that he valued a book particularly. For example, many bits of ephemera bear his signature; but few of his many volumes of Turgenev, Chekhov, Dostoevski, Gorki, Borrow, Lawrence, and Stein, all favorite authors of Anderson's, have his name in them. According to Eleanor Anderson, a large number of volumes now at Ripshin were signed by Sherwood when they were taken as a kind of lending library to a YWCA-sponsored Girls' Industrial Conference in the mid-1930's.

A large number of books in Anderson's library bear a printed bookplate: "Property of the Marion Publishing Co. Library." These books were once part of the lending library which Anderson the newspaper editor and his third wife Elizabeth Prall set up at the Print Shop in Marion in 1928. Some of these books were from Anderson's personal library, but many of them came from other sources. At its peak the Print Shop Library apparently included as many as one thousand volumes. When this lending library was broken up after an existence of about three years, Anderson reclaimed some of the books and left the rest to be taken by other people. Thus we have not considered that any book we have run across bearing the "Marion Publishing Co." plate should be included in a catalog of Anderson's library. We have included only those which, insofar as present evidence will indicate, he claimed or reclaimed and moved back to his shelves at Ripshin.

Some of the books Anderson left on his shelves at Ripshin when he died probably belonged originally to Elizabeth Prall, his third wife. An intellectual and well-educated woman, she had been manager of the Lord and Taylor Bookstore in New York prior to her marriage. Certainly she must have taken some of her own books to Ripshin in 1926. Especially some of the older classics still in the collection may be suspected to have belonged to her. Furthermore, the fact that she left Ripshin in 1929 expecting to return — but ultimately did not — makes it unlikely that she took her books with her. A few books still on the shelves at Ripshin bear her signature. But we have made no attempt to weed out of the list books which may have belonged to Elizabeth Prall because — with the exception of a half dozen or so — there is no way of clearly distinguishing them. Besides, these books were retained by Anderson from 1929 until his death in 1941 and can thus be realistically considered as a part of his own library.

A substantial number of books in Anderson's library bear presentation inscriptions from their authors. These inscriptions, which we have recorded here insofar as we have had access to them, reveal an astonishing range of acquaintance among contemporary writers; and the extreme cordiality and flattering nature of many of the inscriptions serve to document the great esteem in which Anderson was held by writers of his own generation.

We have enjoyed a remarkable degree of cooperation and assistance from several persons, mostly members of Anderson's family, in the course of this attempt to reconstruct Anderson's library. We acknowledge with thanks the assistance of Mrs. Robert L. Anderson, Chapel Hill, North Carolina; Mrs. Marion Anderson Spear, Madison, North Carolina; Mrs. Margaret Anderson Stuart, New York, New York; Mr. John S. Anderson, Chicago, Illinois; Elizabeth C. Anderson, Chapel Hill, North Carolina; Mr. and Mrs. Peter Anderson, Wilmington, Delaware; and Mr. Robert F. Williams, Richmond, Virginia. We wish especially to thank Mrs. Sherwood Anderson of Marion, Virginia, who assisted constantly with the project over a period of almost two years. We are particularly grateful to her for spending several days going over books with us at Ripshin and Rosemont during March and May of 1974 and during August and September of 1975, identifying books which had belonged to her husband.

The Catalog

1. Adams, Cornele B. *National Industrial Organization.* Santurce, Puerto Rico: Cantero Fernández, 1934.

2. Adams, Henry. *The Education of Henry Adams.* Boston: Houghton Mifflin, 1918.

3. —. *Letters to a Niece and Prayer to the Virgin of Chartres.* Boston: Houghton Mifflin, 1920.

4. Adams, James Truslow. *America's Tragedy.* New York: Scribner's, 1935. Inscribed by S. A.: "A curiously good historian whom nevertheless in the end and in spite of all you do not trust — a kind of Stuart Chase among historians. There is a basic vulgarity."

5. Adler, Elmer, ed. *Breaking into Print.* New York: Simon and Shuster, 1937.

6. Aiken, Conrad. *Blue Voyage.* New York: Scribner's, 1927.

7. —, *et al. Prose Quartos,* boxed set of six booklets. New York: Random House, 1930. Includes: Conrad Aiken, *Gehenna;* Sherwood Anderson, *The American County Fair;* Stephen Vincent Benét, *The Litter of Rose Leaves;* Louis Bromfield, *Tabloid News;* Theodore Dreiser, *Fine Furniture;* Carl Van Vechten, *Feathers.*

8. Akers, Dwight. *Drivers Up: The Story of American Harness Racing.* New

York: Putnam's, 1938.

9. *Albatross Book of American Short Stories.* Hamburg: The Albatross, 1935.

10. Anderson, Margaret C. *My Thirty Years' War.* New York: Covici-Friede, 1930.

11. Andreyev, Leonid. *The Seven That Were Hanged.* New York: Boni and Liveright, 1918 (Modern Library).

12. —. *To the Stars,* trans. Maurice Magnus. London: C. W. Daniel, 1921.

13. Angelo, Valenti. *Christmas: A Fragment.* New York, 1938. Inscribed by Valenti: "For Sherwood Anderson 1938."

14. Anthony, Katharine. *Catherine the Great.* New York: Knopf, 1925. Inscribed: "To Elizabeth Anderson, who helped me see New Orleans. Ferdinand Schevill."

15. Apuleius, Lucius. *The Golden Asse,* trans. William Adlington. Boston: Small, Maynard and Co., [1925].

16. [Arno, Peter]. *Peter Arno's Parade.* New York: Liveright, 1929.

17. Arnold, Thurman W. *The Symbols of Government.* New Haven: Yale, 1938. Inscribed: "Presented to Sherwood Anderson to go with Folklore. Thurman Arnold."

18. Artzibashef, Michael. *Breaking-Point.* New York: Huebsch, 1915.

19. —. *Jealousy; Enemies; The Law of the Savage.* New York: Boni and Liveright, 1923.

20. Atherton, Gertrude. *Rezanov.* New York: Boni and Liveright, 1919 (Modern Library).

21. Augustine, Saint. *The Confessions of Saint Augustine,* trans. E. B. Pusey. New York: Dutton, 1913.

22. Aurelius Antoninus, Marcus. *The Thoughts of the Emperor Marcus Aurelius Antoninus,* trans. George Long. New York: T. Nelson, [1928].

23. *Authors Club Manual.* New York, 1925.

24. Babbitt, Irving. *Rousseau and Romanticism.* Boston: Houghton Mifflin, 1928.

25. Bacheller, Irving. *Coming Up the Road.* Indianapolis: Bobbs-Merrill, 1928.

26. Bacon, Francis. *Essays.* Philadelphia: H. Altemus, n.d.

27. Baedeker, Karl. *Spain and Portugal: Handbook for Travellers,* 4th edition. Leipsig: Karl Baedeker, 1913.

28. Bakeless, John E. *Daniel Boone.* New York: William Morrow, 1939. S. A. signature.

29. Balter, Ida C. *Glory Strains.* Chicago: Occult Publishing Co., 1926.

30. Balzac, Honoré de. *Droll Stories.* New York: Carlton House, [1930].

31. —. *Pere Goriot.* [Jacket Library]. Inscribed: "To Sherwood Anderson with kindest regards — Sherman Mittell."

32. —. *Works.* New York: Hearst's International Library Co., 1914 (vols. 13 and 15 only).

33. Basso, Hamilton. *Beauregard, the Great Creole.* New York: Scribner's, 1933.

34. —. *Cinnamon Seed.* New York: Scribner's, 1934. S. A. signature.

35. —. *Court-house Square.* New York: Scribner's, 1936. S. A. signature.

36. —. *Relics and Angels.* New York: Macaulay, 1929.

37. Bates, Sylvia C., ed. *Twentieth Century Short Stories.* Boston: Houghton Mifflin, 1933. S. A. signature.

38. *Battles and Leaders of the Civil War,* Grant-Lee Edition, 4 vols. in 8 parts. New York: Century Co., 1884-1888.

39. Baudelaire, Charles. *Baudelaire: His Prose and Poetry,* ed. T. R. Smith. New York: Boni and Liveright, 1919 (Modern Library). Two copies.

40. —. *Constantin Guys.* Paris: Nilsson, 1925.

41. —. *Flowers of Evil.* New York: Harper, 1936.

42. Beal, Fred E. *Proletarian Journey.* New York: Hillman-Curl, 1937.

43. Beard, Charles A. and Mary R. *The Rise of American Civilization.* New York: Macmillan, 1930.

44. Beard, Mary R. *On Understanding Women.* London: Longmans, Green, 1931. S. A. signature.

45. Beaumont, Francis and John Fletcher. *Select Plays: Beaumont and Fletcher.* New York: Dutton, 1926.

46. Beebe, Charles William. *Jungle Peace.* New York: Modern Library, n.d.

47. Beer, Thomas. *The Mauve Decade.* Garden City, New York: Garden City Publishing Co., 1926.

48. Beery, Jesse. *Prof. Beery's Saddle-Horse Instructions.* Pleasant Hill, Ohio: Jesse Beery, 1909-. Books 2, 4, and 5. Gift of J. H. Wyse.

49. Bein, Albert. *Little Ol' Boy: A Play in Three Acts.* New York: Samuel French, 1929.

50. Bell, Clive. *Since Cézanne.* New York: Harcourt, Brace, 1922.

51. Benét, Stephen Vincent. *John Brown's Body.* Garden City, New York: Doubleday, Doran, 1928.

52. Benét, William Rose. *Merchants from Cathay.* New York: Century Co., 1913.

53. Bercovici, Rion. *For Immediate Release.* New York: Sheridan House, 1937.

54. Berg, Ruben. *Moderna Amerikaner.* Stockholm: Hugo Gebers, 1925.

55. Bishop, John Peale. *Act of Darkness.* New York: Scribner's, 1935. S. A. signature.

56. Black, John. *Songs of the World's Fair.* Boston: Bruce Humphries, 1939.

57. Blackwood, Algernon. *Episodes Before Thirty.* New York: Dutton, 1924.

58. Blake, William. *Poems,* ed. W. B. Yeats. New York: Boni and Liveright, n.d. (Modern Library).

59. Blankenship, Russell, Rollo L. Lyman, and Howard C. Hill, eds. *American Literature.* New York: Scribner's, 1937.

60. Blasco Ibáñez, Vicente. *The Cabin,* trans. F. H. Snow and B. M. Mekota. New York: Boni and Liveright, n.d. (Modern Library).

61. —. *Mare Nostrum,* trans. C. B. Jordan. New York: Dutton, 1919.

62. [Blech, William J.]. *The World Is Mine: The Extravagant Story of a Modern Monte Cristo,* by William Blake (pseud.). New York: Simon and Schuster, 1938. Inscribed: "Dear Anderson — The setting is modern Spain. A melodrama of ideas with a vengeance. Greetings from the Inner Sanctum. M. Lincoln Schuster."

63. Boccaccio, Giovanni. *The Decameron,* 2 vols. London: Privately printed for The Navarre Society, 1921.

64. Boleslavski, Richard and Helen Woodward. *Way of the Lancer.* New York: Literary Guild, 1932.

65. Bolitho, William. *Twelve Against the Gods.* New York: Simon and Schuster, 1929.

66. Boni, Albert, ed. *The Modern Book of French Verse in English Translations.* New York: Boni and Liveright, 1920.

67. Borrow, George. *The Bible in Spain.* New York: Dutton, n.d.

68. —. *Lavengro: The Scholar, the Gypsy, the Priest.* London: Macmillan, 1896.

69. —. Another copy. New York: Putnam's, 1913.

70. —. *The Romany Rye.* New York: Dutton, 1910.

71. —. Another copy. New York: Dutton, 1914.

72. —. *Wild Wales: Its People, Language, and Scenery.* New York: Putnam's, 1907.

73. —. *The Zincali, An Account of the Gypsies in Spain.* New York: Putnam's, 1908.

74. Boswell, James. *Life of Johnson.* Boston: Houghton Mifflin, 1917.

75. Bowen, John Joseph. *The Strategy of Robert E. Lee.* New York: Neale Publishing Co., 1914.

76. Bowers, Claude G. *The Tragic Era.* New York: Literary Guild, 1929.

77. Bowman, Heath. *All Your Born Days.* Indianapolis: Bobbs-Merrill, 1939.

78. Boyd, James. *Bitter Creek.* New York: Scribner's, 1939. Inscribed by Boyd: "To Sherwood Anderson in gratitude and recognition."

79. —. *Marching On.* New York: Scribner's, 1927.

80. Brand, Millen. *The Outward Room.* New York: Simon and Schuster, 1937. Inscribed: "To the Sherwood Andersons with affectionate regards, Millen Brand."

81. Brandeis, Louis D. *Other People's Money.* Washington: National Home

Library Foundation, 1933. Inscribed: "To Sherwood Anderson with kind regards. Sherman Mittell."

82. Breuer, Bessie. *The Daughter.* New York: Simon and Schuster, 1938. S. A. signature.

83. —. *Memory of Love* — page proof. [New York: Simon and Schuster, 1934].

84. Brillat-Savarin, Jean Anthelme. *The Physiology of Taste.* New York: Boni and Liveright, 1926.

85. Brinton, Selwyn J. *The Golden Age of the Medici.* London: Methuen, 1925.

86. Brooks, Van Wyck. *The Life of Emerson.* New York: Dutton, 1932. Inscribed: "For Sherwood and — for auld lang syne, Van Wyck Brooks, Westport, March 21, 1932." A second copy is unsigned.

87. —. *The Pilgrimage of Henry James.* New York: Dutton, 1925.

88. —, *et al.,* eds. *The American Caravan.* New York: Macaulay, 1927.

89. Broun, Heywood and Margaret Leech. *Anthony Comstock.* New York: A. and C. Boni, 1927.

90. Brousson, Jean Jacques. *Anatole France Himself,* trans. John Pollock. Philadelphia: Lippincott, 1925.

91. Brown, Edmund R., ed. *Modern Russian Classics.* Boston: Four Seas Co., 1918.

92. Browne, Waldo R. *Altgeld of Illinois.* New York: Huebsch, 1924.

93. Brownell, Baker. *Earth Is Enough.* New York: Harper, 1933.

94. Brownell, William C., ed. *American Prose Masters.* New York: Scribner's, 1923.

95. Browning, Robert. *A Blot in the 'Scutcheon and Other Poetic Dramas.*

London: W. Scott, 1896.

96. —. *The Complete Poetic and Dramatic Works* (Cambridge Edition). Boston: Houghton Mifflin, 1895.

97. Brush, Albert. *The Dark Tower.* New York: Flying Stag Press, 1925.

98. Bunin, Ivan A. *The Gentleman from San Francisco and Other Stories,* trans. D. H. Lawrence *et al.* New York: Thomas Seltzer, 1934.

99. Burklund, Carl Edwin, ed. *New Michigan Verse.* Ann Arbor: Univ. of Michigan Press, 1940.

100. Burnett, Whit. *The Maker of Signs.* New York: Harrison Smith and Robert Haas, 1934. Inscribed: "For Sherwood Anderson whose Winesburg opened the way for a whole generation & certainly for the stories in this. With gratitude and humility, Whit Burnett." Also S. A. signature.

101. Burroughs, Bryson. *Metropolitan Museum of Art: Catalogue of Paintings,* 8th ed. New York, 1926.

102. Burrow, Trigant. *The Biology of Human Conflict.* New York: Macmillan, 1937. Inscribed: "To Sherwood Anderson in affectionate remembrance and my deep appreciation, Trigant Burrow."

103. Buss, Kate. *Studies in the Chinese Drama.* Boston: Four Seas Co., 1922.

104. Bussard, Léon and Georges Duval. *Arboriculture Fruitière.* Paris: J. -B. Baillière et fils, 1907.

105. Butler, Samuel. *The Way of All Flesh.* New York: Dutton, 1916.

106. —. Another copy. New York: Boni and Liveright, n.d. (Modern Library).

107. Bynner, Witter. *Eden Tree.* New York: Knopf, 1931. Inscribed by Bynner: "Sherwood — Considered? Hal."

108. —. *Against the Cold.* New York: Knopf, 1940.

109. Cabell, James Branch. *Beyond Life.* New York: Robert M. McBride, 1919.

110. —. Two other copies. New York: Boni and Liveright, 1919.

111. —. *The Cream of the Jest.* New York: Robert M. McBride, 1920.

112. —. *Ladies and Gentlemen.* New York: Robert M. McBride, 1934. Inscribed: "For Sherwood Anderson as a fellow Spectator of polite letters, with the best wishes of Branch Cabell 29 September 1934."

113. —. *Smirt.* New York: Robert M. McBride, 1934. Inscribed: "For Sherwood Anderson whom we have long admired as a writer and still desiderate as a visitor. Branch Cabell & James Branch Cabell. 26 February 1934."

114. Cahan, Abraham. *The Rise of David Levinsky.* New York: Harper, 1917.

115. Caldwell, Erskine. *God's Little Acre.* New York: Viking, 1933.

116. —. Galley proofs of *God's Little Acre.* [New York: Viking, 1933].

117. —. *Jackpot.* New York: Duell, Sloan and Pearce, 1940. S. A. signature.

118. Callaghan, Morley. *Such Is My Beloved. New* York: Scribner's, 1934.

119. —. *They Shall Inherit the Earth.* New York: Modern Age, 1937.

120. Calmer, Edgar. *When Night Descends.* New York: Farrar and Rinehart, 1936. Inscribed: "To Sherwood Anderson first American writer of his generation with the author's best wishes. Nov. 10, '36." Also S. A. signature.

121. Calverton, V. F. *For Revolution.* New York: John Day Co., 1932. Inscribed: "To Sherwood, Revolutionarily, George."

122. —. *The Liberation of American Literature.* New York: Scribner's, 1932.

123. —. *The Man Inside.* New York: Scribner's, 1936. Inscribed: "To Sherwood in all affection, George Calverton."

124. —. *The Newer Spirit*. New York: Boni and Liveright, 1925.

125. —. *Three Strange Lovers*. New York: Macaulay, 1930. Inscribed: "To Sherwood in all admiration and affection - George VFC."

126. — and S. D. Schmalhausen, eds. *Sex in Civilization*. New York: Macaulay, 1929. Inscribed by Calverton: "To Sherwood merrily and mercifully."

127. Canby, Henry S. *Classic Americans*. New York: Harcourt, Brace, 1931.

128. —. *Definitions: Essays in Contemporary Criticism*. New York: Harcourt, Brace, 1922. Inscribed: "To Sherwood Anderson from his friend Henry S. Canby." A second copy is unsigned.

129. Carman, Bliss. *Songs of the Sea Children*. Boston: L. C. Page, 1903.

130. Carneal, Georgette. *The Great Day*. New York: Liveright, 1932.

131. Carnevali, Emanuel. *A Hurried Man:* —. Paris: Three Mountains Press, 1925.

132. Cellini, Benvenuto. *The Memoirs of Benvenuto Cellini*, trans. Anne MacDonell. New York: Dutton, 1925.

133. Cervantes Saavedra, Miguel de. *Don Quixote*. New York: American Book Exchange, 1880.

134. —. Another copy. Philadelphia: Porter and Coates, [1891].

135. —. Another copy. New York: Modern Library, 1930.

136. Chamberlin, William H. *Russia's Iron Age*. Boston: Little, Brown, 1934.

137. Charnwood, Godfrey R. B., lst Baron. *Abraham Lincoln*. New York: Holt, 1917.

138. Chase, Cleveland B. *Sherwood Anderson*. New York: Robert M. McBride, 1927.

139. Chateaubriand, François René. *Memoirs,* trans. A. T. De Mattos. London: Freemantle and Co., 1902 (Vol. I only).

140. Chekhov, Anton. *The Horse-Stealers and Other Stories,* trans. Constance Garnett. New York: Macmillan, 1921.

141. —. *The Plays of Anton Tchekov,* trans. Constance Garnett. New York: Modern Library, n.d.

142. —. *Stories of Russian Life,* trans. Marian Fell. New York: Scribner's, 1915.

143. Chesterton, G. K. *The Man Who Was Thursday.* New York: Boni and Liveright, 1917 (Modern Library).

144. Clark, Barrett H. *Oedipus or Pollyanna.* Seattle: University of Washington Book Store, 1927. Inscribed: "To Sherwood Anderson with regards from Barrett H. Clark — 31 May '27."

145. —, ed. *Great Short Novels of the World.* New York: Robert M. McBride, 1927.

146. —, ed. *Great Short Novels of the World,* 2 vols. New York: A. and C. Boni, 1932. Inscribed to Eleanor Anderson by S. A.

147. — and Maxim Lieber, eds. *Great Short Stories of the World.* New York: Robert M. McBride, 1926.

148. Claudel, Paul. *The City: A Play,* trans. J. S. Newberry. New Haven: Yale, 1920.

149. —. *The Tidings Brought to Mary.* New Haven: Yale, 1916.

150. Cleaton, Irene and Allen. *Books and Battles: American Literature, 1920-1930.* Boston: Houghton Mifflin, 1937.

151. Clemens, Samuel L. *The American Claimant and Other Stories and Sketches.* New York: Harper, 1897.

152. —. *Life on the Mississippi.* New York: Harper, 1901.

153. —. *Personal Recollections of Joan of Arc.* New York: Harper, 1896.

154. —. *The Prince and the Pauper.* New York: Harper, 1901.

155. — and Charles Dudley Warner. *The Gilded Age.* Hartford, Connecticut: American Publishing Co., 1890.

156. Clifford, Sir Hugh. *The Downfall of the Gods.* New York: Dutton, 1911.

157. Coblentz, Stanton A., ed. *Modern British Lyrics.* New York: Minton, Balch, 1925.

158. Cochran, Louis. *Boss Man.* Caldwell, Idaho: Caxton Printers, 1939. Signed by author.

159. —. *Son of Haman.* Caldwell, Idaho: Caxton Printers, 1937. Inscribed: "To Sherwood Anderson in appreciation — Louis Cochran — St. Louis 8-7-39."

160. Cole, Arthur Charles. *The Irrepressible Conflict, 1850-1865.* New York: Macmillan, 1934.

161. Colony, Horatio. *Birth and Burial.* Boston: Meador Publishing Co., 1939.

162. Conkle, E. P. *Loolie and Other Short Plays.* New York: Samuel French, 1935.

163. Conklin, Groff, ed. *The New Republic Anthology, 1915-1935.* New York: Dodge Publishing Co., 1936.

164. Connick, Charles J. *Adventures in Light and Color: An Introduction to the Stained Glass Craft.* New York: Random House, 1937.

165. Conrad, Joseph. *The Secret Agent.* Leipzig: Bernhard Tauchnitz, 1907.

166. —. *Suspense.* Garden City, New York: Doubleday, Page, 1925.

167. Conroy, Jack. *The Disinherited.* New York: Covici-Friede, 1933.

168. Coppard, Alfred E. *Yokohama Garland and Other Poems.* Philadelphia: Centaur Press, 1926.

169. *Copyright Law Symposium.* New York: American Society of Composers, Authors and Publishers, [1939].

170. Cournos, John. *Autobiography.* New York: Putnam's, 1935.

171. —. *Grandmother Martin Is Murdered.* New York: Farrar and Rinehart, 1930.

172. —. *Hear, O Israel.* London: Methuen and Co., 1938. Inscribed: "To Sherwood with warm affection and admiration from John, August 1, 1938."

173. —, ed. *The Fifteen Finest Short Stories.* New York: Dodd, Mead, 1928.

174. Covarrubias, Miguel. *Island of Bali.* New York: Knopf, 1937.

175. Cowley, Malcolm, ed. *After the Genteel Tradition: American Writers Since 1910.* New York: Norton, 1937. S. A. signature.

176. Cox, Sidney and Edmund Freeman, eds. *Prose Preferences.* New York: Harper, 1926.

177. Crane, Stephen. *Men, Women and Boats.* New York: Boni and Liveright, 1921. Two copies.

178. —. *The Red Badge of Courage.* New York: D. Appleton, 1900. With early bookplate bearing inscription: "Sherwood Burton Anderson His Book."

179. —. *The Work of Stephen Crane,* ed. Wilson Follett, 12 vols. New York: Knopf, 1925-1927.

180. Cronin, Archibald J. *The Stars Look Down.* Boston: Little, Brown, 1935. S. A. signature.

181. Crowninshield, Frank, ed. *Short Stories from Vanity Fair, 1926-1927.* New York: Liveright, 1928. Inscribed to S. A. by Crowninshield.

182. Cullen, John Paul. *Hello, Wisconsin!* Boston: Meador Publishing Co., 1931. Inscribed: "To Sherwood Anderson (in appreciation) John Paul Cullen 11-18-31." Also a second inscribed copy.

183. Cummings, E. E. . . . *Is 5.* New York: Boni and Liveright, 1926.

184. —. *Tulips and Chimneys.* New York: Thomas Seltzer, 1923.

185. Curtis, Newton M. *From Bull Run to Chancellorsville.* New York: Putnam's, 1906.

186. Dahlberg, Edward. *Bottom Dogs.* New York: Simon and Schuster, 1930. Author's inscription to S. A.

187. —. *Those Who Perish.* New York: John Day, 1934. Inscribed: "For Sherwood Anderson who has influenced all of us who are writing today with admiration for his genius. Edward Dahlberg."

188. Dana, Charles A., ed. *Fragments from Parnassus,* 3rd edition. Woodstock, Vermont: Elm Tree Press, 1922.

189. Dana, Richard Henry. *Two Years Before the Mast.* Boston: James R. Osgood and Co., 1873. S. A. signature.

190. D'Annunzio, Gabriele. *The Child of Pleasure.* New York: Boni and Liveright, 1925 (Modern Library).

191. —. *Tales of My Native Town.* Garden City, New York: Doubleday, Page, 1920.

192. —. *The Triumph of Death.* New York: Boni and Liveright, 1923 (Modern Library).

193. [Dargan, Olive Tilford]. *A Stone Came Rolling,* by Fielding Burke (pseud.). New York: Longmans, Green, and Co., 1935. S. A. signature.

194. Daudet, Alphonse. *Sapho: Manon Lescaut.* New York: Boni and Liveright, 1919 (Modern Library).

195. [Davies, Arthur B.] . *The Etchings and Lithographs of Arthur B. Davies,*

compiled by F. N. Price. New York: Mitchell Kennerley, 1929.

196. Davis, Jefferson. *The Rise and Fall of the Confederate Government.* New York: D. Appleton and Co., 1881. Volume II only.

197. [Davis, Varina]. *Jefferson Davis: Ex-President of the Confederate States of America, A Memoir by His Wife.* New York: Belford Co., 1890. Volume I only.

198. Davison, Edward L. *Collected Poems 1917-1939.* New York: Harper, 1940. Inscribed: "To Sherwood and Eleanor affectionately presented."

199. —. *Nine Poems.* New York: Privately printed, 1937.

200. —. *The Ninth Witch and Other Poems.* New York: Harper, 1932. Inscribed: "Sherwood and Eleanor Anderson in Friendship from Edward Davison."

201. Defoe, Daniel. *Captain Singleton.* New York: Dutton, 1916.

202. —. *A Journal of the Plague Year.* London: Routledge and Sons, 1884.

203. —. *Moll Flanders and History of the Devil.* London: George Bell and Sons, 1892.

204. —. *Moll Flanders.* London: Simkin, Marshall, Hamilton, Kent, 1924. Inscribed: "Elizabeth Prall Anderson."

205. —. Another copy. New York: Greenberg, [1925].

206. De Goncourt, Edmond and Jules. *The Goncourt Journals 1851-1870,* trans. Lewis Galantière. Garden City, New York: Doubleday, Doran, 1937. Inscribed: "For Sherwood with the accumulated affection of twenty years of constant friendship. Lewis Galantière." Also S. A. signature.

207. —. *Renée Maupérin.* New York: Boni and Liveright, n.d. (Modern Library).

208. De La Mare, Walter J. *The Listeners and Other Poems.* New York: Holt, 1916.

209. —. *Memoirs of a Midget.* New York: Knopf, 1922.

210. —. *The Return.* New York: Knopf, 1922.

211. Dell, Floyd. *Looking At Life.* New York: Knopf, 1924.

212. —. *Moon-Calf.* New York: Knopf, 1920. Inscribed: "To Sherwood Anderson, historian of the American romance — gratefully, Floyd Dell, October, 1920."

213. De Maupassant, Guy. *Bel-Ami.* New York: French Library Syndicate, 1917.

214. —. *Love, and Other Stories,* trans. Michael Monahan. New York: Boni and Liveright, n.d. Two copies.

215. —. *Mademoiselle Fifi and Twelve Other Stories.* New York: Boni and Liveright, 1917 (Modern Library).

216. De Palencia, Isabel. *I Must Have Liberty.* New York: Longmans, Green and Co., 1940. Inscribed: "For Sherwood Anderson and Ellinor hoping it will bring back memories of the Spain we spoke of in Tampa. Very cordially, Isabel de Palencia."

217. Derleth, August. *Country Growth.* New York: Scribner's, 1940. Inscribed: "To Sherwood Anderson, August Derleth, 12/7/40 in New York."

218. Desti, Mary. *The Untold Story: Life of Isadora Duncan, 1921-1927.* New York: Liveright, 1929.

219. Dickson, George. *Peter Rae.* London: George Allen and Unwin, 1925. Inscribed: "To Sherwood Anderson for what he has meant to me. With great respect from George Dickson."

220. Dorado, Carolina Marcial. *Primeras Lecciones de Español.* Boston: Ginn and Co., 1918.

221. Dorfman, Joseph. *Thorstein Veblen and His America.* New York: Viking Press, 1934.

222. Dos Passos, John. *Manhattan Transfer*. New York: Harper, 1925.

223. Dostoevsky, Fyodor. *The Brothers Karamazov*, trans. Constance Garnett. New York: Macmillan, 1915.

224. —. *An Honest Thief and Other Stories*, trans. Constance Garnett. New York: Macmillan, 1919.

225. —. *The Possessed*, trans. Constance Garnett. New York: Macmillan, n.d.

226. —. *A Raw Youth*, trans. Constance Garnett. New York: Macmillan, 1916.

227. Dreiser, Theodore. *An American Tragedy*, 2 vols. New York: Boni and Liveright, 1925.

228. —. *A Book About Myself*. New York: Boni and Liveright, 1922.

229. —. *Dawn*. New York: Liveright, 1931.

230. —. *The Financier*. New York: A. L. Burt, 1912.

231. —. Another copy. New York: Boni and Liveright, [1925?]. S. A. signature.

232. —. Another copy. New York: Boni and Liveright, 1927.

233. —. *Free and Other Stories*. New York: Boni and Liveright, 1918.

234. —. Another copy. New York: Boni and Liveright, 1923.

235. —. *Sister Carrie*. New York: Boni and Liveright, 1917.

236. —. *Tragic America*. New York: Liveright, 1931.

237. Drinkwater, John. *Abraham Lincoln, A Play*. Boston: Houghton Mifflin, 1919.

238. Dumas, Alexandre. *Memoirs of a Physician*. New York: A. L. Burt, n.d.

239. Duncan, Isadora. *My Life.* New York: Boni and Liveright, 1927.

240. Dunsany, Lord [Edward J. M. D. Plunkett]. *A Dreamer's Tales and Other Stories.* New York: Boni and Liveright, n.d.

241. Durtain, Luc. *Quarantième Étage.* Paris: Librairie Gallimard, 1927. Author's inscription to S. A.

242. Eckenrode, Hamilton J. *Bottom Rail on Top.* New York: Greenberg, 1935. S. A. signature.

243. Eddy, Sherwood and Kirby Page. *Creative Pioneers.* New York: Association Press, 1937.

244. Edmunds, Abe C. *Poems.* Lynchburg, Virginia: Little Bookshop, 1931.

245. Elam, Samuel M. *George Borrow.* New York: Knopf, 1929.

246. Eliot, T. S. *The Idea of a Christian Society.* New York: Harcourt, Brace, 1940. S. A. signature.

247. —. *Poems.* New York: Knopf, 1920.

248. Elliot, Frances M. *Old Court Life in France.* Leipzig: Bernhard Tauchnitz, 1873. Vol. I only.

249. Ellis, Anne. *The Life of an Ordinary Woman.* Boston: Houghton Mifflin, 1929.

250. Ellis, Harold Milton, Louise Pound, and G. W. Spohn, eds. *A College Book of American Literature.* New York: American Book Co., 1940.

251. Ellis, Havelock. *The New Spirit.* New York: Boni and Liveright, 1921.

252. Embree, Edwin R. *Prospecting for Heaven.* New York: Viking Press, 1932.

253. Emerson, Ralph Waldo. *Essays.* New York: Thomas Nelson, n.d.

254. Ervine, St. John G. *The Mountain and Other Stories.* New York: Mac-

millan Co., 1928.

255. Ethridge, Willie Snow. *As I Live and Breathe.* New York: Frederick A. Stokes, 1937. Inscribed: "For Sherwood Anderson, who discerningly knows the 'roommate' of this book has more sense than the writer of it. Willie Snow Ethridge."

256. —. *Mingled Yarn.* New York: Macmillan, 1938. Inscribed: "For Sherwood Anderson and Mrs. with sincere affection, from Willie Snow Ethridge. May 5, 1938."

257. Fabre, Jean Henri. *The Life of the Caterpillar,* trans. A. T. de Mattos. New York: Boni and Liveright, 1916 (Modern Library). S. A. signature.

258. Fagin, Nathan Bryllion. *The Phenomenon of Sherwood Anderson.* Baltimore: Rossi-Bryn, 1927.

259. Farrar, John C., ed. *The Literary Spotlight.* New York: George H. Doran, 1924.

260. Farrell, James T. *No Star Is Lost.* New York: Vanguard Press, 1938.

261. Faulkner, William. *Mosquitoes.* New York: Boni and Liveright, 1927.

262. —. *Sanctuary.* New York: J. Cape and H. Smith, 1931.

263. —. *Sartoris.* New York: Harcourt, Brace, 1929.

264. —. *Soldiers' Pay.* New York: Boni and Liveright, 1926. Inscribed to S. A. by Faulkner. Also a second copy.

265. —. *The Sound and the Fury.* New York: J. Cape and H. Smith, 1929.

266. —. *This Earth: A Poem,* with drawings by Albert Heckman. New York: Equinox, 1932.

267. —. *The Wild Palms.* New York: Random House, 1939.

268. Feibleman, James K. *Death of the God in Mexico.* New York: Liveright, 1931. Inscribed by S. A.: "To Eleanore - Sherwood Anderson."

269. —. *In Praise of Comedy.* New York: Macmillan, 1939. Inscribed: "For Sherwood and Eleanor Anderson with love — Jimmy Feibleman."

270. Fielding, Henry. *A Journey from this World to the Next and A Voyage to Lisbon.* London: Dent, 1902.

271. —. *The Life and Death of Tom Thumb the Great and Some Miscellaneous Writings.* London: Dent, 1902.

272. —. *The Works of Henry Fielding,* ed. George Saintsbury. New York: Nottingham Society, n.d. Volumes I, II, V, and VI.

273. Figgis, Darrell. *The Return of the Hero.* New York: Charles Boni, 1930.

274. Fishman, Joseph F. *Sex in Prison.* New York: National Library Press, 1934.

275. Flanagan, Dorothy Belle. *Dark Certainty.* New Haven: Yale, 1931.

276. Flaubert, Gustave. *Madame Bovary,* trans. E. M. Aveling. New York: Modern Library, n.d. Two copies.

277. —. *The Temptation of St. Anthony.* New York: Boni and Liveright, n.d. (Modern Library).

278. Flower, Sydney B. *The Goat-Gland Transplantation.* Chicago: New Thought Book Dept., 1921.

279. Foerster-Nietzsche, Elizabeth, ed. *The Nietzsche-Wagner Correspondence,* trans. C. V. Kerr. New York: Boni and Liveright, 1921.

280. Forster, E. M. *A Passage to India.* New York: Harcourt, Brace, 1924.

281. France, Anatole. *The Crime of Sylvestre Bonnard.* New York: Harper, 1890.

282. —. Another copy. New York: Boni and Liveright, n.d. (Modern Library).

283. —. *L'Anneau D'Améthyste.* Paris: Calmann-Lévy, 1917.

284. —. *On Life and Letters,* 4th series, trans. Bernard Miall. London: John Lane, 1924.

285. —. *Penguin Island.* London: John Lane, 1921. Two copies.

286. —. *The Queen Pedauque,* trans. J. A. V. Stritzko. New York: Boni and Liveright, 1923 (Modern Library).

287. —. *The Red Lily.* New York: Boni and Liveright, 1917 (Modern Library).

288. —. *Revolt of the Angels.* London: John Lane, 1914. Inscribed: "S. A. from A. E. H."

289. —. *La Rôtisserie de la Reine Pédauque.* Paris: Calmann-Lévy, n.d.

290. —. *Thaïs,* trans. Ernest Tristan. New York: Boni and Liveright, n.d. (Modern Library).

291. Frank, Waldo. *The Bridegroom Cometh.* New York: Doubleday, Doran, 1939.

292. —. *The Dark Mother.* New York: Boni and Liveright, 1920. Inscribed: "To Sherwood with love Waldo."

293. —. *The Death and Birth of David Markand.* New York: Scribner's, 1934.

294. —. *Our America.* New York: Boni and Liveright, 1919.

295. —. *Rahab.* New York: Boni and Liveright, 1922.

296. —. *The Unwelcome Man.* Boston: Little, Brown, 1917.

297. —, et al., eds. *America and Alfred Stieglitz.* Garden City, New York: Doubleday, Doran, 1934. S. A. signature.

298. Franklin, Benjamin. *Autobiography.* Philadelphia: Henry Altemus, n.d.

299. Freeman, Douglas Southall. *R. E. Lee: A Biography,* 4 vols. New York:

Scribner's, 1935. Inscribed by S. A. In Vol. I: "This book belongs to Sherwood Anderson and is loaned not given to one A. Funk of Marion, Va. - Sherwood Anderson."

300. Freeman, Joseph. *An American Testament.* New York: Farrar and Rinehart, 1936. S. A. signature.

301. Frenssen, Gustav. *Jörn Uhl,* trans. F. S. Delmer. New York: Boni and Liveright, 1913 [?].

302. Freud, Sigmund. *The Problem of Lay-Analyses.* New York: Brentano's, 1927.

303. Friend, Julius W. and James Feibleman. *Science and the Spirit of Man.* London: George Allen and Unwin, 1933. Inscribed: "To Sherwood Anderson - Julius W. Friend and James Feibleman."

304. *From the American Mercury 1927.* New York: Knopf, 1928.

305. Fuller, Major-General John F. C. *Grant and Lee: A Study in Personality and Generalship.* New York: Scribner's, 1933. Inscribed by S. A.: "Grant — man of singular beauty of personality. A rather prejudiced book, not enough background out of which he came taken into consideration, but good as a counter irritant against the rather silly adoration of Lee."

306. Gaboriau, Émile. *File No. 113.* New York: J. H. Sears, 1928.

307. Galsworthy, John. *Swan Song.* New York: Scribner's, 1928.

308. Galt, William E. *Phyloanalysis.* London: Kegan Paul, Trench, Trubner, 1933.

309. Garnett, David, Francis Meynell, *et al. The Week-End Book.* New York: Dial Press, 1924.

310. Gauguin, Paul. *Paul Gauguin's Intimate Journals,* trans. Van Wyck Brooks. New York: Boni and Liveright, 1921.

311. —. *Noa-Noa.* New York: Nicholas L. Brown, 1920.

312. Gautier, Théophile. *Mademoiselle de Maupin.* New York: Modern Library, 1925.

313. Gay, John. *The Beggar's Opera.* New York: Huebsch, 1920.

314. George, Walter L. *A Bed of Roses.* New York: Boni and Liveright, 1919. Two copies.

315. Gessner, Robert. *Upsurge.* New York: Farrar and Rinehart, 1933.

316. Gide, André. *L'École Des Femmes.* Paris: Librairie Gallimard, 1929. Inscribed: "a Sherwood Anderson, en attentif hommage, André Gide."

317. Gilbert, Sir William S. *H. M. S. Pinafore and Other Plays.* New York: Modern Library, 1925.

318. —. *The Mikado and Other Plays.* New York: Boni and Liveright, 1917 (Modern Library). S. A. signature.

319. Giles, Herbert A. *A History of Chinese Literature.* New York: Appleton, 1923. Inscribed: "Christmas 1923 - To Sherwood from Max [Radin?]."

320. —, translator. *Strange Stories from a Chinese Studio.* London: T. Werner Laurie, 1916.

321. Gilman, Mildred E. *Divide By Two.* New York: Harcourt, Brace, 1938.

322. Godchaux, Elma. *Stubborn Roots.* New York: Macmillan, 1936.

323. Gogol, Nikolai. *Dead Souls.* London: Dent, 1915.

324. —. *The Overcoat and Other Stories.* New York: Knopf, 1923.

325. Gold, Michael. *Jews Without Money.* New York: Liveright, 1932.

326. Goldman, Emma. *Living My Life,* 2 vols. New York: Knopf, 1931.

327. Goll, Ivan, ed. *Les Cinq Continents, Anthologie Mondiale de Poésie Contemporaine.* Paris: La Renaissance Du Livre, 1922.

328. Gorky, Maxim. *Bystander*, trans. B. G. Guerney. New York: Literary Guild, 1930.

329. —. *Foma Gordyeeff*, trans. I. F. Hapgood. New York: Scribner's, 1901.

330. —. *Orloff and His Wife*, trans. I. F. Hapgood. New York: Scribner's, 1901.

331. —. *Reminiscences of Leo Nikolaevich Tolstoy*, trans. S. S. Koteliansky and Leonard Woolf. New York: Huebsch, 1920.

332. —. *The Story of A Novel and Other Stories*, trans. M. Zakrevsky. New York: Dial Press, 1925. S. A. signature.

333. —. *Tales of Two Countries.* New York: Huebsch, 1914.

334. Gosse, Edmund. *Books on the Table.* New York: Scribner's, 1921.

335. Grahame, Kenneth. *Dream Days.* New York: John Lane Co., 1909.

336. —. *The Golden Age.* New York: John Lane Co., 1910.

337. Grant, Ulysses S. *Personal Memoirs of U. S. Grant*, 2 vols. New York: Charles L. Webster and Co., 1885. S. A. signature.

338. Green, Horace. *General Grant's Last Stand.* New York: Scribner's, 1936.

339. Green, Paul. *Out of the South.* New York: Harper, 1939. Inscribed: "For Sherwood Anderson - Affectionately, Paul Green."

340. —. *Roll Sweet Chariot.* New York: Samuel French, 1935. S. A. signature.

341. Griffith, William, ed. *American Scrap Book.* New York: Forum Press, 1930.

342. Gruenberg, Louis. *Four Diversions for String Quartet Small Score.* New York: Cos Cob Press, n.d.

343. Guedalla, Philip. *The Second Empire.* New York: Putnam's, 1922.

344. Hackett, Francis. *Horizons.* New York: Huebsch, n.d.

345. Hallgren, Mauritz A. *Seeds of Revolt.* New York: Knopf, 1933. S. A. signature.

346. Hammond, John L. and Barbara. *The Skilled Labourer, 1760-1832.* London: Longmans, Green and Co., 1920.

347. Hamsun, Knut. *Growth of the Soil,* trans. W. W. Worster, 2 vols. New York: Knopf, 1921.

348. *Handbook to Paris and Its Environs.* London: Ward, Lock and Co., n.d.

349. Hanline, Maurice A. *The Sympathy of the Moon.* Contemporary Verse, 1922.

350. Hansen, Harry. *Midwest Portraits.* New York: Harcourt, Brace, 1923.

351. Hardy, Thomas. *Desperate Remedies.* New York: Harper, 1896.

352. —. *The Mayor of Casterbridge.* New York: Boni and Liveright, n.d. (Modern Library).

353. —. *The Trumpet-Major.* New York: Harper, 1896.

354. —. *Under the Greenwood Tree.* New York: A. & C. Boni, 1925.

355. *Harlan Miners Speak.* New York: Harcourt, Brace, 1932. S. A. signature.

356. Harris, Bernice Kelly. *Purslane.* Chapel Hill: Univ. of N. C. Press, 1939. S. A. signature.

357. Harrison, Joseph Shea. *Recessional.* Cincinnati: N. A. Powell, 1936. Inscribed: "To Sherwood Anderson - whose own work has meant so very much to me for many years. Sincerely, Joe Shea Harrison."

358. Harrison, Salomay L. *México Simpático: Tierra de Encantos.* Boston:

D. C. Heath, 1929.

359. Harrow, Benjamin, ed. *Contemporary Science.* New York: Boni and Liveright, 1921 (Modern Library).

360. Hartsock, Ernest. *Narcissus and Iscariot.* Atlanta: Bozart Press, 1927.

361. Haslip, Joan. *Parnell: A Biography.* New York: Frederick A. Stokes, 1937. S. A. signature.

362. Hatcher, Harlan. *Creating the Modern American Novel.* New York: Farrar and Rinehart, 1935.

363. Hauptmann, Gerhart. *The Sunken Bell.* New York: Doubleday, 1904.

364. Hawthorne, Nathaniel. *The Blithedale Romance.* New York: J. H. Sears and Co., [1925]. Inscribed: "To Sherwood Anderson from Dwight Macdonald, Spring 1929. This was written by a fellow craftsman of letters." S. A. has written in pencil: "Too many Elizabeths."

365. —. *The Marble Faun.* New York: Hurst and Co., n.d.

366. Hazlitt, William. *The Plain Speaker.* London: George Bell and Sons, 1900.

367. —. *The Round Table; Northcote's Conversations; Characteristics.* London: George Bell and Sons, 1894.

368. —. *Sketches and Essays; Winterslow.* London: George Bell and Sons, 1900.

369. Hecht, Ben. *A Book of Miracles.* New York: Viking, 1939.

370. —. *Count Bruga.* New York: Boni and Liveright, 1926.

371. —. *Erik Dorn.* New York: Boni and Liveright, 1924.

372. —. *A Thousand and One Afternoons in Chicago.* Chicago: Covici-McGee, 1922.

373. Heiden, Konrad. *Hitler: A Biography,* trans. Winifred Ray. New York: Knopf, 1936. S. A. signature.

374. Heijermans, Herman. *The Good Hope,* trans. Lillian Saunders and Caroline Heijermans-Houwink. New York: Samuel French, 1928.

375. Hemingway, Ernest. *Green Hills of Africa.* New York: Scribner's, 1935. S. A. signature.

376. —. *In Our Time.* New York: Boni and Liveright, 1925.

377. —. *The Sun Also Rises.* New York: Modern Library, 1930.

378. —. *The Torrents of Spring.* New York: Scribner's, 1926. Two copies.

379. Henry, Martin M. *To Fair Lucille.* Dayton, Ohio: Belles-Lettres Editions, 1939.

380. Hergesheimer, Joseph. *Wild Oranges.* New York: Knopf, 1919. Inscribed [by Knopf?] : "Is for Miss Elizabeth Prall."

381. Herndon, William H. and Jesse W. Weik. *Abraham Lincoln,* 2 vols. New York: D. Appleton and Co., 1917.

382. Hertz, Emanuel. *Abraham Lincoln: A New Portrait,* 2 vols. New York: Liveright, 1931.

383. Heyward, Duncan C. *Seed from Madagascar.* Chapel Hill: Univ. of N. C. Press, 1937.

384. Hicks, Granville. *John Reed: The Making of A Revolutionary.* New York: Macmillan, 1936. Inscribed: "Sherwood Anderson with warm regard, Granville Hicks." Also S. A. signature.

385. Hielscher, Kurt. *Picturesque Yugo-Slavia.* New York: Brentano's, 1926.

386. *Holy Bible.* New York: Lane and Scott, 1851.

387. Housman, Laurence. *Angels and Ministers.* New York: Harcourt, Brace, 1922.

388. Howard, Sidney C. *Yellow Jack.* New York: Harcourt, Brace, 1934.

389. Huddleston, Sisley. *France.* London: Ernest Benn, 1926.

390. Hudson, William H. *Green Mansions.* New York: Boni and Liveright, 1916 (Modern Library).

391. Hughes, Richard A. *The Innocent Voyage.* New York: Harper, 1929.

392. Hugo, Victor M. *Selections from the Poetical Works of Victor Hugo.* New York: Crowell, 1899. Inscribed: "To Elizabeth Prall from Aunt Lil."

393. Hurst, Fannie. *A President Is Born.* New York: Harper, 1928.

394. Hurston, Zora Neale. *Mules and Men.* Philadelphia: Lippincott, 1935. S. A. signature.

395. Huysmans, Joris K. *The Cathedral,* trans. Clara Bell. London: Kegan Paul, Trench, Trubner and Co., 1922.

396. —. *Down There (La Bas),* trans. Keene Wallis. New York: A. and C. Boni, 1924.

397. Ibsen, Henrik. *A Doll's House and Two Other Plays.* London: Dent, 1912.

398. —. *Eleven Plays of Henrik Ibsen.* New York: Modern Library, [193-?].

399. —. *Ghosts and Two Other Plays.* New York: Dutton, 1914.

400. —. *Ghosts; An Enemy of the People; The Wild Duck,* ed. W. Archer. New York: Scribner's, 1906.

401. —. *The Master Builder; Pillars of Society; Hedda Gabler.* New York: Boni and Liveright, 1917 (Modern Library). Two copies.

402. —. *Plays.* New York: Macmillan, 1927.

403. *The Illustrated Horse Doctor.* Philadelphia: Lippincott, 1872.

404. Irving, Washington. *The Works of Washington Irving*, 3 vols. New York: Collier, n.d.

405. James, William. *The Letters of William James*, ed. by his son Henry James. Boston: Atlantic Monthly Press, 1920. Vol. II only.

406. Jeffers, Robinson. *Return, An Unpublished Poem.* San Francisco: Grabhorn Press, 1934.

407. —. *Roan Stallion, Tamar, and Other Poems.* New York: Boni and Liveright, 1925.

408. Jessup, Alexander, ed. *The Best American Humorous Short Stories.* New York: Boni and Liveright, 1920 (Modern Library).

409. Johnson, James Weldon. *God's Trombones: Seven Negro Sermons in Verse.* New York: Viking, 1927. Inscribed: "For Sherwood, with great admiration, James Weldon Johnson."

410. Johnson, R. Brimley, ed. *Popular British Ballads.* London: Dent, 1894. Vols. I and II only. Signature of Tennessee Mitchell.

411. Johnson, Rossiter. *Campfire and Battlefield: An Illustrated History of the Campaigns and Conflicts of the Great Civil War.* New York: Williams and Cox, n.d.

412. —. Another copy. New York: Bryan, Taylor, [1895].

413. Jolas, Eugène. *Cinema, Poems,* introduction by Sherwood Anderson. New York: Adelphi, 1926. Inscribed: "To Elizabeth and Sherwood, with love and deepest gratitude, Eugène Jolas, Paris, Christmas 1926." A second copy is unsigned.

414. —. *Planets and Angels.* Mt. Vernon, Iowa: Cornell College English Club, 1940. Inscribed: "To Sherwood Anderson with the admiration and friendship of Gene Jolas."

415. Jones, Henry Festing. *Samuel Butler, Author of Erewhon.* London: Macmillan, 1919.

416. Jones, Howard Mumford. *They Say the Forties.* New York: Holt, 1937. Inscribed: "I was *not* Sherwood Anderson's secretary, but O how I wish I had been! Howard Mumford Jones."

417. Jordan, Louis F. *Memoirs of a Criminal Lawyer.* Staunton, Virginia: Beverley Press, 1935. Inscribed: "For Sherwood Anderson, Compliments, Louis F. Jordan."

418. Joyce, James. *Dubliners.* New York: Huebsch, 1917. Two copies.

419. —. *Ulysses,* 4th printing. Paris: Shakespeare and Company, 1924. Inscribed in S. A.'s wife Eleanor's hand: "Sherwood Anderson, Marion, Va."

420. Karsner, David. *Horace Traubel: His Life and Work.* New York: Egmont Arens, 1919. Long inscription by Karsner to S. A. in 1925. Also S. A. signature.

421. —. *Sixteen Authors to One.* New York: Lewis Copeland, 1928.

422. Kemp, Harry. *Don Juan's Note-Book.* New York: Privately printed, 1929.

423. Kennedy, Millard F. and Alvin F. Harlow. *Schoolmaster of Yesterday.* New York: McGraw-Hill, 1940. S. A. signature.

424. Keyserling, Count Hermann, ed. *The Book of Marriage.* New York: Harcourt, Brace, 1926.

425. Komroff, Manuel. *The Fool and Death.* Privately printed, 1930. Inscribed by Komroff: "For Sherwood Anderson with all best wishes."

426. —. *The Grace of Lambs.* New York: Boni and Liveright, 1925. Inscribed: "To Sherwood Anderson, master narrator and pilot of 'young America.' Sincerely, Manuel Komroff."

427. —. *Juggler's Kiss.* New York: Boni and Liveright, 1927. Two copies.

428. —, ed. *Tales of the Monks.* New York: Dial Press, 1928. Inscribed: "This ancient collection of tales for Sherwood Anderson in friendship -

Manuel Komroff."

429. Konody, Paul G., ed. *Modern War; Paintings by C. R. W. Nevinson.* New York: Robert McBride, 1917. Signature of Elizabeth Prall.

430. Koskull, Marie Luise. *Damals in Russland.* Leipzig: Koehler and Amelang, 1931.

431. Kozlenko, William, ed. *Contemporary One-Act Plays.* New York: Scribner's, 1938.

432. Krause, Herbert. *Wind Without Rain.* Indianapolis: Bobbs-Merrill, 1939. S. A. signature.

433. [Krebs, Richard J. H.]. *Out of the Night,* by Jan Valtin (pseud.). New York: Alliance Book Corporation, 1940. S. A. signature.

434. Kreymborg, Alfred. *The Four Apes.* New York: Raley, 1939. Inscribed: "To Sherwood A. from Alfred K. — vide page 143. 54 Charles St., 10/26/39."

435. —. *Troubador: An Autobiography.* New York: Boni and Liveright, 1925.

436. —, *et al.,* eds. *The Second American Caravan.* New York: Macaulay, 1928.

437. —, Lewis Mumford, and Paul Rosenfeld, eds. *The New Caravan.* New York: Norton, 1936.

438. Lamb, Harold. *Genghis Khan: The Emperor of All Men.* Garden City, New York: Garden City Publishing Co., 1927.

439. Lamon, Harry M. and Rob R. Slocum. *Turkey Raising.* New York: Orange Judd, 1924.

440. Lankes, Julius J. *Virginia Woodcuts.* Newport News, Virginia: Virginia Press, 1930.

441. —. *A Woodcut Manual.* New York: Holt, 1932.

442. Lardner, Ring. *Works,* 5 vols. (including *Gullible's Travels, What Of It?, How to Write Short Stories with Samples, The Big Town,* and *You Know Me Al).* New York: Scribner's, 1925. Each volume has S. A. signature.

443. —. *Roundup.* New York: Scribner's, 1929.

444. Latzko, Andreas. *Men in War.* New York: Boni and Liveright, 1918.

445. Lawrence, D. H. *Aaron's Rod.* New York: Thomas Seltzer, 1922.

446. —. *Apocalypse.* New York: Viking, 1932.

447. —. *Assorted Articles.* New York: Knopf, 1930.

448. —. *The Letters of D. H. Lawrence,* ed. Aldous Huxley. New York: Viking, 1932. S. A. signature.

449. —. *The Lost Girl.* New York: A. and C. Boni, 1930.

450. —. *The Man Who Died.* New York: Knopf, 1928. S. A. signature.

451. —. *The Plumed Serpent.* New York: Knopf, 1926.

452. —. *The Rainbow.* New York: Modern Library, 1915[?].

453. —. *Reflections on the Death of a Porcupine and Other Essays.* Philadelphia: Centaur Press, 1925.

454. —. *Sons and Lovers.* New York: Boni and Liveright, 1922 (Modern Library).

455. —. *The Virgin and the Gipsy.* New York: Knopf, 1930.

456. —. *Women in Love.* New York: Viking, 1933 [?].

457. Leech, Walter Stuart. *The Great Crystal Fraud or the Great P. J.* Chicago: Occult Publishing Co., 1926.

458. Le Gallienne, Richard, ed. *The Le Gallienne Book of American Verse.*

New York: Boni and Liveright, 1925.

459. Le Sage, Alain René. *Asmodeus; or, the Devil on Two Sticks*, trans. Joseph Thomas. New York: G. H. Doran, 1926. Inscribed: "To Sherwood Anderson artist-mystic-teller of tales on his fiftieth birthday this humble expression of gratitude for his many works. Laverne W. Colwell. September 13, 1926."

460. Levin, Meyer. *The Old Bunch*. New York: Viking, 1937.

461. Levy, Melvin P. *The Last Pioneers*. New York: Alfred H. King, 1934.

462. Lewis, Sinclair. *Main Street*. New York: Harcourt, Brace and Howe, 1920. Inscribed: "Tennessee M. Anderson."

463. – and John C. Moffitt. *It Can't Happen Here*. New York: Dramatists Play Service, 1938.

464. Lewis, D. B. Wyndham. *François Villon: A Documented Survey*, with preface by Hilaire Belloc. New York: Literary Guild, 1928.

465. Lewis, Wyndham. *Tarr*. New York: Knopf, 1918.

466. Lewisohn, Ludwig. *The Case of Mr. Crump*. Paris: Edward W. Titus, 1926.

467. –. *Mid-channel: An American Chronicle*. New York: Harper, 1929.

468. –, ed. *A Modern Book of Criticism*. New York: Boni and Liveright, 1919. Two copies.

469. [Lincoln, Abraham]. *An Autobiography of Abraham Lincoln*, ed. N. W. Stephenson. Indianapolis: Bobbs-Merrill, 1926. S. A. signature.

470. Lindsay, Vachel. *The Litany of Washington Street*. New York: Macmillan, 1929. S. A. signature.

471. Linn, James W. and Houghton W. Taylor. *A Foreword to Fiction*. New York: Appleton-Century, 1935.

472. Lippmann, Walter. *A Preface to Morals.* New York: Macmillan, 1929.

473. Llona, Victor, *et al.*, eds. *Les Romanciers Américains.* Paris: Denoël et Steele, 1931.

474. Lodge, Henry Cabot, ed. *The Best of the World's Classics;* Volume I: *Greece.* New York: Funk and Wagnalls, 1909.

475. — and Francis W. Halsey, eds. *The Best of the World's Classics;* Volume II: *Rome.* New York: Funk and Wagnalls, 1909.

476. Loeb, Harold. *The Chart of Plenty.* New York: Viking, 1935. S. A. signature.

477. Lovett, Robert Morss and Howard Mumford Jones, eds. *The College Reader.* Boston: Houghton Mifflin, 1936.

478. Lowry, Robert J. *Hutton Street.* Cincinnati: The Little Man, 1940.

479. Luhan, Mabel Dodge. *Lorenzo in Taos.* New York: Knopf, 1932. Two copies.

480. Lumpkin, Katharine Du Pre and Dorothy Wolff Douglas. *Child Workers in America.* New York: Robert McBride, 1937.

481. Lyman, George D. *Ralston's Ring.* New York: Scribner's, 1937.

482. —. *The Saga of the Comstock Lode.* New York: Scribner's, 1934.

483. MacDonald, Lois. *Southern Mill Hills.* New York: Alex Hillman, 1928.

484. MacDougall, Curtis D., ed. *National Almanac and Year Book for 1938.* Chicago: National Survey and Sales Corporation, 1937. S. A. signature.

485. McFee, William. *Command.* Garden City, New York: Doubleday, Page, 1922.

486. McIlvaine, Charles. *One Thousand American Fungi.* Indianapolis: Bowen-Merrill, 1900.

487. McKee, Philip. *Big Town,* with a foreword by Sherwood Anderson. New York: John Day, 1931. With McKee's signature.

488. Maeterlinck, Maurice. *A Miracle of Saint Anthony and Five Other Plays.* New York: Boni and Liveright, 1917 (Modern Library).

489. Mann, Thomas. *Children and Fools,* trans. H. G. Scheffauer. New York: Knopf, 1928.

490. March, Joseph M. *The Set-Up.* New York: Covici-Freide, 1928.

491. Marcus, Shmuel, ed. *Anthology of Revolutionary Poetry,* ed. Marcus Graham (pseud.). New York: The Active Press, 1929.

492. Marcuse, Ludwig. *Heine: A Life Between Love and Hate,* trans. L. M. Sievelking and Ian Morrow. New York: Farrar and Rinehart, 1933. S. A. signature.

493. [Marshak, I. I.]. *Men and Mountains,* by M. Ilin (pseud.), trans. Beatrice Kinkead. Philadelphia: Lippincott, 1935. S. A. signature.

494. Masefield, John. *Poems and Plays.* New York: Macmillan, 1918.

495. —. *The Trial of Jesus.* New York: Macmillan, 1925.

496. Masereel, Frans. *Geschichte Ohne Worte: 60 Holzschnitte von Frans Masereel.* München: Kurt Wolff, 1927.

497. —. *Landschaften und Stimmungen: 60 Holzschnitte von Frans Masereel.* München: Kurt Wolff, 1929.

498. —. *Mein Studenbuch.* München: Kurt Wolff, 1926.

499. Masters, Edgar Lee. *The Great Valley.* New York: Macmillan, 1916.

500. Masters, Herbert. *Look in Thy Heart.* Brooklyn, New York: Privately printed, 1939.

501. Mathews, Basil J. *The Jew and the World Ferment.* London: Edinburgh House, 1934.

502. Maugham, W. Somerset. *Liza of Lambeth*. London: T. Fisher Unwin, 1915.

503. —. *The Moon and Sixpence*. New York: Grosset and Dunlap, 1919.

504. —. *Of Human Bondage*. New York: Literary Guild, 1937.

505. Maurois, André. *The Next Chapter: The War Against the Moon*. New York: Dutton, 1928.

506. Maverick, Maury. *In Blood and Ink*. New York: Starling Press, 1939. Inscribed: "To my good friends the Sherwood Andersons on their visit to San Antonio from Maury Maverick (I knew the Andersons when I was in Congress. Now I'm Mayor of San Antonio. December 11, 1939)."

507. Meier-Graefe, Julius. *Vincent van Gogh, A Biographical Study*, trans. J. H. Reece, 2 vols. London: Medici Society, 1922.

508. Melville, Herman. *Moby Dick*. New York: Scribner's, 1899.

509. —. *Some Personal Letters of Herman Melville and a Bibliography by Meade Minnigerode*. New York: Brick Row Book Shop, 1922.

510. —. *Typee*. Philadelphia: David McKay, 1930.

511. Mencken, H. L. *Prejudices: Sixth Series*. New York: Knopf, 1927.

512. Meredith, George. *Diana of the Crossways*. New York: Boni and Liveright, n.d. (Modern Library).

513. Merezhkovskii, Dmitrii S. *The Romance of Leonardo da Vinci*, trans. Bernard G. Guerney. New York: Modern Library, 1928.

514. *Message from the President of the United States Transmitting a Report of the Secretary of Agriculture in Relation to the Forests, Rivers, and Mountains of the Southern Appalachian Region*. Washington: Government Printing Office, 1902.

515. Meynell, Alice. *Collected Poems*. New York: Scribner's, 1913. Inscribed: "E. Prall."

516. Michaud, Régis. *Panorama de la Littérature Américaine Contemporaine.* Paris: Kra, 1926. Inscribed by Michaud: "To Sherwood Anderson with deep sympathy and admiration this modest contribution to the glory of American letters whom he so highly illustrates."

517. —. *Le Roman Américain D'Aujourd'hui.* Paris: Boivin, 1926.

518. Millet, Fred B. *Contemporary American Authors.* New York: Harcourt, Brace, 1940.

519. Milton, John. *Paradise Lost.* New York: Hurst and Co., n.d.

520. Minor, Charles L. C. *The Real Lincoln,* 4th edition. Gastonia, North Carolina: Atkins-Rankin Co., 1928.

521. Mitchell, Broadus. *William Gregg: Factory Master of the Old South.* Chapel Hill: Univ. of N. C. Press, 1928.

522. Moberg, Vilhelm. *Memory of Youth.* New York: Simon and Schuster, 1937. S. A. signature.

523. Molière. *Plays.* New York: Boni and Liveright, 1924. Two copies.

524. Monroe, Harriet and Alice C. Henderson, eds. *The New Poetry.* New York: Macmillan, 1936.

525. Moore, George. *Avowals.* New York: Boni and Liveright, 1926.

526. —. *Confessions of a Young Man.* New York: Modern Library, 1925.

527. —. *Evelyn Innes.* New York: Modern Library, [19-?].

528. —. *Works* (Carra Edition), 21 vols. New York: Boni and Liveright, 1922-1924.

529. Moore, Julia A. *The Sweet Singer of Michigan, Poems by Mrs. Julia A. Moore,* ed. Walter Blair. Chicago: P. Covici, 1928.

530. Morand, Paul. *Ouvert la Nuit.* Paris: Editions de la Nouvelle Revue Française, 1922.

531. Morison, Samuel E. and Henry S. Commager. *The Growth of the American Republic.* New York: Oxford Univ. Press, 1930.

532. —. Another copy, 2 vols. New York: Oxford Univ. Press, 1937. S. A. signature.

533. Morley, Christopher. *Old Loopy.* Chicago: Argus Book Shop, 1935. S. A. signature.

534. —, ed. *Modern Essays, Second Series.* New York: Harcourt, Brace, 1924. Inscribed: "Sherwood Anderson with gratitude from Christopher Morley."

535. Morris, William. *Selected Writings,* ed. G. D. H. Cole. New York: Random House, 1934.

536. Mumford, Lewis. *The Golden Day.* New York: Boni and Liveright, 1926.

537. Munz, Charles C. *Land Without Moses.* New York: Harper, 1938.

538. *My Chinese Marriage* [by "M. T. F."]. New York: Duffield, 1921.

539. Nathan, George Jean. *The Bachelor Life.* New York: Reynal and Hitchcock, 1941. Inscribed: "To Sherwood Anderson with all the old, warm regard of George Jean Nathan, Feb. 26, 1941."

540. —. *Land of the Pilgrims' Pride.* New York: Knopf, 1927.

541. —. *The Theatre of the Moment.* New York: Knopf, 1936. Inscribed: "To Sherwood Anderson — In affectionate friendship, George Jean Nathan."

542. —, Sherwood Anderson, *et al.,* eds. *American Spectator Yearbook.* New York: Frederick A. Stokes Co., 1934. S. A. signature.

543. Nekrassov, Nicholas. *Who Can Be Happy and Free in Russia?* trans. J. M. Soskice. London: Oxford Univ. Press, 1917.

544. Nevinson, Henry W. *Farewell to America.* New York: Huebsch, 1922.

545. Newman, Frances. *The Short Story's Mutations from Petronius to Paul Morand*. New York: Huebsch, 1924.

546. Nicholson, Daniel H. S. and A. H. E. Lee, eds. *The Oxford Book of English Mystical Verse*. Oxford: Clarendon Press, 1921.

547. Nietzsche, Friedrich. *Thus Spake Zarathustra*. New York: Boni and Liveright, 1917 (Modern Library).

548. —. *The Genealogy of Morals*, trans. H. B. Samuel. New York: Boni and Liveright, 1918. Two copies.

549. O'Brien, Edward J., ed. *The Best Short Stories of 1920 and the Yearbook of the American Short Story*. Boston: Small, Maynard and Co., 1921. Also similar volumes for 1921, 1922, 1925, 1927, 1928, and 1940.

550. —, ed. *50 Best American Short Stories, 1915-1939*. Boston: Houghton Mifflin, 1939.

551. O'Brien, Frederick. *White Shadows in the South Seas*. New York: Century Co., 1920.

552. Ockerson, J. A. *The Mississippi River from St. Louis to the Sea*. St. Louis, 1892.

553. O'Donnell, Edwin P. *Green Margins*. Boston: Houghton Mifflin, 1936. S. A. signature.

554. O'Flaherty, Liam. *The Black Soul*. London: Jonathan Cape, 1928.

555. Omar Khayyam. *Rubaiyat*, trans. Edward Fitzgerald. New York: Crowell, 1896.

556. —. Another copy. London: William Heinemann, 1909.

557. O'Neil, Raymond. *The Triumph of the Egg, A Drama in One Act*. Chicago: Dramatic Publishing Co., 1932. Two copies.

558. O'Neill, Eugene. *The Emperor Jones*. New York: Boni and Liveright, 1928.

559. —. *The Emperor Jones; The Straw.* New York: Boni and Liveright, 1921.

560. —. *The Moon of the Caribbees and Six Other Plays of the Sea.* New York: Boni and Liveright, 1923 (Modern Library). Two copies.

561. Ossendowski, Ferdinand. *Slaves of the Sun.* New York: Dutton, 1928.

562. "Ouida" [Marie Louise de la Ramée]. *In A Winter City.* New York: Boni and Liveright, 1923 (Modern Library).

563. Overton, Grant M., ed. *Great Modern Short Stories.* New York: Modern Library, 1930.

564. Ovid. *Metamorphoses,* trans. F. J. Miller, 2 vols. New York: Putnam's, 1916.

565. *Pages from The Nation.* New York: Nation Press, 1928.

566. Paine, Albert Bigelow. *Mark Twain, A Biography,* 3 vols. New York: Harper, 1912.

567. Paine, Thomas. *Selections from the Writings of Thomas Paine,* ed. Carl Van Doren. New York: Boni and Liveright, 1922 (Modern Library). Two copies.

568. Pancoast, Henry S., ed. *Standard English Poems.* New York: Holt, 1899.

569. Papini, Giovanni. *Figure Umane.* Florence: Stabilimenti Grafici Vallecchi, 1940.

570. Parkman, Francis. *La Salle and the Discovery of the Great West.* Boston: Little, Brown, 1918.

571. Pastor, Antonio, *et al. Linguaphone: Curso de Conversación Español.* Linguaphone Institute, n.d.

572. Pater, Walter. *Marius the Epicurean.* New York: Boni and Liveright, 1921 (Modern Library). Two copies.

573. —. Another copy. New York: A. L. Burt, n.d.

574. Peattie, Donald C. *A Prairie Grove.* New York: Literary Guild, 1938.

575. Pendleton, William C. *History of Tazewell County and Southwest Virginia, 1748-1920.* Richmond: W. C. Hill Printing Co., 1920.

576. —. *Political History of Appalachian Virginia 1776-1927.* Dayton, Virginia: Shenandoah Press, 1927. Inscribed by the author.

577. Pepys, Samuel. *Passages from the Diary of Samuel Pepys,* ed. Richard Le Gallienne. New York: Boni and Liveright, 1921 (Modern Library).

578. Percy, William Alexander. *Enzio's Kingdom and Other Poems.* New Haven: Yale, 1924. Inscribed: "For Sherwood Anderson with a lot of liking. William Alexander Percy. October, 1924."

579. Perkins, Frances. *People At Work.* New York: John Day Co., 1934.

580. Peterkin, Julia. *Black April.* Indianapolis: Bobbs-Merrill, 1927.

581. —. *Scarlet Sister Mary.* Indianapolis: Bobbs-Merrill, 1928.

582. Peters, Lulu Hunt. *Diet and Health.* Chicago: Reilly and Lee Co., 1934.

583. Peterson, Arnold. *Karl Marx and Marxism.* New York: Labor News Co., 1933.

584. Petronius Arbiter. *The Satyricon,* ed. C. K. Scott-Moncrieff. London: Simpkin, Marshall, Hamilton, Kent, n.d.

585. Pinckney, Josephine. *Sea-Drinking Cities: Poems.* New York: Harper, 1927. Inscribed: "For Sherwood Anderson with salutations and regards — Josephine Pinckney."

586. Pirandello, Luigi. *The One-Act Plays of Luigi Pirandello.* New York: Dutton, 1928.

587. Poe, Edgar A. *The Best Tales of Edgar Allan Poe.* New York: Boni and Liveright, 1924 (Modern Library).

588. Pope, Alexander and William Collins. *The Poetical Works of Pope and Collins,* 4 vols. in 2. Boston: Houghton Mifflin, 1882.

589. Porter, Katherine Anne. *Flowering Judas and Other Stories.* New York: Harcourt, Brace, 1935. S. A. signature.

590. Powys, John Cowper. *Wolf Solent: A Novel,* 2 vols. New York: Simon and Schuster, 1929.

591. Powys, Llewelyn. *Black Laughter.* New York: Harcourt, Brace, 1924.

592. Prezzolini, Giuseppe. *Nicolo Machiavelli.* New York: Brentano's, 1928.

593. Price, Margaret. *The Negro Voter in the South.* Atlanta: Southern Regional Council, n.d.

594. Priestley, J. B., ed. *The Mercury Story Book.* London: Longmans, Green, 1929.

595. *Prohibition As We See It: Opinions Expressed by Clergymen in a Nation Wide Poll of the Episcopal Church in the United States.* New York: Church Temperance Society, 1928.

596. Proust, Marcel. *The Guermantes Way,* 2 vols., trans. C. K. Scott Moncrieff. New York: Thomas Seltzer, 1925.

597. —. *Swann's Way,* introduction by Lewis Galantiere. New York: Modern Library, 1928.

598. —. *Within A Budding Grove,* trans. C. K. Scott Moncrieff. New York: Thomas Seltzer, 1924. S. A. signature. A second copy unsigned.

599. Quiller-Couch, Sir Arthur T., ed. *The Oxford Book of English Verse, 1250-1900.* Oxford: Clarendon Press, 1907.

600. Ransom, John Crowe. *God Without Thunder: An Unorthodox Defense of Orthodoxy.* New York: Harcourt, Brace, 1930.

601. Rascoe, Burton. *Before I Forget.* New York: Literary Guild, 1937.

602. —. *Morrow's Almanack for 1928.* New York: William Morrow, 1927.

603. Reed, John. *Ten Days That Shook the World.* New York: International Publishers, 1926. S. A. signature.

604. Reitmeister, Louis A. *If Tomorrow Comes.* New York: Walden Press, 1934.

605. Remarque, Erich M. *All Quiet on the Western Front.* Boston: Little, Brown, 1929.

606. Remlap, L. T. [pseud. of Loomis T. Palmer]. *Grant and His Travels.* New York: Hurst and Co., 1885. Volume I only.

607. Rey, Robert. *Gauguin.* New York: Dodd, Mead, 1924.

608. Rhys, Jean. *Voyage in the Dark.* New York: W. Morrow, 1935.

609. Rickel, Harry, ed. *The Wisdom of Balzac.* New York: Putnam's, 1923. Inscribed: "To Sherwood Anderson, a great literary artist, with compliments from Harry Rickel."

610. Riggs, Lynn. *Green Grow the Lilacs, A Play.* New York: Samuel French, 1931.

611. Ringel, Frederick J., ed. *America As Americans See It.* New York: Literary Guild, 1932. S. A. signature.

612. —, ed. Another copy. New York: Harcourt, Brace, 1932.

613. River, Walter L. *The Torguts.* New York: Frederick A. Stokes, 1939.

614. Roberts, Elizabeth Madox. *The Great Meadow.* New York: Viking, 1930.

615. Rogers, Virginia Horton. *Chaff and Wheat.* Fort Atkinson, Wisconsin: Privately printed, 1936.

616. *Roget's Thesaurus,* new edition. New York: Thomas Y. Crowell, 1879.

617. Rolland, Romain. *The Fourteenth of July, and Danton: Two Plays of the French Revolution.* New York: Holt, 1918.

618. —. *Mother and Son.* New York: Holt, 1927.

619. Romains, Jules. *The Death of a Nobody,* trans. Desmond MacCarthy and Sydney Waterlow. New York: Huebsch, 1914.

620. Rorty, James. *Children of the Sun.* New York: Macmillan, 1926.

621. —. *Where Life Is Better: An Unsentimental American Journey.* New York: Reynal and Hitchcock, 1936. Inscribed: "For Sherwood Anderson who has travelled farther and I suspect seen more. James Rorty."

622. Rose, Héloïse Durant. *Dante: A Dramatic Poem.* New York: Oxford Univ. Press, 1921.

623. Rosenbaum, Nathan. *Each In His Time.* Philadelphia: Ariel Publishing Co., 1925. Inscribed: "To the author of 'Dark Laughter' — Nathan Rosenbaum."

624. Rosenfeld, Paul. *The Boy in the Sun.* New York: Macaulay Co., 1928.

625. —. *Discoveries of a Music Critic.* New York: Harcourt, Brace, 1936. Inscribed: "To my dear Sherwood and Eleanor — much love from Paul."

626. —. *Men Seen: Twenty-four Modern Authors.* New York: Dial Press, 1925. Inscribed: "To the Sun Man Sherwood Anderson Love and greetings. P. R."

627. —. *Musical Chronicle (1917-1923).* New York: Harcourt, Brace, 1923. Inscribed: "For Sherwood and Elizabeth with much love. Paul — Sept. 17 '23."

628. —. *Musical Portraits.* New York: Harcourt, Brace and Howe, 1920. Inscribed: "To Sherwood Anderson and Tennessee Mitchell with love — Paul Rosenfeld 5/17/20."

629. —. *Port of New York.* New York: Harcourt, Brace, 1924.

630. Rosskam, Edwin. *San Francisco: West Coast Metropolis,* introduction by William Saroyan. New York: Longmans, Green, 1939. S. A. signature.

631. Rosskam, Edwin and Ruby A. Black, eds. *Washington Nerve Center.* New York: Alliance Book Corporation, 1939.

632. Rothermell, Fred. *To Raise These Halt.* New York: Lee Furman, 1936. Inscribed: "For Eleanor and Sherwood Anderson — Fred Rothermell, New York, September, 1936."

633. Russell, Bertrand. *Marriage and Morals.* New York: Liveright, 1929.

634. —. *Political Ideals.* New York: Century, 1917.

635. —. *Selected Papers.* New York: Modern Library, 1927.

636. Russell, Mrs. Bertrand (Dora). *The Right to Be Happy.* New York: Harper, 1927.

637. Ryttenberg, Lillie and Beatrice Lang, eds. *Samples: A Collection of Short Stories.* New York: Boni and Liveright, 1927.

638. Samuels, Samuel H. *The First Book of Poems.* Brooklyn, New York: Privately printed, 1926.

639. Sandburg, Carl. *Abraham Lincoln: The Prairie Years,* 2 vols. New York: Harcourt, Brace, 1926.

640. —. *Rootabaga Stories.* New York: Harcourt, Brace, 1922. Inscribed: "Sherwood — ﹏go to it, old horse thief ﹏ — yours zigzag — Carl Sandburg."

641. —. *Selected Poems,* ed. Rebecca West. New York: Harcourt, Brace, 1926.

642. Santayana, George. *Little Essays.* New York: Scribner's, 1921.

643. —. *Soliloquies in England and Later Soliloquies.* New York: Scribner's, 1923. Inscribed: "To Sherwood Anderson with all good wishes, Ralph Church — June 30."

644. Sassoon, Siegfried L. *The Memoirs of George Sherston.* New York: Literary Guild, 1937.

645. Saxon, Lyle. *Children of Strangers.* Boston: Houghton Mifflin, 1937. S. A. signature.

646. —. *Father Mississippi.* New York: Century Co., 1927.

647. Sayler, Oliver M. *Moscow Art Theatre Series of Russian Plays,* 2 vols. New York: Brentano's, 1922.

648. Schnitzler, Arthur. *Fraülein Else.* New York: Simon and Schuster, 1925. Inscribed: "To Elizabeth with love, Sherwood."

649. —. *Green Cockatoo and Other Plays.* Chicago: A. C. McClurg, 1913.

650. —. *The Road to the Open,* trans. Horace Samuel. New York: Knopf, 1923.

651. Scott, Evelyn. *The Wave.* New York: J. Cape and H. Smith, 1929.

652. Scott, Robert, compiler. *The War of the Rebellion: A Compilation of the Official Records of the Union and Confederate Armies* (Series I, Vol. XXXII, Part III — Correspondence). Washington: Government Printing Office, 1891.

653. Seabrook, William B. *The Magic Island.* New York: Harcourt, Brace, 1929.

654. Segond, Louis, translator. *La Sainte Bible.* New York: Oxford Univ. Press, 1892.

655. Seligmann, Herbert J. *D. H. Lawrence: An American Interpretation.* New York: Thomas Seltzer, 1924.

656. Seltzer, Thomas, ed. *Best Russian Short Stories.* New York: Boni and Liveright, 1918. Two copies.

657. Sender, Ramon J. *Seven Red Sundays.* New York: Liveright, 1936.

658. Sergel, Roger L. *Arlie Gelston.* New York: Huebsch, 1923. Inscribed: "For Sherwood Anderson, who has, written more truly and deeply than this generation yet dreams, from Roger L. Sergel."

659. Sergel, Ruth, ed. *The Woman in the House.* New York: The Womans Press, 1938.

660. Shakespeare, William. *Complete Works,* ed. W. G. Clark and W. A. Wright. New York: Grosset and Dunlap, 1911.

661. —. *Shakespeare's Principal Plays,* ed. Tucker Brooke and John W. Cunliffe. New York: Century Co., 1924.

662. —. *Antony and Cleopatra.* London: Dent, 1906.

663. —. *Comedy of Errors.* London: Dent, 1897.

664. —. *Henry IV, Part Two.* London: Dent, 1914.

665. —. *Henry VI, Part One.* London: Dent, 1913.

666. —. *King Lear.* London: Dent, 1904.

667. —. *Macbeth.* London: Dent, 1899.

668. —. *Merchant of Venice.* London: Dent, 1898.

669. —. *Much Ado About Nothing.* London: Dent, 1899.

670. —. *Richard III.* London: Dent, 1916.

671. —. *Romeo and Juliet.* London: Dent, 1899.

672. —. *Sonnets.* London: Dent, 1919.

673. Shaw, George Bernard. *Candida.* New York: Brentano's, 1913. S. A. wrote "psychology" on first page.

674. Shaw, Lloyd. *Cowboy Dances: A Collection of Western Square Dances.* Caldwell, Idaho: Caxton Printers, 1939. Inscribed: "For Sherwood

Anderson most gratefully! Lloyd Shaw."

675. Shelley, Percy B. *Poetical Works.* London: Oxford Univ. Press, 1905.

676. Sherman, Stuart P. *Critical Woodcuts.* New York: Scribner's, 1926. S. A. signature. A second copy unsigned.

677. Sherman, William T. *Memoirs of General William T. Sherman.* New York: D. Appleton, 1875. Volume I only.

678. Shipley, Joseph T., ed. *Modern French Poetry,* An Anthology. New York: Greenberg, 1926. Inscribed: "To Elizabeth and Sherwood Anderson in deep and affectionate admiration — Maria and Eugene Jolas."

679. Shipman, Evan. *Free for All.* New York: Scribner's, 1935. S. A. signature.

680. Sigmund, Jay G. *Drowsy Ones.* Cedar Rapids, Iowa: Prairie Publishing Co., 1925. With author's signature.

681. —. *Merged Blood, The Attic Chest,* [and other titles]. Des Moines: Maizeland Press, 1929.

682. —. *Wapsipinicon Tales.* Cedar Rapids, Iowa: Prairie Publishing Co., 1927. Inscribed: "For Sherwood Anderson, who great as he is, is not too big to hear the voice of a lesser singer, piping by the roadside. Jay G. Sigmund, Nov. 14, 1927." A second copy is unsigned.

683. Sinclair, Upton. *The Way Out.* New York: Farrar and Rinehart, 1933. S. A. signature.

684. Sklar, George and Albert Maltz. *Peace on Earth, An Anti-War Play,* with a foreword by Sherwood Anderson. New York: Samuel French, 1934.

685. Smith, Chard Powers. *Annals of the Poets.* New York: Scribner's, 1935.

686. Smith, Henry Justin. *Deadlines.* Chicago: Covici-McGee, 1923. Inscribed: "For Sherwood Anderson with sincere friendship, Henry Justin Smith, Nov., 1923."

687. Soboleff, Leonid. *Romanoff,* trans. Alfred Fremantle. New York: Longmans, Green, 1935. S. A. signature.

688. Sologub, Feodor. *The Old House and Other Tales,* trans. John Cournos. New York: Knopf, 1916.

689. Soule, George H. *The Coming American Revolution.* New York: Macmillan, 1934.

690. *Special Report on Diseases of the Horse.* Washington: Government Printing Office, 1903.

691. Spratling, William P. *Little Mexico.* New York: J. Cape and H. Smith, 1932. Inscribed by Spratling to S. A.

692. —. *Old Plantation Houses in Louisiana.* New York: William Helburn, 1927. Inscribed: "For Sherwood and Elizabeth with love and no apologies. Bill. New Orleans, Dec. 16, 1927."

693. — and William Faulkner. *Sherwood Anderson and Other Famous Creoles.* New Orleans: Pelican Bookshop, 1926. Inscribed to Anderson by Faulkner.

694. Stalin, Joseph, *et al. Soviet Union 1935.* Moscow: Cooperative Publishing Society, 1935.

695. Stallings, Laurence. *Plumes.* New York: Grosset & Dunlap, 1925.

696. Steffens, Joseph Lincoln. *The Autobiography of Lincoln Steffens,* 2 vols. New York: Harcourt, Brace, 1931.

697. Stein, Emanuel, *et al. Labor and the New Deal.* New York: F. S. Crofts, 1934.

698. Stein, Gertrude. *Four Saints in Three Acts.* New York: Random House, 1934. Two copies.

699. —. *Geography and Plays,* with introduction by Sherwood Anderson. Boston: Four Seas Co., 1922.

700. —. *How to Write.* Paris: Plain Edition, 1931. Two copies.

701. —. *Lectures in America.* New York: Random House, 1935. Inscribed: "To Sherwood with all my love, Gertrude."

702. —. *The Making of Americans.* New York: A. and C. Boni, 1926.

703. —. *Paris France.* New York: Scribner's, 1940.

704. —. *Tender Buttons: Objects, Food, Rooms.* New York: Claire Marie, 1914.

705. —. *Useful Knowledge.* New York: Payson and Clarke, 1928.

706. Steinberg, Noah. *God's Dust.* New York: Combo Press, 1939. S. A. signature.

707. Stendhal [Marie Henri Beyle]. *The Red and the Black,* trans. C. K. Scott-Moncrieff, 2 vols. New York: Boni and Liveright, 1926.

708. Stephenson, Nathaniel W. *Lincoln.* Indianapolis: Bobbs-Merrill, 1922. S. A. signature.

709. Stetsky, A., *et al.,* eds. *Our Country.* Moscow: Cooperative Publishing Society, 1937.

710. [Stettheimer, Ettie]. *Philosophy: An Autobiographical Fragment,* by Henrie Waste (pseud.). London: Longmans, Green, 1917. S. A. signature.

711. Stevens, Glendon A. *Roses in the Little Garden.* Boston: Little, Brown, 1926.

712. Stevens, James. *Paul Bunyan.* New York: Knopf, 1925. Inscribed: "To Sherwood Anderson, for a memorable day and evening — James Stevens."

713. Stevenson, Robert Louis. *Treasure Island.* New York: Boni and Liveright, [192-?] (Modern Library).

714. Stokes, Thomas L. *Chip Off My Shoulder.* Princeton: Princeton Univ. Press, 1940. S. A. signature.

715. *Stories From the Dial.* New York: Dial Press, 1924.

716. Strachey, John. *Literature and Dialectical Materialism.* New York: Covici-Friede, 1934.

717. —. *The Nature of Capitalist Crisis.* New York: Covici-Friede, 1935.

718. Strachey, Lytton. *Books and Characters.* New York: Harcourt, Brace, 1922.

719. —. *Elizabeth and Essex.* New York: Harcourt, Brace, 1928.

720. Strindberg, August. *Miss Julie and Other Plays.* New York: Boni and Liveright, 1918.

721. —. *On the Seaboard.* New York: Grosset and Dunlap, 1913.

722. Stringer, Arthur. *Irish Poems.* New York: Mitchell Kennerley, 1911.

723. Stuart, Jesse. *Man With A Bull-Tongue Plow.* New York: Dutton, 1934. S. A. signature.

724. —. *Tim: A Story By Jesse Stuart, With A Cover Illustration by Charles Atkinson.* Cincinnati: The Little Man, 1939.

725. Sudermann,Hermann. *Dame Care.* New York: Boni and Liveright, 1918 (Modern Library).

726. Sweeney, Ed. *Poorhouse Sweeney,* with a foreword by Theodore Dreiser. New York: Boni and Liveright, 1927.

727. Swift, Jonathan. *The Choice Works of Dean Swift in Prose and Verse.* New York: John W. Lovell Co., n.d.

728. —. *Journal to Stella.* New York: Dutton, n.d.

729. Swinburne, Algernon Charles. *Poems.* New York: Boni and Liveright,

n.d. (Modern Library).

730. —. *Poetical Works.* New York: Thomas Y. Crowell, 1884.

731. Symons, Arthur. *Cities and Sea-coasts and Islands.* New York: Brentano's, 1919.

732. —. *The Symbolist Movement in Literature.* New York: Dutton, 1919.

733. Synge, John M. *The Dramatic Works of John M. Synge.* Dublin: Maunsel and Co., 1915. Inscribed by Waldo Frank: "The works of the most vital, singing soul of modern British annals — To Sherwood Anderson, to whom it is most appropriate to give them. Waldo F."

734. Talley, Thomas W., ed. *Negro Folk Rhymes.* New York: Macmillan, 1922.

735. Tarkington, Booth. *The Plutocrat.* Garden City, New York: Doubleday, Page, 1927.

736. Tate, Allen, *et al. I'll Take My Stand: The South and the Agrarian Tradition,* by Twelve Southerners. New York: Harper, 1930.

737. Tennyson, Alfred. *Maud.* East Aurora, New York: Roycrofters Press, 1900.

738. Terrell, John Upton. *Sunday Is the Day You Rest.* New York: Coward-McCann, 1939. S. A. signature.

739. Terry, Thomas Philip. *Terry's Short Cut to Spanish.* Boston: Houghton Mifflin, 1938.

740. Thomas, Dorothy. *Ma Jeeter's Girls.* New York: Knopf, 1933. S. A. signature.

741. Thomas, William Sturgis. *Field Book of Common Gilled Mushrooms.* New York: Putnam's, 1928.

742. Thompson, Francis. *Complete Poetical Works.* New York: Boni and Liveright, 1918 (Modern Library).

743. Thoreau, Henry D. *Walden.* New York: Dutton, 1912.

744. —. *A Week on the Concord and Merrimac Rivers.* New York: Scribner's, 1921.

745. Tippett, Tom. *Horse Shoe Bottoms* (uncorrected proofs). New York: Harper, 1935.

746. —. *When Southern Labor Stirs.* New York: J. Cape and H. Smith, 1931. S. A. signature.

747. Tolstoy, Leo. *The Death of Ivan Ilyitch.* New York: Boni and Liveright, n.d. (Modern Library). S. A. signature.

748. —. *The Devil,* trans. Aylmer Maude. New York: Harper, 1926.

749. —. *Redemption, and Two Other Plays.* New York: Boni and Liveright, 1919 (Modern Library).

750. —. *Resurrection,* trans. Louise Maude. New York: Grosset and Dunlap, n.d.

751. —. *War and Peace,* 4 vols. in 2, trans. Leo Wiener. Boston: Dana Estes and Company, 1904. S. A. signature.

752. —. *What Is Art?,* trans. Aylmer Maude. New York: Thomas Y. Crowell, 1899.

753. Tomlinson, Henry M. *The Sea and the Jungle.* New York: Modern Library, 1928.

754. Toomer, Jean. *Cane.* New York: Boni and Liveright, 1923. Inscribed: "For Sherwood Anderson whose rich glow and beauty opened those emotions which in this book are most pure. Jean Toomer."

755. Townsend, William B. *Observations from a Peak in Lumpkin,* ed. A. F. Dean. Privately printed, n.d. Inscribed: "May 8, 1939 — To Sherwood Anderson, a writer, from one who wishes he was. Austin F. Dean."

756. Trollope, Anthony. *The Warden, and Barchester Towers.* New York:

Modern Library, 1936.

757. Tully, Jim. *Beggars of Life.* New York: A. and C. Boni, 1924.

758. Turgenev, Ivan. *Fathers and Sons.* New York: Boni and Liveright, 1917 (Modern Library). Two copies.

759. —. *Memoirs of A Sportsman; A Nobleman's Nest,* trans. I. F. Hapgood. Boston: Jefferson Press, n.d.

760. —. *Rudin,* trans. Constance Garnett. New York: Macmillan, 1917.

761. —. *Smoke,* trans. W. F. West. New York: Thomas Y. Crowell, n.d.

762. —. Another copy, trans. Constance Garnett. New York: Macmillan, 1917.

763. —. Another copy. New York: Boni and Liveright, 1919 (Modern Library).

764. —. *A Sportsman's Sketches,* trans. Constance Garnett, 2 vols. New York: Macmillan, 1920.

765. Turner, Frederick Jackson. *The Frontier in American History.* New York: Holt, 1937.

766. Undset, Sigrid. *Kristin Lavrans-Datter: A Trilogy (The Bridal Wreath, The Mistress, The Cross),* 3 vols. New York: Knopf, 1927.

767. Vanderbilt, Cornelius. *Farewell to Fifth Avenue.* New York: Simon and Schuster, 1935.

768. Vandercook, John W. *Black Majesty.* New York: Harper, 1928.

769. Vane, Sutton. *Outward Bound.* New York: Boni and Liveright, 1924.

770. Van Gogh, Vincent. *The Letters of Vincent Van Gogh to His Brother, 1872-1886,* 2 vols. London: Constable, 1927. S. A. signature.

771. —. *Further Letters of Vincent Van Gogh to His Brother, 1886-1889.*

Boston: Houghton Mifflin, 1930. S. A. signature.

772. —. *Letters to An Artist, from Vincent van Gogh to Anton Ridder van Rappard, 1881-1885,* trans. R. Van Messell. New York: Viking, 1936. S. A. signature.

773. Varney, John C. *First Wounds.* New York: F. Bianco, 1926.

774. Veblen, Thorstein. *The Place of Science in Modern Civilisation and Other Essays.* New York: Huebsch, 1919.

775. Veiby, John. *Jingo.* South Bend, Indiana, 1927.

776. Vorse, Mary Heaton. *Labor's New Millions.* New York: Modern Age Books, 1938.

777. Waley, Arthur, translator. *A Hundred and Seventy Chinese Poems.* New York: Knopf, 1919.

778. Ward, Thomas H., ed. *The English Poets.* New York: Macmillan, 1901-1918. Vol. V only: *Browning to Rupert Brooke* (1918).

779. Wason, Robert A. *Babe Randolph's Turning Point: An Episode of the Civil War.* Chicago: Old Dominion Shop, 1904.

780. Wassermann, Jakob. *Bula Matari: Stanley, Conqueror of A Continent.* New York: Liveright, 1933. S. A. signature.

781. —. *Worlds' Ends: Five Stories,* trans. Lewis Galantière. New York: Boni and Liveright, 1927.

782. Waters, Frank. *The Wild Earth's Nobility.* New York: Liveright, 1935.

783. Weaver, John V. A. *In American — Poems.* New York: Knopf, 1921.

784. Weigall, Arthur E. *Nero, The Singing Emperor of Rome.* New York: Garden City Publishing Co., 1930. S. A. signature.

785. Weil, Oscar. *Letters and Papers.* San Francisco: Book Club of California, 1923.

786. Weinberg, Louis. *The Art of Rodin.* New York: Boni and Liveright, 1918 (Modern Library).

787. Weinper, Zishe. *At the Rich Man's Gate,* trans. Morton Deutsch. New York: Coward-McCann, 1935. Inscribed: "As a token of regards and friendship to Mr. and Mrs. Sherwood Anderson, Z. Weinper."

788. Wells, H. G. *Ann Veronica.* New York: Boni and Liveright, 1909.

789. —. *The New Machiavelli.* New York: Duffield, 1919.

790. —. *The War in the Air.* New York: Boni and Liveright, 1917.

791. Werner, Morris R. *Tammany Hall.* Garden City, New York: Doubleday, Doran, 1928.

792. West, Rebecca. *The Judge.* New York: George H. Doran, 1922.

793. Whitman, Walt. *Leaves of Grass,* introduction by Sherwood Anderson. New York: Crowell, 1933.

794. —. *The Patriotic Poems of Walt Whitman.* Garden City, New York: Doubleday, Page, 1918.

795. Whitsett, George. *Jealous Mountains.* Philadelphia: Centaur Press, 1933.

796. Wiese, Erich. *Paul Gauguin: Zwei Jahrzehnte nach Seinem Tode.* Leipzig, 1923.

797. Wilde, Oscar. *An Ideal Husband; A Woman of No Importance.* New York: Boni and Liveright, 1919 (Modern Library).

798. —. *Intentions.* New York: Boni and Liveright, n.d. (Modern Library).

799. —. *The Picture of Dorian Gray.* New York: Boni and Liveright, 1918 (Modern Library).

800. —. Another copy. New York: Brentano's, 1910.

801. —. *Poems.* New York: Boni and Liveright, n.d. (Modern Library).

802. —. *Salome; The Importance of Being Earnest; Lady Windermere's Fan.* New York: Boni and Liveright, 1919 (Modern Library).

803. Wilder, Thornton. *The Cabala.* New York: A. and C. Boni, 1926.

804. Williams, Albert Rhys. *The Russian Land.* New York: New Republic, Inc., 1928. Two copies.

805. Williams, Blanche Colton, ed. *O. Henry Memorial Award Prize Stories of 1925.* Garden City, New York: Doubleday, Page, 1926.

806. —, ed. *O. Henry Memorial Award Prize Stories of 1929.* New York: Doubleday, Doran, 1929. S. A. signature.

807. Williamson, Henry. *Tarka the Otter.* New York: Dutton, 1928.

808. Wilson, Goodridge. *Smyth County History and Traditions.* Kingsport, Tennessee: Kingsport Press, 1932. Three copies.

809. Wilson, James Harrison. *The Life of John A. Rawlins.* New York: Neale Publishing Co., 1916.

810. Wilstach, Paul. *Tidewater Virginia.* Indianapolis: Bobbs-Merrill, 1929.

811. Winkler, John K. *The Dupont Dynasty.* New York: Blue Ribbon Books, 1938.

812. Winston, Robert W. *Andrew Johnson, Plebeian and Patriot.* New York: Holt, 1928.

813. Winter, Ella. *Red Virtue: Human Relationships in the New Russia.* New York: Harcourt, Brace, 1933. Inscribed: "Sherwood Anderson — Hoping this will prove an added temptation to go see Ella Winter. New York, May 1st, 1933."

814. Winter, Lois F. *Fable in Gothic.* Caldwell, Idaho: Caxton Printers, 1940. Inscribed: "To Sherwood Anderson, with recollection of Writers' Conference, Boulder, Colo., Lois F. Winter."

815. Wodehouse, P. G. *Heavy Weather.* New York: A. L. Burt, 1933. S. A. signature.

816. Wolf, Friedrich. *The Sailors of Cattaro.* New York: Samuel French, 1935.

817. Wood, William C. H. *Elizabethan Sea-Dogs.* New Haven: Yale, 1921.

818. Woodruff, Hiram W. *The Trotting Horse of America,* 19th edition. Philadelphia: Porter and Coates, 1874.

819. Woodward, Helen. *Queen's in the Parlor.* Indianapolis: Bobbs-Merrill, 1933. Inscribed: "For Sherwood Anderson hoping he will find it true fun. Helen Woodward. August 21st, 1933."

820. Woodward, William E. *Meet General Grant.* New York: Liveright, 1928.

821. Woolf, Virginia. *A Room of One's Own.* London: Hogarth Press, 1929.

822. —. *To the Lighthouse.* New York: Harcourt, Brace, 1927.

823. Wylie, Elinor. *Mr. Hodge and Mr. Hazard.* New York: Knopf, 1928.

824. Young, Arthur H. *On My Way.* New York: Liveright, 1928.

825. Young, James C. *Marse Robert, Knight of the Confederacy.* New York: Rae D. Henkle, 1929.

826. Young, Stanley. *Robin Landing: A Play in Three Acts.* New York: Farrar and Rinehart, 1938.

827. —. *Sons Without Anger.* New York: Farrar and Rinehart, 1939. Inscribed: "For Sherwood Anderson, great friend and great writer, Stanley Young." Also S. A. signature.

828. Young, Stark. *Encaustics.* New York: New Republic, Inc., 1926. Inscribed: "To Sherwood and Miss Elizabeth from Stark with love."

829. —. *The Flower in Drama.* New York: Scribner's, 1923. Inscribed: "To Sherwood Anderson, with love and admiration, from Stark Young, 1923."

830. —. *Glamour.* New York: Scribner's, 1925. Inscribed: "To Sherwood and Miss Elizabeth from Stark Young 1925."

831. Zhdanov, A., Maxim Gorky, *et al. Problems of Soviet Literature.* Moscow: Co-operative Publishing Society, 1935.

832. Zostchenko, Mikhail. *Russia Laughs,* trans. Helena Clayton. Boston: Lothrop, Lee and Shepard, 1935. S. A. signature.

833. Zugsmith, Leane. *Goodbye and Tomorrow.* New York: Liveright, 1931. Inscribed: "For Sherwood Anderson with warm regards. Leane — Jan. 29, 1932."

834. —. *Never Enough.* New York: Liveright, 1932.

835. —. *The Reckoning.* New York: H. Smith and R. Haas, 1934.

836. [Zuloaga, Ignacio]. *Exhibition of Paintings by Ignacio Zuloaga,* with introduction and bibliography by Christian Brinton. New York: Redfield-Kendrick-Odell, 1916.

837. Zweig, Arnold. *The Case of Sergeant Grischa.* New York: Viking, 1928.

CRITICAL ESSAYS

ADDENDA TO SHEEHY AND LOHF'S *SHERWOOD ANDERSON:*
COPYRIGHT INFORMATION AND LATER PRINTINGS

G. Thomas Tanselle

The list which follows records two kinds of information not included in
Eugene P. Sheehy and Kenneth A. Lohf's *Sherwood Anderson: A Bibliography* (Los Gatos: Talisman Press, 1960). (1) First is the information available in the copyright records: the official publication date of each book (by
law the copyright date), here preceded by the abbreviation *Pub*; the date of
deposit *(Dep)* of two copies in the Copyright Office; and the official date
of the completion of printing *(Pr)*, as reported to the Copyright Office, with
the names of the printer and binder *(Bd)*. (2) The second kind of data con-
sists of the dates of some of the later printings of the books, as stated on the
copyright pages of the books themselves. This information has been taken
from the copies of the later printings in The Newberry Library and in my
own collection. Only later impressions by the original publishers are listed,
because Sheehy and Lohf do attempt to include later printings which represent changes of publishers' imprints (the Grosset & Dunlap *Many Marriages*
and *Dark Laughter*, for instance, are listed as "reprints," though the number
of earlier Huebsch and Boni & Liveright impressions from the same plates is
not specified). The record offered here for the original publishers may not
be complete, since it is limited to copies available in two collections; but it
is a start, which can be supplemented from holdings elsewhere.

A word must be said about one item not recorded in Sheehy and Lohf
at all. The first entry in Sheehy and Lohf is *Windy McPherson's Son* (1916);
but the copyright records reveal the existence of a 1909 pamphlet of 30

145

pages:

An Idea to Establish a Commercial Democracy. Pub 22 Oct. 1909; *Dep* 29 Dec.; *Pr & Bd* 20 Oct., Republican Printing Co., Elyria, Ohio.

Apparently no copies of this pamphlet are known to have survived; but the record of the copyright deposit leaves no doubt that the pamphlet did exist. William A. Sutton, in *The Road to Winesburg* (Metuchen: Scarecrow, 1972), describes what little can be conjectured about *Commercial Democracy,* which Anderson called a "magazine" in his *Memoirs* (Sheehy and Lohf's entry 392 thus places *Commercial Democracy* in a list of "Serial Publications Edited by Anderson," with the notation that no file has been located). But, as Sutton reports, Harry J. Crandall remembered *Commercial Democracy* as an "advertising pamphlet" for Anderson's company, and Anderson's brother Karl referred to a pamphlet of sketches "distributed as advertisements" (see Sutton, pp. 170-72). Whether both a pamphlet and a magazine existed or only this pamphlet—now known to have had the title *An Idea to Establish a Commercial Democracy*—is impossible to say at present; and whether this pamphlet could be the "Book on Socialism" which Anderson called his "first experience as a writer" (Sutton, p. 176) cannot be speculated about without seeing the pamphlet. In the light of this copyright entry, new inquiries are now being made in an effort to locate a copy.

The remaining items are listed below according to their Sheehy-Lohf numbers (although in one instance the numbering places a book—item 21—out of chronological order):

1. *Windy McPherson's Son* (Lane). *Pub* 1 Sept. 1916; *Dep* 22 Sept.; *Pr* 8 Aug., Little & Ives, New York; *Bd* H. Wolff Estate, New York.[1]

4. *Marching Men* (Lane). *Pub* 14 Sept. 1917; *Dep* 18 Sept.; *Pr & Bd* 23 Aug., Little & Ives, New York.

7. *Mid-American Chants* (Lane). *Pub* 12 April 1918; *Dep* 15 April; *Pr & Bd* 26 March, Little & Ives, New York.

9. *Winesburg, Ohio* (Huebsch). *Pub* 8 May 1919; *Dep* 17 Nov.; *Pr* 28 April, Van Rees Press, New York (from plates set by Plimpton Press, Norwood, Mass.); *Bd* H. Wolff Estate, New York.
   1st printing: April 1919

2nd printing: Dec. 1919
3rd printing: Jan. 1921
4th printing: Dec. 1921
5th printing: March 1922[2]

13. *Poor White* (Huebsch). *Pub* 27 Oct. 1920; *Dep* 4 April 1921; *Pr* 20 Sept. 1920, Vail-Ballou Press, Binghamton, New York; *Bd* Robert Rutter & Son, New York.
    1st printing: Sept. 1920
    2nd printing: Feb. 1921
    3rd printing: Dec. 1921

17. *The Triumph of the Egg* (Huebsch). *Pub* 24 Oct. 1921; *Dep* 8 Dec.; *Pr* 3 Oct., Burr Printing House, New York; *Bd* H. Wolff Estate, New York.
    1st printing: Oct. 1921
    2nd printing: Dec. 1921
    3rd printing: Feb. 1922
    4th printing: Aug. 1924

21. *Horses and Men* (Huebsch). *Pub* 26 Oct. 1923; *Dep* 11 Feb. 1924; *Pr* 16 Oct. 1923, Vail-Ballou Press, Binghamton, New York; *Bd* H. Wolff Estate, New York.

25. *Many Marriages* (Huebsch). *Pub* 20 Feb. 1923; *Dep* 13 April; *Pr* 7 Feb., Vail-Ballou Press, Binghamton, New York; *Bd* H. Wolff Estate, New York.
    1st printing: 20 Feb. 1923
    2nd printing: 20 Feb. 1923
    3rd printing: March 1923

29. *A Story Teller's Story* (Huebsch). *Pub* 15 Oct. 1924; *Dep* 24 Oct., 4 Nov.; *Pr* 1 Oct., Vail-Ballou Press, Binghamton, New York; *Bd* H. Wolff Estate, New York.
    1st printing: Oct. 1924
    2nd printing: Oct. 1924
    3rd printing: Dec. 1924
    4th printing: Feb. 1927 (Viking)

33. *Dark Laughter* (Boni & Liveright). *Pub* 15 Sept. 1925; *Dep* 14 Oct.;

Pr & Bd 8 Sept., Van Rees Press, New York.
1st printing: Sept. 1925
2nd printing: Sept. 1925
3rd printing: Oct. 1925
4th printing: Oct. 1925
5th printing: Nov. 1925
6th printing: Nov. 1925
7th printing: Dec. 1925
8th printing: May 1926
9th printing: Oct. 1926[3]

37. *The Modern Writer* (Lantern Press). *Pub* 10 Dec. 1925; *Dep* 15 July 1926; *Pr & Bd* 1 Dec. 1925, Grabhorn Press, San Francisco.

38. *Sherwood Anderson's Notebook* (Boni & Liveright). *Pub* 14 May 1926; *Dep* 8 July; *Pr & Bd* 4 May, Van Rees Press, New York.
1st printing: April 1926
2nd printing: Sept. 1926

39. *Tar: A Midwest Childhood* (Boni & Liveright). *Pub* 20 Nov. 1926; *Dep* 26 Nov.; *Pr & Bd* 9 Nov., Van Rees Press, New York.
1st printing: Nov. 1926
2nd printing: Dec. 1926
Bonibooks, No. 2 (Albert & Charles Boni)
1st printing: July 1930
2nd printing: Nov. 1930[4]

43. *A New Testament* (Boni & Liveright). *Pub* 15 June 1927; *Dep* 30 July; *Pr* 9 June, Advertising Agency Service, New York; *Bd* Montauk Bindery, New York.
1st printing: May 1927
2nd printing: June 1927

45. *Hello Towns!* (Liveright). *Pub* 17 April 1929; *Dep* 20 April; *Pr & Bd* 2 April, Van Rees Press, New York.
1st printing: April 1929
2nd printing: April 1929

47. *Nearer the Grass Roots* (Westgate Press). *Pub* 30 July 1929; *Dep* 14 May 1930; *Pr & Bd* 20 July 1929, Grabhorn Press, San Francisco.

48. *The American County Fair* (Random House). *Pub* 27 Dec. 1930; *Dep* 29 Jan. 1931; *Pr & Bd* 20 Dec. 1930, Southworth Press, Portland, Maine.

49. *Perhaps Women* (Liveright). *Pub* 15 Sept. 1931; *Dep* 26 Sept.; *Pr & Bd* 3 Sept., Van Rees Press, New York.

50. *Beyond Desire* (Liveright). *Pub* 19 Sept. 1932; *Dep* 10 Oct.; *Pr & Bd* 8 Sept., Montauk Book Manufacturing Co., New York (from plates set by Van Rees Press, New York).
   1st printing: Sept. 1932
   2nd printing: Sept. 1932
   3rd printing: Sept. 1932

52. *Death in the Woods* (Liveright). *Pub* 8 April 1933; *Dep* 25 Aug.; *Pr & Bd* 7 April, Van Rees Press, New York.

53. *No Swank* (Centaur Press). *Pub* 3 Dec. 1934; *Dep* 8 July 1935; *Pr & Bd* 28 Nov. 1934, Haddon Craftsmen, Camden, New Jersey.

54. *Puzzled America* (Scribner). *Pub* 29 March 1935; *Dep* 4 April; *Pr & Bd* Scribner Press, New York.

55. *Kit Brandon* (Scribner). *Pub* 9 Oct. 1936; *Dep* 21 Oct.; *Pr & Bd* Scribner Press, New York.

59. *Plays* (Scribner). *Pub* 9 Sept. 1937; *Dep* 15 Sept.

60. *A Writer's Conception of Realism* (Olivet College). *Pub* 20 Jan. 1939; *Dep* 20 March; *Pr & Bd* 20 Jan., Optic Press, Olivet, Michigan.

61. *Home Town* (Alliance Book Corp.). *Pub* 21 Oct. 1940; *Dep* 23 Oct.; *Pr* 25 Sept., Photogravure & Color Co., New York; *Bd* American Book-Stratford Press, New York.

62. *Sherwood Anderson's Memoirs* (Harcourt Brace). *Pub* 9 April 1942; *Dep* 14 April; *Pr & Bd* 12 March, Quinn & Boden, Rahway, New Jersey.

NOTES

[1] The *National Union Catalog* also records a 1917 Lane impression.

[2] The *National Union Catalog* lists two succeeding printings by Viking: a 6th in 1927 (March, according to Phillips) and a 7th in June 1931. For a discussion of the distinguishing features of the first impression, see William L. Phillips, "The First Printing of Sherwood Anderson's *Winesburg, Ohio,*" *SB*, 4 (1951-52), 211-13.

[3] And to Sheehy-Lohf 35 ("reprints") may be added the Pocket Books edition printed in March 1952 and published in May.

[4] These Bonibooks printings antedate Sheehy-Lohf 41, a 1931 printing attributed to Boni & Liveright. This is the only instance I have noticed in which Sheehy and Lohf give an entry number to a "reprint" by the original publisher; the imprint here is presumably erroneous, for the Boni & Liveright firm became simply "Horace Liveright" in 1928, and the *Cumulative Book Index* records a Bonibooks (Albert & Charles Boni) hard-cover issue in 1931.

THE EDITIONS OF *WINESBURG, OHIO*

William L. Phillips

About twenty-five years ago I ventured into the special territory of the bibliographers with a note about the first edition of *Winesburg, Ohio*.[1] A complaint by one of the early reviewers of the book about Anderson's use of "lay " when "lie" was called for had led me to check my "first edition, first issue," for the offending sentence. It was not there; but my "first edition, second issue," of course, did have it. Armed with what seemed to me to be indisputable evidence of the priority of the printings (soon we would call them impressions), and not a little annoyed at the price which I had paid from my veteran's benefits for the "first printing" because the dealer had read Merle Johnson's *High Spots of American Literature* and Whitman Bennett's *A Practical Guide to American Book Collecting*, I submitted a note to *Studies in Bibliography* which pointed out that the correction of Anderson's error in usage, and not broken or unbroken type, would establish the order of the two impressions.

The publication of my note and an approving notice of it by Jacob Blanck in *The Antiquarian Bookman* two months later[2] led to a barrage of letters from collectors and librarians, some to *Studies in Bibliography*, some to Mr. Blanck, and some to me; all confirmed the "lay" reading for the first issue, but some raised further questions about binding and top edge color, various type irregularities, and collation. The following summary of the characteristics of the several printings which extends and corrects the 1951 note may be useful to collectors of Anderson's work.

The first and second printings (impressions) of *Winesburg* carry identical dates on the title page ("MCMXIX") and identical notices on the copyright page ("COPYRIGHT, 1919, BY B. W. HUEBSCH / PRINTED IN U.S.A."). The third printing (impression) carries the date "MCMXXI" on the title page, but only the original copyright notice for 1919 on the copyright page. Beginning with the *fourth* printing, however, not only does the title page carry the date in Roman numerals on the title page, but also a list of printings appears on the copyright page. The latest I have seen, the sixth printing, lists the following dates for the first six printings:

> First printing, April, 1919
> Second printing, December, 1919
> Third printing, January, 1921
> Fourth printing, December, 1921
> Fifth printing, March, 1922
> Sixth printing, March, 1927

Some of the correspondents concerning the *SB* note argued that their copies with "lie" readings must be first editions, since there was no evidence to the contrary on the copyright page. They sometimes quoted Boutell's *First Editions of Today and How to Tell Them* in which representatives of Viking Press had stated: "Our first editions can be distinguished by the fact that there is no indication to the contrary on the copyright page. That is, we indicate the date and number of each reprinting . . . . The policy of B. W. Huebsch, regarding first editions, was the same as the present policy of The Viking Press."[3] Correspondence with B. W. Huebsch settled the matter; in March, 1952, he examined his personal copies of *Winesburg* (a first printing and a third printing which had no printing date on the copyright page) and wrote:

> This copy is evidence, too, that Boutell received erroneous information from this office concerning my practice when publishing under my own name regarding the manner of distinguishing successive printings. I had no "policy" but, generally, altered the date on the title page to conform to the year of the new printing and added on the copyright page the number and year of that printing. The absence of such notation on the copyright page of the copy in question proves that my practice was not rigid.

> The reason for the omission in the cases of, perhaps,

the second and third printings may have been the need for haste in replenishing stock; it is not impossible that I compromised with myself on a single evidence of a new printing in order to reduce the delay in going to press. The alterations on title and copyright pages were often something of a nuisance, for there were fewer complete bookmaking plants in 1920 than there are today, and I remember that often I would have composition done in one office, electrotyping in another and presswork in still another. Both composing room and foundry hated these little jobs of correcting dates and they generally did them badly.[4]

The points which characterize the first impression are the following: orange or yellow cloth; top edge stained orange-yellow or yellow;[5] a perfect title page frame; extraneous "of" p. 4, second line from the bottom; "lay," p. 86, 1. 5; perfect type in "his," p. 196, 1. 9; and perfect type in "cutting," p. 260, 1. 9. Most copies of the first impression have the map of Winesburg as a pasted-down end paper; two copies which can be shown from inscriptions to have been early copies, however, do not have the map, and both are missing two leaves.

The points which characterize the second impression are a yellow cloth cover; top edge white; a break in the lower right side of the title page frame; p. 4, 11. 1 and 2 *infra* reset to remove the extraneous "of"; "lie," p. 86, 1. 5; perfect type in "the," p. 251, 1. 3; and *ut* depressed in "cutting," p. 260, 1. 9. In about one half the copies of this impression which I have seen, the type is depressed in "his," p. 196, 1. 9; this type-wear, given the small number of copies in the second printing and the perfect "his" in the first and third printings, probably marks these copies as late in the impression.

The third impression can be distinguished by the appearance of the date "MCMXXI" on the title page. Otherwise it has the same points as the second impression, except that the broken type in "his" and "cutting" have been repaired. The title page frame remains broken. Subsequent impressions are indicated on the copyright page.

Since the sales and other records of the B. W. Huebsch publishing house have long since been destroyed, it is not possible to be certain about the quantity of each printing, but an estimate can be made from other evidence. Huebsch provided a statement to Anderson on May 1, 1921, which listed sales of 1754 copies from May through October 31, 1919. Since Anderson wrote to Huebsch in November, 1920, expressing the hope that *Poor White* would "not get out of print at Christmas time as Winesburg did," it can be supposed that the initial printing did not exceed 1800 copies and had run out in the late fall of 1919. The same report listed sales of only 775 copies for the year beginning November, 1919, which approximates the period between the second printing (December, 1919) and the third (January, 1921); thus the second printing surely did not exceed 1000 copies. Anderson's remark in 1927 that Winesburg "was two years selling 5,000" exaggerated its early sale.[6]

The quality of the editorial work and the typography of *Winesburg* certainly did not match the quality of the authors which B. W. Huebsch's small firm was publishing in 1919 (Joyce and Lawrence among them). Scattered through the text are extraneous periods or dots and imperfect type which remain through all the printings;[7] margins and running titles are poorly aligned in several copies I have seen; and a single quotation mark on the running title of "Queer" (p. 229) never was corrected. Since the Modern Library editions and the English edition by Jonathan Cape in 1922 were printed from the Huebsch plates, a number of errors remained in the text until Malcolm Cowley prepared the Compass Edition for The Viking Press in 1960. Cowley made approximately 75 minor editorial changes, about half of them insertions of a comma to improve the sense of a line.[8] He also corrected Anderson's faulty usage ("was," p. 13, l. 2 *infra*; "were," p. 72, l. 6 *infra*; "whom," p. 194, l. 12; and "returned," p. 301, l. 5); made consistent Anderson's spelling of some of his characters' names (Tom Sinnings, Ned Winters, Hern's Grocery, Mrs. Kate McHugh, Wacker's Cigar Store, Wesley Moyer, and Turk Smollet);[9] and corrected several obvious typographical errors. His edition is the first to present the text as it should have been printed in 1919, and it should be considered standard.

Cowley's care with his edition did not, oddly enough, correct one faulty passage which has remained since the first edition. In the catalog of "truths" which the old man in "The Book of the Grotesque" lists in his book, Anderson carefully set up a series of opposite "truths," the devotion to any one of which may lead one to grotesqueness: virginity-passion, wealth-poverty, and thrift-profligacy. All editions of *Winesburg*, including Cowley's, permit the final pair of opposites to read "carelessness and abandon." The Newberry manuscript of *Winesburg* reads "carefullness" (sic), the early magazine version of the story reads "carefulness,"[10] and "carefulness" it should be in any future editions of *Winesburg, Ohio*.

NOTES

[1]William L. Phillips, "The First Printing of Sherwood Anderson's *Winesburg, Ohio,*" *SB,* 4 (1951-1952), 211-213.

[2]"That Difference of Opinion," February 9, 1952, pp. 639-640.

[3]H. S. Boutell, ed. Roger Boutell (Philadelphia, 1937), p. 64.

[4]Letter to William L. Phillips, March 17, 1952.

[5]Of the fourteen copies of the first impression on which this list is based, only three have a distinctly yellow binding and top edge to match; inconclusive evidence from inscriptions suggests that they were bound after those with the orange cloth. For information about copies in their possession I am indebted to Mr. Campbell R. Coxe, Mr. Jacob Blanck, and the Humanities Research Center, the University of Texas at Austin.

[6]Anderson Collection, The Newberry Library. The Huebsch statement, Anderson's November, 1920 letter to Huebsch, and his 1927 letter (to N. Bryllion Fagin) are cited in William A. Sutton, *The Road to Winesburg* (Metuchen, N. J., 1972), p. 450.

[7]See, e.g., p. 20, l. 27; p. 97, ll. 3 and 8; p. 251, l. 1; and p. 303, ll. 2 and 12.

[8]Cowley listed his textual changes in a two-page transcript, "A Note for Sherwood Anderson's Bibliographers."

[9]Cowley missed one incorrect variant of Tom Sinnings' name, p. 27, l. 10 *infra,* which appears as p. 41, l. 10 *infra* of the Compass edition.

[10]*Masses,* 8 (February, 1916), 17. This periodical contribution was omitted from Eugene P. Sheehy and Kenneth A. Lohf, *Sherwood Anderson: A Bibliography* (Los Gatos, California, 1960).

SHERWOOD ANDERSON'S CLYDE, OHIO

Thaddeus B. Hurd

In March 1884 Irwin Anderson, a harnessmaker, with his wife and children, moved to Clyde, Ohio. The children were Carl age 10, Stella 8, Sherwood 7, Irving 5 and Ray 10 months. A son Earl was born in Clyde in June 1885, and a daughter Fern, who died age 2, in December 1890. Carl (Karl) became a prominent painter and member of the National Academy of Design. Sherwood became a well known author.

Mrs. Anderson, the former Emma Smith, died in Clyde in May 1895 and is buried in the local cemetery. Stella, a schoolteacher in Clyde, kept the family together for a short time thereafter, but they were gone from Clyde by about 1899.

The family was thus in Clyde about 15 years, while the children were growing up. Sherwood's writing career did not begin until some years after he left Clyde, but this town of his boyhood, adolescence and young manhood had much influence on his writings. In them he has left us a vivid picture of the small midwest American town in the closing years of the last century.

What sort of town was Clyde? Towns, like people, have individuality, formed by place, time and events. The Clyde of Sherwood's years was prosperous, located in a rich agricultural area, a big small town, friendly, of mixed cultural background and colorful history.

Clyde lies in the fertile plain that borders the south shore of Lake Erie. Driving west from Pennsylvania across the state line into Ohio, the low mountains on the southern horizon give way to high hills and the coastal plain widens. Lying high above Lake Erie, it is deeply cut by valleys of

156

creeks and rivers flowing north into the lake. South of Cleveland the Ohio Turnpike now soars high above the wide valley of the Cuyahoga River. At Elyria the Black River cuts a narrow gorge through a flat countryside. Thence west the level plain extends through Oberlin and Norwalk on to Bellevue, marked by lines of sand dunes that once bordered the shore of an ancient and larger Lake Erie.

At Bellevue you are about half way across northern Ohio and at the west boundary of the old Connecticut Western Reserve. Eight miles west lies Clyde. The level road cuts through old sand dunes. At Birdseye's Corners it crosses the South Ridge road, an old Indian trail and ancient lake shore line. The land now drops gently. Ahead the trees and buildings of Clyde cluster on the horizon. You drive across flat land that was once Lake Erie bottom and enter Clyde.

From Bellevue the straight highway, now U. S. 20, is the east part of the old Maumee and Western Reserve Turnpike, a pioneer road once filled with covered wagons headed west to Michigan and Indiana. As it enters Clyde, the road crosses another old Indian trail, the North Ridge road, now Maple Street, last ancient shore line of old Lake Erie. Here, when the "Pike" was opened in 1827, a crossroads village quickly appeared. William Hamer's tavern, a log building on a high sand dune, now gone, gave the name of Hamer's Corners to the little settlement.

A few rods west of the Corners the road again drops slightly. Here one entered the great Black Swamp country, stretching north to Sandusky Bay on Lake Erie and westward into Indiana and Michigan. The Pike was cut through its dense forests. Felled logs laid side by side to make a corduroy road sank out of sight in the muck. The Pike from here west became known far and wide as the worst road in America.

Hamer's Corners prospered as a small trading center and travelers' rest. Stagecoach and covered wagon trade brought prosperity. The village soon had another tavern, two stores, William McPherson's blacksmith shop, a doctor, a cemetery, two religious societies, a church and several houses both at the Corners and scattered along the North Ridge road. The time was 1830 through 1850.

The Ohio canal boom in these years had not affected north central Ohio. On the east the Cuyahoga-Muskingum canal and on the west the Maumee-Miami canal linked Lake Erie to the Ohio River, bringing new cities and great prosperity. The proposed Sandusky-Scioto canal for central Ohio was never built. But in 1850 new forces were astir in the land. The railroads were coming. Hamer's Corners lay in their path.

Ohio's first railroad was the Mad River line, begun in 1838, running

157

south from Sandusky City on Lake Erie to Dayton on the Mad River, thence on to Cincinnati on the Ohio River. Its first roadbed through Bellevue was soon abandoned for a shorter route that brought it right past William Hamer's front door. Meanwhile plans were afoot for an east-west line, the Toledo and Norwalk, extended almost at once on to Cleveland. The summer of 1852 was one of great excitement at the Corners. Construction crews of both lines raced toward an intersection, crossing on the North Ridge road on Lyman Miller's farm, a stone's throw south of the Corners. The east-west line reached the junction first, thus gaining forever the crossing right of way.

The junction was of great importance. Travelers from Cleveland or Toledo headed for Dayton or Cincinnati all had to change trains here. Excitement ran high. A great city would develop. To properly name it, local citizens met at Hamer's Tavern. Centerville was suggested, for this would be the hub of commerce in northern Ohio. A former resident of Clyde, New York, suggested that name. Others were proposed, but the final vote favored Clyde. Some teamsters stopping at the tavern took part in the voting.

Thus Clyde was born. A boom was on. Lyman Miller's heirs rushed to lay out their farm into streets and lots. Speculators bought and platted land near the crossing. The Junction House hotel of wood construction was quickly erected, followed by two fine brick hotels, the Nichols House and the St. Vincent. A row of stores soon lined the old North Ridge road, Maple Street. All clustered around the crossing where an elegant passenger depot of Victorian wooden Gothic style was erected, built L-shaped along both railroads. A few rods east of the crossing a little north-south lane was widened to become Main Street. Hamer's Corners was forgotten, some buildings moved bodily to Main Street. The years 1852-1890 saw the building of Main Street and all the older part of present Clyde.

Northwest Ohio was Indian country until 1817, when by the Treaty of the Maumee, near present Toledo, the Indians ceded the last of their Ohio lands to the federal government, retaining only a few scattered reservations. These lands, nearly a fourth of the present state, were surveyed in 1820 and put on sale in 1822.

During the War of 1812, military action, the "War in the West," had centered here and had broken the grip of the British and Indians who had controlled the area since the close of the Revolution. General William Henry Harrison successfully weathered the siege of Fort Meigs at present Perrysburg in May-July 1813. Young Major George Croghan with a handful of Kentucky regulars repulsed the British and Indians in the Battle of Fort Stephenson at present Fremont in August 1813. In September 1813 Commodore Oliver H. Perry destroyed the British fleet in the Battle of Lake Erie. Harrison's invasion of Upper Canada (Ontario) followed in October 1813 and here in the Battle of the Thames the British were decisively defeated and Tecumseh, leader of the Indian forces, was killed. British control of the Northwest Territory (Ohio, Indiana, Illinois, Michigan and Wisconsin) was forever ended.

Before the war, a few traders and squatters had come into the area, most clustered about Fort Stephenson. All fled east and south when Detroit fell in 1812. After the war many returned, and with them newcomers from the Western Reserve on the east and the mid-Ohio country on the south. In 1820 the Ohio legislature divided northwest Ohio into counties, and when the lands went on sale in 1822 the trickle of settlers became a flood. The best land was quickly sold at $1.25 per acre and by 1840 the country was settled.

Hamer's Corners, now Clyde, in Sandusky County, lay only eight miles west of the Connecticut Western Reserve where the settlers were largely of New England stock, either first generation direct or second generation after a stopover in New York state. The first settlers of the lands between Bellevue and Hamer's Corners were mostly from the Reserve or from New York, bringing New England customs, traditions and religion.

Thus the Corners and surrounding countryside became a bit of transplanted New England. Yet the location of the Corners on the Pike, main highway west, brought an assortment of frontier types and made it a frontier town. It early acquired the nickname of "Bang-All" because of the frequent fights at William Hamer's tavern.

The character of the Corners changed little in the first 25 years. The dense forests of the surrounding countryside were gradually cleared, great primeval logs of walnut, butternut, cherry, maple, oak and other hardwoods rolled into huge piles and burned. The land was very fertile. The farmers prospered as did the tradesmen at the Corners. Life was rural and the work day never ended, but the people felt themselves fortunate to be in a land so blessed by the Creator.

The coming of the railroads brought changes, economic and cultural. The big Irish migration to America in the 1840's had brought an abundance of labor to build the railroads. Some settled in Clyde, mostly in the southeast part of town. With them came the first Catholic church, St. Mary's. The first mass was said in Clyde in 1853. The first church building was a small white wood structure in the northwest part of town. A graveyard, the present St. Mary's cemetery, developed around it. The present imposing brick Gothic church edifice dates from 1890.

The railroads brought great prosperity. The industrial revolution was sweeping America, bringing a hitherto undreamed-of abundance of manufactured goods at low prices. Their distribution to the consumer gave rise to a new social class, the retail merchants. Stores soon lined Main Street. Goods flowed in quickly and cheaply by rail, and through the stores to the prosperous farm population. It was the day of the businessman. Their families formed a social upper class in the town. The factory had not yet come to Clyde, though the village boasted two steam powered flour mills.

Railroads were the lifeblood of the new town. Passengers and freight in abundance flowed east and west, north and south, with much interchange between the two lines. Trains ran constantly day and night, especially on the east-west New York to Chicago line. The depot was the hub of village life, and watching the trains come and go a major entertainment.

Population changes came with the railroads. A stream of traveling salesmen, "drummers," serviced the village merchants. People from many areas now flowed into town. Some became permanent residents. Others, the "floaters," stayed briefly then moved on.

A major change facilitated by the railroads was the German migration. The old Black Swamp lands north of Clyde were still largely forest, the last land to be had at earlier low prices. Here these Germans settled, families arriving daily at the depot with little more than a handbag and a featherbed. Frugal and hard working, they cleared the forests, drained the swamps, brought large areas under productive cultivation, and became prosperous farmers. Some were Catholic and joined the Irish in St. Mary's church. Most were Lutherans. They bought the little white Universalist church building on West Forest Street in Clyde where their buggies and wagons filled the churchyard each Sunday while they listened to services in German.

Industry came slowly to Clyde. The Hunter brothers established their Edge Tool Works at an early date. This later became the Clyde Cutlery Company, for many years the small but prosperous mainstay of Clyde manufacturing. The Wilder brothers packed sauerkraut in wood kegs, later in tin cans, and gave Clyde the nickname of "Sauerkrautville." A factory to manufacture parlor organs was built just as the piano was coming into vogue. It went into bankruptcy soon after it opened. The building was later occupied by a bicycle factory.

Commerce and trade were the mainstay of Clyde's economic life. To them the modest manufacturing added strength. The town was prosperous and supported a substantial group of doctors, lawyers and bankers. All this may have persuaded Irwin Anderson to settle in Clyde, but ironically just at the time when factory-made harness equipment was putting the craftsman harnessmaker out of business.

This is the Clyde in which young Sherwood Anderson grew up and to which he returns so often in his writings. The creative urge which later matured in him may well have been born here. Along with its material prosperity Clyde had a stimulating cultural life. There was a publishing house which issued dramatic plays, there were professional and amateur theatricals, several debating societies, a circle of artists talented in painting and drawing, Spiritualist and freethinker groups, a public school with unusual leadership, and the established churches. Their influence on young Sherwood, his brother Carl, and other young people of town was considerable, and worthy of another story.

A BORROWING FROM BORROW

Walter B. Rideout

According to his essay "To George Borrow" in *No Swank,* Sherwood
Anderson was introduced to the work of this odd Victorian writer by a
chance meeting in Elyria, Ohio with a woman "Borrovian" while he was
still a businessman but after he had begun to write himself. In the essay
Anderson declares that he felt the charm of the book the woman was hold-
ing — it was *The Bible in Spain* — before she even handed it to him to read.
Considering the use Anderson made of passages in another book by Borrow,
as shortly to be described, one may suspect that his report of this preter-
natural feeling owed something to the British writer's own account in
Lavengro, quoted in the essay, of how as a boy he sensed the significance
to himself of Defoe's *Robinson Crusoe* before he even picked it out of a
package of books set down on a table in his home. As Anderson admits,
"None but Borrovians will believe this tale" of how "I was introduced to
that great master of prose, Mr. George Borrow."[1] There is no question at
all, of course, that the "great master" did become one of his favorite authors, for the fact is attested to by a number of admiring references to
Borrow in Anderson's books and correspondence. Writing to Van Wyck
Brooks in the spring of 1918, for example, Anderson remarked that he
"always coupled Mark Twain with George Borrow" in his mind because he
felt "the same quality of honesty in them, the same wholesome disregard
of literary precedent"; and a year later he wrote to Waldo Frank to name
some of his long-held literary interests, which included the Bible and Shakespeare:

A BORROWING FROM BORROW

The Bible I've always read and I read also the
marvelous prose of De Foe and Geo Borrow. Do
you know dear old Borrow. I've read Lavengro and
Romany Rye twenty - times.[2]

Anderson was attracted to Borrow, the man and his writings, for a number of reasons. In "To George Borrow," he addressed him as "sweet master
of the trivial, of the everyday little adventures of living, hater of sham respectability!"[3] Both men enjoyed traveling about, often on foot, meeting
ordinary and extra ordinary people by chance on the way, hearing and later
retelling in their own fashion the personal experiences that these people
told them. Borrow's books mix autobiographical fact with fanciful invention; a form of the picaresque, they are episodic in structure; and they are
told in the first person in a narrative style, the forthrightness and simplicity
of which tend to conceal the writer's skill. In sum, *The Bible in Spain,
Lavengro,* and *The Romany Rye* have literary traits and express an attitude
toward life that make it easy to understand why the Ohio story teller read
and referred to them again and again.

Curiously, however, Anderson seems never to have mentioned in any
of his published works or letters yet another volume by Borrow which he
read, the less well known *Wild Wales* (1862), an account of a walking tour
the author took through Wales in the summer of 1854. Although none of
the "adventures" Borrow recounts in *Wild Wales* is so exciting as, say, the
episode in *Lavengro* of his desperate fistfight with the Flaming Tinman, still
Anderson must have responded to Borrow's enthusiastic descriptions of
Welsh scenery, his tales of rogues, "queer characters," and other less flam-
boyant people met on the road, and the general sense that Borrow well
conveys of being footloose in the open air. Anderson must have admired too
the story of the grotesquely tumbling, "bedivilled woman," Johanna Col-
gan, as told by her to Borrow and made by him into one of his greatest tales
in, so to speak, the Anderson manner. One says "must have," for it is certain that Anderson read, or at least dipped deep into, *Wild Wales.* In fact he
was so much impressed by what he read that he drew directly on a section
of this book in order to create an appropriate ancestor for the hero of "An
Ohio Pagan," the long tale first published as the conclusion to *Horses and
Men.*

"An Ohio Pagan" and " 'Unused,' " another long tale first published
in this remarkable volume, are self-contained parts of a projected novel,
tentatively titled *Ohio Pagans,* which Anderson worked on over several
years and then abandoned. References in letters he wrote in the summer of

1920 suggest the kinds of materials he was using. Writing to Frank from a vacation cottage by the little town of Ephraim, Wisconsin, on the shore of Lake Michigan's Green Bay, Anderson refers to

> a tale I began a year or two ago, about a boy,
> grandson of a Welsh poet, named Twm o'r Nant.
> The boy's name was Tom Edwards.
>   I took that yarn up again, and it is expand-
> ing into a novel of country people and their ef-
> forts to find God, a tale of barnyards and fields
> and the back yards of village house[s] , ice cut-
> ters on a bay, etc.[4]

In a letter to Marietta Finley (later Mrs. E. Vernon Hahn) he specifically names the heroine of " 'Unused' " and the Hero of "An Ohio Pagan" as the central figures of the novel, and identifies the principal setting as the area near his home town of Clyde.[5]

As the latter comments imply, he was drawing on personal experience, especially in "An Ohio Pagan." Like the story's youthful protagonist, Tom Edwards, young Sherwood Anderson had been for a while a "swipe," or groom, in the employ of a physically huge "sporting farmer" named White-head. Like the Harry Whitehead of the story, the real Thomas Whitehead had moved with his equally huge wife from his farm into Clyde — called Bidwell in the story as in *Poor White* — had purchased an abandoned factory building, and in a lordly gesture had converted it into a stables for his blooded harness-race horses.[6] Like Tom Edwards, Anderson in his youth had been an unskilled laborer in grimy cities and had detested them; and in 1899 in a summer of golden weather just before his final year of formal schooling, that at Wittenberg Academy, Anderson, again like his hero, had worked with a man who operated a threshing outfit and who moved slowly from farm to farm over the country stretching northward from Clyde to Sandusky and the Lake Erie shore.[7] Perhaps something of Tom Edwards's pagan attitude toward nature existed already in Anderson himself that summer of 1899 when he was intensely happy merely to exist in such land-scape and such weather; but in any case two decades later, in the summer of 1920 at Ephraim, the middle-aged Anderson was going through a conscious phase of anti-"Puritanism" and of paganry at the same time he was writing Tom Edwards's story. A University of Chicago professor who summered nearby could amusedly recall Anderson one sunny morning coming up a hill by the blue waters of Lake Michigan, fully clothed, to be sure, but with his shaggy head crowned by a wreath of field flowers.[8]

As happened so often in Anderson's writing, then, lived experience got into the story; but in creating a grandfather for his hero he drew on another form of experience, his reading, specifically what he had read in Chapters LIX and LX of *Wild Wales* about the historical Thomas Edwards (1739-1810), Welsh poet and writer of dramatic interludes, known to his countrymen as "Twm o'r Nant," which, as both Borrow and Anderson explain, means "Tom of the Dingle." At the end of Chapter LVIII of *Wild Wales* Borrow tells how during his walking tour of Wales he found at Llangollen "a kind of chapbook" containing "the life of Twm O'r Nant, written by himself in choice Welsh," and one of his interludes, *Riches and Poverty.* Calling the former "probably the most remarkable autobiography ever penned," Borrow in the fourteen pages of his Chapter LIX summarizes Twm's life, quoting extensively in his own English translation from the Welsh poet's account.

Clearly the actual Thomas Edwards was a figure attractive to Borrow and, by way of Borrow, to Anderson. Born on a farm of poor parents, Twm learned to read and write both Welsh and English largely through his own efforts after only a few weeks of schooling. Very early he was seized with "a rage or madness for poetizing," and he quickly made a name for himself as a writer of interludes, moral plays like those in English dramatic history, combining allegorical characters with considerable realism of action. Partly because he " 'wrote in common verse and in the language of the present day,' " Twm's interludes became so popular that after his death he was widely, if exaggeratedly, known, according to Borrow, as "The Welsh Shakespeare." During much of his life, however, he supported himself, not from his poetry but, being physically strong and knowledgeable about horses, from the trade of carter, or teamster; and Borrow pays much attention in Chapter LIX to Twm's tales of his adventures in this trade. In fact, having devoted the following Chapter LX to a discussion of the interlude form and a detailed summary, with quotations, of *Riches and Poverty,* Borrow concludes of Twm that he "was greater as a man than as a poet, and that his fame depends more on the cleverness, courage and energy, which it is evident by his biography that he possessed, than on his interludes."[9]

Just as Borrow had delighted in reading Twm o'r Nant's autobiography, so Anderson seems to have delighted in reading Borrow's summary of it, so much so that two-thirds of the second paragraph of "An Ohio Pagan" is a kind of summary of that summary.

The first Thomas Edwards was a gigantic fig-

ure in the history of the spiritual life of the Welsh.
Not only did he write many stirring interludes concerning life, death, earth, fire and water but as a
man he was a true brother to the elements and to
all the passions of his sturdy and musical race. He
sang beautifully but he also played stoutly and beautifully the part of a man. There is a wonderful tale,
told in Wales and written into a book by the poet
himself, of how he, with a team of horses, once
moved a great ship out of the land into the sea,
after three hundred Welshmen had failed at the task.
Also he taught Welsh woodsmen the secret of the
crane and pulley for lifting great logs in the forests,
and once he fought to the point of death the bully
of the countryside, a man known over a great part
of Wales as The Cruel Fighter.[10]

Observing only the second half of this quotation, one finds that the
moving of the ship, the lifting of the logs, and the fight are three of the
four feats that Borrow chooses in order to prove Twm o'r Nant's greatness
"as a man," emphasizing them in his summary by quoting in full Twm's
own account of the events and referring to them again at the conclusion to
Chapter LX on the interludes: "A time will come when his interludes will
cease to be read, but his making ink out of elderberries, his battle with the
'cruel fighter,' his teaching his horses to turn the crane, and his getting the
ship to the water, will be talked of in Wales till the peak of Snowdon
shall fall down."[11]

What is particularly significant about Anderson's borrowing, however,
is not simply his indebtedness to a literary source but the way he adapts
that source to his own creative purpose. A comparison of his and Borrow's
— that is, Twm o'r Nant's — accounts of these three feats shows that Anderson deliberately magnified each of them and gave it a legendary, even a
mythic, quality. Anderson writes that Twm, working only with the aid of
a team of horses, moved "a great ship out of the land into the sea," whereas
in Twm's own story the "carter poet," as Borrow terms him at one point,
flatly calls it " 'a small ship' " which he managed to get from the wood
where it had been built to " 'the river Towy' " a mile and a quarter away,
using not only a team of four horses and an ingenious arrangement of rope
and pulleys but also the assistance of a " 'lad' " and " 'three or four men.' "
In Twm's account, furthermore, a crowd of people in a holiday mood had

earlier left the ship in a ditch after pushing it only a short distance, but Anderson, echoing legend or myth, specifies a magic number of "three hundred" men who had "failed at the task" despite, by implication, their best efforts. As for the second feat, Twm, telling of how he was the first carter in Wales or England to hitch horses to a crane for loading wood in the forest, emphasizes simply the mechanics of the process and the relative ease of labor it gave him and his pregnant wife who was helping him as well as she could. Anderson, on the other hand, omits the wife and makes Twm a kind of Welsh Daedalus. As for the third feat, Twm describes a bloody enough battle between himself and a young neighboring man " 'who was a cruel fighter,' " but who in this instance sought to punish Twm for using " 'scurrilous language' " against the man's sister. Both men were indeed badly hurt, Twm's opponent recovering only after " 'many thought he would die.' " Anderson, however, transforms this quite local, rather discreditable fight into an heroic struggle by Twm against a near-national oppressor.[12]

Nor do Anderson's magnifying and mythifying of his hero's grandfather end with his reworking of the three feats. In Chapter LIX of *Wild Wales* Borrow is quite willing to admit Twm's human defects. For example, he delights in Twm's tales of how, while keeping a tollgate on a turnpike at one point in his career, he often saw phantom hearses and funeral processions pass " 'through the gate without paying toll' "; but Borrow lets the reader know that he thinks Twm a better story teller than truth teller. Elsewhere in *Wild Wales,* too, he reports one Welshman's word that Twm was " 'very satirical' " as well as " 'very clever' " and another's that, like all writers of interludes, Twm was a " 'blackguard' " and a " 'scamp,' " the judgment of "scamp" not being out of keeping with some of the other events he mentions in Twm's life.[13] Nevertheless, Anderson, ignoring all such reservations, grandly describes this "first Thomas Edwards" as "a gigantic figure in the history of the spiritual life of the Welsh" and asserts that he not only wrote "many stirring interludes" concerning the traditional elements, "earth, fire and water," but "as a man was a true brother" to them. In short, Borrow's very human figure of Twm o'r Nant is turned by Anderson into an heroic Welsh Bard.

Anderson, as good a story teller as Borrow or Twm o'r Nant, knew what he was about in all this magnification and mythmaking. By providing young Tom Edwards of Bidwell, Ohio with such a grandfather, he prepares his readers to accept as believable the intense poetic nature of his unsophisticated, rather inarticulate hero and also to accept as believable of Tom the metamorphic visions that come to him at the end of each of the two chapters into which "An Ohio Pagan" is divided.

Both visions are in every sense extraordinary. In the first chapter, one learns, Tom is orphaned early and is taken into Harry Whitehead's home. As he grows into adolescence, he drops gladly out of school, much preferring to gain knowledge in the world of harness racing as a swipe for Whitehead's trotters and pacers. At "the great spring race meeting at Columbus, Ohio," this loving, intuitive knowledge of horses enables the sixteen-year-old "boy with the blood of Twm O'r Nant in his veins," when put into the sulky, to guide to a record victory Whitehead's black stallion Bucephalus, who had been given this name out of Classic legend by "John Telfer, our town poetry lover" because " 'It was the name of the mighty horse of a mighty man.' "[14] Despite this success Tom runs away from Bidwell when the local truant officer convinces Whitehead that Tom must return to school. After working unhappily for some months in an ugly industrial city, Tom takes a job with a threshing outfit working through Northern Ohio between the fictitious Bidwell and the real Sandusky on Lake Erie. Each day he rejoices at driving a team of horses through "the yellow sunwashed fields" to fetch water and fuel for the big steam threshing machine, and each night he listens sympathetically as the owner of the thresher prays to Jesus for continued fair weather. The work, the weather, and the praying turn Tom to thoughts "of God and of the possibilities of God's part in the affairs of men." Uninstructed in Christian doctrine, he conceives of Jesus as some unknown power in nature itself and imagines him "as a young god walking about over the land." The "blood of the old poet Twm O'r Nant [awakes] in him," and in a magnificently mythopoeic paragraph Anderson demonstrates how myth, religion, nature, and the daily task flow together in the mind of this youth who had once "driven Bucephalus . . . to victory."

> The water boy for the threshing crew rode the
> horse Pegasus down through the lanes back of the
> farm houses in Erie County, Ohio, to the creeks
> where the threshing tanks must be filled. Beside
> him on the soft earth in the forest walked the young
> god Jesus. At the creek Pegasus, born of the springs
> of Ocean, stamped on the ground. The plodding
> farm horses stopped. With a dazed look in his eyes
> Tom Edwards arose from the wagon seat and pre-
> pared his hose and pump for filling the tank. The
> god Jesus walked away over the land, and with a

wave of his hand summoned the smiling days.[15]

Tom's initial vision comes at the end of Chapter I when, after a brief shower one early Sunday evening, he looks across a field toward "a low grass-covered hill," hoping to see an incarnation of Jesus there.

> The long slanting rays of the evening sun fell
> on the crest of the hill and touched with light the
> grass stalks, heavy with drops of rain and for a
> moment the hill was crowned as with a crown of
> jewels. A million tiny drops of water, reflecting
> the light, made the hilltop sparkle as though set
> with gems. "Jesus is there," muttered the boy.
> "He lies on his belly in the grass. He is looking at
> me over the edge of the hill."

However bizarre the vision, it is appropriate to a randomly-educated youth descended from a grandfather who was poet, great "spiritual" figure among his countrymen, and greatly passionate, almost superhuman man.

Tom's first vision, quasi-religious in form and content, has been sensuous but not sensual; the second is thoroughly erotic, as might be expected in a story by an author for whom a concept of paganism involved a rejection of the sexual repressiveness he associated with Puritanism. In Chapter I Tom had "—for the first and last time in his life—" attended a church on the outskirts of "a village called Castalia" and during the minister's sermon had dreamily confused the temptation of Jesus by Satan on the Mount with an imagined temptation of Jesus by Mary Magdalene, who offers her body to him.[16] Stirred by his still virginal fascination with sex between men and women, he now in the early fall is filled with a strong, if unfocused, sexual desire that makes him pray to Jesus to bring him a woman and that colors his perception of the whole landscape.

> All through those bright warm clear fall days
> a restless feeling, it seemed to Tom ran through
> everything in nature. In the clumps of woodland
> still standing on the farms flaming red spread it-
> self out along the limbs of trees and there was one
> grove of young maple trees, near a barn, that was
> like a troop of girls, young girls who had walked
> together down a sloping field, to stop in alarm at

> seeing the men at work in the barnyard. Tom stood
> looking at the trees. A slight breeze made them
> sway gently from side to side. Two horses standing
> among the trees drew near each other. One nipped
> the other's neck. They rubbed their heads together.

On yet another Sunday's day of rest the chance sight of a mother feeding her baby at her breast stirs "the grandson of the Welsh poet." As he walks out into the country, the "passion that could not find expression through his body [goes] up into his mind and he [begins] to see visions." As he looks about, "everything in nature [becomes] woman" — apple trees are like women's arms, the apples are like women's breasts, the fences around fields fall "into the forms of women's bodies." Climbing "the highest [hill] in all that part of the country" — that is, the Mount of Temptation — Tom looks out over Sandusky Bay, and in his eyes the bay itself assumes "the form and shape of a woman's head and body," tempting him as he had pictured Mary Magdalene physically tempting Jesus. Turning his eyes toward the sky, Tom sees the clouds take on the faces of a giant man and a giant woman, the faces merging in ecstasy. Looking out on the fields, he sees the land with its rounded hills become a reclining woman, the eyes black puddles of water "shining invitingly up at him." Bay, sky, fields — water, air, earth. If Twm o'r Nant was "a true brother to the elements," his visionary grandson is one with them in passion.

This scene on the high hill brings one back to Twm o'r Nant's life and writings a final time. That one of Twm's interludes was entitled "A Vision of the Course of the World" may have had something to do, along with his tales of phantoms at the tollgate, with Anderson's making his Ohio pagan a visionary, just as Twm's development, very late in life, of "strong religious convictions . . . about a Saviour" may have had something to do with the Ohio Tom Edwards's special interest in Jesus.[17] Such suggestions are highly conjectural, but it is less conjectural why Tom's metamorphic visions should involve the elements of water, air, and earth. As Borrow twice explains and then illustrates by lengthy quotation, the most important passage in the interlude *Riches and Poverty* is a debate between Captain Riches and Captain Poverty which characterizes each "according to the rule of the four elements, Water, Fire, Earth, and Air."[18] Here, done by Borrow into galloping English verses, are the relevant sections of dialogue from the one interlude by Twm o'r Nant that Borrow had ever found to read, but which Anderson, consistent in his manner of borrowing, magnified into "many stirring interludes concerning life, death, earth, fire and water":

RICHES

. . .

Of elements four did our Master create
The earth and all in it with skill the most great;
Need I the world's four materials declare —
Are they not water, fire, earth, and air?
. . .

POVERTY

In the marvellous things, which to me thou hast told
The wisdom of God I most clearly behold,
And did He not also make man of the same
Materials He us'd when the world He did frame?

RICHES

Creation is all, as the sages agree,
Of the elements four in man's body that be;
Water's the blood, and fire is the nature,
Which prompts generation in every creature.

The earth is the flesh which with beauty is rife
The air is the breath, without which is no life;
So man must be always accounted the same
As the substances four which exist in his frame.

And as in their creation distinction there's none
'Twixt man and the world, so the Infinite One
Unto man a clear wisdom did bounteously give
The nature of everything to perceive.[19]

Doubtless the poetry of "The Welsh Shakespeare" loses something in translation; but enough may have been left in such lines as, "The earth is the flesh which with beauty is rife," to catch Anderson's eye and ear, and certainly the sense of the passage is clear. In its argument that God created mankind and the world out of identical elements lies sufficient, though perhaps not sole, cause for the creator of "An Ohio Pagan" to make God-seeking, sex-suffused Tom Edwards "perceive" the "nature of everything" in erotic human form.[20]

171

NOTES

[1]*No Swank* (Philadelphia: The Centaur Press, 1934), p. 43.

[2]*Letters of Sherwood Anderson,* edited by Howard Mumford Jones, in association with Walter B. Rideout (Boston: Little, Brown and Company, 1953), p. 31; unpublished letter to Waldo Frank, May, 1919. Quotations from unpublished letters by permission of Eleanor Copenhaver Anderson and the Newberry Library.

[3]*No Swank,* p. 39.

[4]*Letters,* pp. 60-61.

[5]Letter dated August 6, 1920 from Ephraim. Anderson's extremely informative letters to Marietta Finley are being edited for publication by William A. Sutton, who obtained them from her for the Newberry Library.

[6]Anderson's fiction reverses the actual sequence of these events. In April, 1891, Whitehead was turning "the old novelty works" into a stables, but it was not until four years later that he announced his intention to move into Clyde from his farm in the spring of 1896 (*The Clyde Enterprise,* April 16, 1891, p. 3; July 19, 1895, p. 1).

[7]See William A. Sutton, *The Road to Winesburg: A Mosaic of the Imaginative Life of Sherwood Anderson* (Metuchen, N. J.: The Scarecrow Press, 1972), p. 88.

[8]Interview with David H. Stevens, Ephraim, August 24, 1956.

[9]Quotations are from George Borrow, *Wild Wales: Its People, Language, and Scenery* (New York: G. P. Putnam's Sons, 1900), pp. 397, 77, 74, 401, 413.

[10]*Horses and Men* (New York: B. W. Huebsch, 1923), p. 315. All

quotations from "An Ohio Pagan" are from this edition.

11*Wild Wales*, p. 413. As a boy the historical Tom Edwards was inspired by his few weeks of formal schooling to teach himself to write, and made ink from elderberries for that purpose. Presumably Anderson omitted this "feat" as out of keeping with his fictional grandson's dislike of the several years of schooling he receives.

12For Twm's own accounts, see *Wild Wales*, pp. 398-399 (the fight); p. 399 (the lifting of the logs); pp. 402-404 (the moving of the ship). Anderson reversed the order of these feats, possibly in order to end with, and thereby emphasize, Twm's presumed role as national hero.

13*Wild Wales*, pp. 401, 353, 121.

14The name Bucephalus is one of several Classic references in the story, though it is interesting to note that *The Clyde Enterprise* for August 3, 1893 (p. 3) announced that a pacer named Bucephus*[sic]* would race at the Clyde Fair Grounds on August 10. Tom Whitehead's stallion, actually named Solarion, took first, second, or third place in harness races at Toledo, Sandusky, Fremont, Cleveland, and Bellevue in September-October, 1895. (See *The Clyde Enterprise, passim.)*

15In Greek mythology the winged horse Pegasus is usually said to have sprung from the blood of Medusa when Perseus cut off her head; but Anderson may have again been borrowing and adapting, this time from part of the entry on Pegasus in the Eleventh Edition of the *Encyclopedia Britannica* (1911), Vol. 21, p. 56: "The erroneous derivation [of the name from the Greek word for] 'a spring of water' may have given birth to the legends which connect Pegasus with water; *e.g.* that his father was Poseidon, that he was born at the springs of Ocean, and that he had the power of making springs rise from the ground by a blow of his hoof."

16Castalia is the name of an actual village lying between Clyde and Sandusky and built around a spring-fed pool. Anderson might have learned from the *Encyclopedia Britannica* that in Greek mythology it was the name also of a fountain on Mt. Parnassus sacred to Apollo and the Muses and believed to be a source of inspiration.

17*Wild Wales*, pp. 400-402, 406.

[18]*Wild Wales*, p. 409. See also p. 410.

[19]*Wild Wales*, pp. 410-411.

[20]Since Anderson demonstrably drew on Borrow's summary of Twm o'r Nant's autobiography in writing "An Ohio Pagan," there is a possibility that he was also indebted to Chapter LIX of *Wild Wales* for a suggestion toward the title, perhaps even toward the central event, of one of his more famous stories, "Death in the Woods." On p. 402 of *Wild Wales* occurs a paragraph, quoted in translation from Twm's Welsh, which immediately follows the passage on his seeing phantoms at the tollgate and immediately precedes his account of moving the ship:

> "Another time there happened a great wonder connected with an old man of Carmarthen, who was in the habit of carrying fish to Brecon, Menny, and Monmouth, and returning with the poorer kind of Gloucester cheese: my people knew he was on the road and had made ready for him, the weather being dreadful, wind blowing and snow drifting. Well, in the middle of the night, my daughters heard the voice of the old man at the gate, and their mother called to them to open it quick, and invite the old man to come in to the fire! One of the girls got up forthwith, but when she went out there was nobody to be seen. On the morrow, lo and behold! the body of the old man was brought past on a couch, he having perished in the snow on the mountain of Tre 'r Castell. Now this is the truth of the matter."

Despite obvious differences between Twm's anecdote and Anderson's story, one notes here that an old person, apparently poor, who is in the habit of taking one kind of food to market and returning home with another, dies at night in the snow under eerie circumstances. At the beginning of Chapter LIX, p. 394, a collection of twelve subheads announces the chapter's contents. The first of these is "History of Twm O'r Nant"; the fourth is "The Cruel Fighter"; the eighth, startlingly, is "Death in the Snow."

"T.M.": THE FORGOTTEN MUSE OF
SHERWOOD ANDERSON AND EDGAR LEE MASTERS

John H. Wrenn and Margaret M. Wrenn

Sherwood Anderson's Winesburg, Ohio, is part of an archipelago of geographical microcosms rising in this century in Maine and then in Illinois and Ohio and culminating in Mississippi. Tilbury Town, Spoon River, Winesburg, Yoknapatawpha County are the major islands. A visit to any one of them is worth a world-tour. But, though you may find a little Illinois river called the Spoon and even an actual Winesburg, Ohio (unknown to Anderson when he titled his book), you'll look in vain on the map for the village-islands of this archipelago. They aren't there. "True places," as Melville observed, "never are."

Various critical Baedekers and Cooks have provided guidebooks to each of the major islands and even to such gull roosts as Farmington and Gopher Prairie apart from the major chain. But precious little is said about the connections between one island and the next. We hope to establish the possibilities of communication between the two central islands.

Spoon River and Winesburg, Ohio, may properly be called islands because of their distinct insularity. They are often considered to be part of the "village" tradition of American literature, specifically the village the author is supposed to have revolted from. Related to this tradition is the autobiographical novel *Farmington* (1904) by Clarence Darrow, the famous criminal lawyer and Edgar Lee Masters' Chicago law partner from 1893 to 1911. The town Farmington has many resemblances to Masters' village depicted in *Spoon River Anthology* (1914, 1915), which also resembles Tilbury Town in E. A. Robinson's *The Town Down the River* (1910) and earlier volumes.

175

The Gopher Prairie of Sinclair Lewis' *Main Street* (1920) has antecedents in the villages of *Farmington, Spoon River,* and *Winesburg, Ohio* (1919). William Faulkner's town of Jefferson in Yoknapatawpha County, Mississippi, of *Sartoris* (1929) and later volumes is directly connected to Winesburg and indirectly to the others.

Both Edgar Lee Masters and Sherwood Anderson declined to be included in the revolt-from-the-village school. August Derleth in *Three Literary Men: A Memoir . . .* (New York: Candlelight Press, 1963, pp. 34-35, 42) reports Masters' insistence in 1940 that *he* never revolted from Petersburg, Illinois, the ur-Spoon River, and that Anderson, interviewed in his turn, insisted there *was* no such school and if there were he hadn't revolted from the village of Clyde, the prototype of Winesburg. They are both probably right. The pigeon hole is too neat and too narrow.

Yet the village of Spoon River has another antecedent than Petersburg, where Masters spent a happy childhood near the farm of his revered grandparents, Squire Davis and Lucinda (Matlock) Masters. This other village was Lewistown, where the Masters family moved when Lee Masters was eleven. It was much more urban and mercantile and northern than Petersburg; Masters hated it. To a large extent he did revolt from Lewistown, finally fleeing to Chicago when he was twenty-two. All of the more distasteful episodes and characters of *Spoon River Anthology* come from Masters' memories of Lewistown.

In response to a query from August Derleth about his "revolt" Anderson "laughed derisively . . . .'There wasn't anything to this revolting. I liked Clyde. I saw it the way it was and I put it down the way it was. I didn't run away from Clyde. The time came and I went' " (Derleth, p. 34). Of course there were things about Clyde that he didn't like, and he put down those things too in *Winesburg, Ohio.* One of the things that made it both attractive and unattractive was its very insularity. In a small town, most people can know one another. They become interdependent. Often they know one another too well. Having few contacts with the outside world, they become preoccupied with one another's affairs; jealousies and misconceptions incubate and hatch. Grotesques emerge.

Masters lived in Petersburg from 1869 to 1881. On the 4th of July 1881 he moved to Lewistown where he lived until he belatedly asserted his independence in 1892 by moving to Chicago after his mother hit him over the head with a rolled-up window shade. Anderson was born in Camden, Ohio, in the centennial year 1876; his family settled in Clyde while he was still a child. He made his first break for independence much earlier in life, but at about the same time as Masters, and in the same place, Chicago, just about the time the Columbia Exposition opened in 1893.

In 1898 Masters married for the first time. In 1910 he asked his wife to release him, which she refused to do, so that he might marry Tennessee Mitchell, who had been piano instructor to his two nieces. From 1909 to 1911, Masters was engaged in a tumultuous love affair with Miss Mitchell. The dates are Masters'. They occur in the title of his poem, "Ballade of Ultimate Shame: T.M., August 20, 1909-May 23, 1911." He published this poem, with others based on their affair, under the pseudonym Webster Ford in *Songs and Sonnets, Second Series* (Chicago: Rooks Press, 1912).

Masters returned to this central relationship in his literary career again and again in individual poems, novels and plays, and most explicitly in his autobiography *Across Spoon River* (New York: Farrar & Rinehart, 1936), where he quaintly indexes under his own name some sixteen "love affairs" (the index is incomplete here and elsewhere), with "Deirdre"—who is Tennessee Mitchell—inconspicuously listed in alphabetical order: "Deirdre, 295-314." There is no question that Tennessee Claflin Mitchell, or "T.M." in the "Ballade" mentioned above is Deirdre. In the chapter he devotes to her in *Across Spoon River*, Chapter XIV, Masters mentions the feminists "the Claflin sisters" (she was named for Tennessee Claflin) as well as accurate details of her early life (pp. 297-298). In a letter of 25 May 1949, Masters dictated to his second wife her response to a researcher, William L. Phillips, asserting that Miss Mitchell was indeed the Deirdre of *Across Spoon River*. More recently Mrs. Masters has said of her, "Tennessee Mitchell was a very intelligent and courageous woman—a real person."[1] In Tennessee's chapter, one finds, as often in Masters, considerable bitterness that people and events failed to work out as they might have. Yet in commenting on one of Tennessee's final letters he says, ". . . it was full of her best self, and that was perhaps the only self of her that there was. Her other selves may have been the creation of my imagination, my jealous dreads" (p. 309). Then he says,

> It was three years before I extirpated [Tennessee's] [2] poison from my blood, extirpated it as immediate sickness and agony; for the rest, does one ever get well of a poisoning? Rarely has a sensitive man had a love affair like this without great disaster; and literature is full of their descriptions. . . . They may, however, be rich schoolings for the mind and heart. . . . I learned through [Tennessee] the secrets and agonies of

all the world's lovers. . . . My emotional powers
were enormously deepened by [Tennessee] . I
was enabled through her to reread every word of
Shakespeare's plays of passion under a light which
reflected up and out of the printed page every
meaning, and even more than he was able to set
down. (pp. 312-313)

Writing a quarter of a century after the events, he asserts that "What [Ten-
nessee] did was to give me understanding" (p. 405). And he remains so
convinced of her effect on his powers of insight and sympathy as an artist
that he insists, "I could not have written 'Tomorrow Is My Birthday' " — a
favorite poem of Masters' from which he selected his epitaph — "if I had not
had the experience with [Tennessee] ; nor could I have written many other
poems without this severe schooling" (p. 313). He could not in fact have
written *Spoon River Anthology.*

The first seeds of Masters' greatest work were planted in 1909, in his
final visit to his grandmother, the one constant source of love and affection
of his childhood.

This autumn [1909] . . . my grandmother
celebrated her ninety-fifth birthday anniversary; and in the state of mind I was in on
account of [Tennessee] it seemed to me that
there would be healing in communing with
this venerable woman who dated back to my
childhood with infinite memories of happiness
and peace. So I journeyed down to Petersburg,
leaving [Tennessee] . . . .
And so she went on [about "Henry Houghton
. . . Flora Kincaid . . . Branson, the best lawyer in
Petersburg"] with perfect memory and reason
talking of many things both those of recent years
and of the last few months, and those of the long
ago. She even mentioned her old grandmother
Rebecca Wasson. . . . (pp. 302-304)

Both Masters' grandmother, under the name Lucinda Matlock, and Rebecca
Wasson are principal portraits in *Spoon River Anthology*; the other surnames appear there also. Masters continues, "I sat there listening to her as

she talked and talked. I was thinking of [Tennessee]" (p. 304). So the stories of Petersburg and later, by association, of nearby Lewistown came to Masters in his state of emotional hypersensitivity, conscious that he "was taking a last look" (p. 304) at his beloved grandmother and that he could never reconcile his love for Tennessee with his marriage, his children, his career as a lawyer. With his mind in Chicago, doubtless he scarcely heard his grandmother's words but absorbed the pictures and characters directly into his memories of what was to become the composite village Spoon River.

"It was three years" from the end of the affair on "May 23, 1911" till Masters had "extirpated [Tennessee's] poison" (for "poison" read 'enduring emotional effects'), at least "as immediate . . . agony." Art, whatever else it may be, is for the artist in part catharsis. As it had seemed to him "that there would be healing" in 1909 in traveling "down to Petersburg," so he found relief in 1914 in the imaginative journey to Spoon River. In May 1914, three years to the month, the first of his Spoon River epitaphs appeared in *Reedy's Mirror*. In August, the fifth anniversary of the affair, appeared the epitaph "Tennessee Claflin Shope" — spoken by a voice of indeterminate sex who has found peace. Ten years after their parting, Masters celebrated Tennessee as Calypso in the poem "Ulysses" from *The Open Sea* (1921). Speaking as Ulysses, he asks, "What's a woman?" and answers, "She is . . . the Muse."

ii

In the same year, 1914, in which Masters found a cure in writing his masterwork *Spoon River Anthology*, Sherwood Anderson met Tennessee Mitchell in Chicago. She was "a very dear friend"[3] of Cornelia Anderson, Sherwood's first wife from whom he was now separated. Sherwood spent the summer of 1915 with Tennessee at Lake Chateaugay in the Adirondacks. In the fall his wife granted him a divorce, which became final in July 1916. On 31 July 1916 he married Tennessee Mitchell. Between fall 1915 and his marriage to Tennessee he wrote most of the stories of *Winesburg, Ohio*.[4]

For Anderson as for Masters, Tennessee was a breath of freedom. Named after the feminist Tennessee Claflin, independent of family and self-supporting, attractive, understanding, mature — she was thirty-five when Masters met her, forty when she met Anderson — she was perhaps the ideal lover for an aspiring artist. What an escape for both men! — from a conditioned village morality, from a boring, conventional marriage, from their children, from the workaday life of the professional man (Masters the attorney) or businessman (Anderson the salesman, paint-manufacturer, advertising writer). By the time she met Masters, Tennessee was already a liberated woman as her unfinished manuscript autobiography[5] and, in fact, Masters' account in *Across Spoon River* indicate. For these two artists she was in quite different ways a great liberating force.

For Masters she was a mental, emotional, imaginative stimulus—an irritant, an "agony" that found a cure in his greatest work, *Spoon River Anthology.* For Anderson she was a release for his emotional and physical needs, a shield against distractions, a guardian of his solitude. Even after their marriage Anderson and Tennessee lived apart, Tennessee continuing to use her own name and to support herself (and, to a small degree, supporting Cornelia Anderson and the children) so that Sherwood could maintain the solitude that his craft required and have the encouragement of an affectionate wife as well. Whereas Masters in *Across Spoon River* saw her as a "demon" (p. 307), "a cold, uncanny, farsighted mind" (p. 306), to Anderson, as he revealed to his friends in letters quoted by William Sutton (p. 42), she was a "princess," who was "unspeakably bully," with the "blessed flavor" of "understanding people—Tennessee is one of them." He was fully aware, at the time, of her beneficent, direct effect on his work.

But the influence of Tennessee on *Winesburg, Ohio* was at least as much indirect, through her influence on Masters, as direct, through her immediate effect on Anderson. Walter Havighurst in *The Heartland: Ohio, Indiana, Illinois* (New York: Harper, 1956, p. 332) relates that "in the spring of 1915, a friend had given Anderson a copy of the Masters poems [*Spoon River Anthology*], which he read all night. A few months later he began working freshly on the Winesburg book." Anderson by 1915 was writing as a poet his free-verse *Mid-American Chants* (1918). Both he and Tennessee could very well have missed the free-verse epitaphs published in 1914 in *Reedy's Mirror* by "Webster Ford," even though Tennessee would have known the identity of Webster Ford as Masters, who had published *Songs and Sonnets* (1910) under that name at the height of their affair. It was in many ways her book, about their relationship. But neither Anderson nor Tennessee could have missed for long the furor in Chicago and elsewhere which greeted the book-publication of Masters' *Spoon River Anthology* by Macmillan in 1915. Tennessee herself might have called Anderson's attention to Masters' book. For Anderson knew of her earlier connection with Masters, explaining on one occasion, "We were both after the same girl, and I won out" (Derleth, p. 32); similarly Masters reports in *Across Spoon River*

Tennessee's early frankness with him regarding *his* predecessor, "her former lover" (p. 302).

Spoon River and Winesburg, Ohio, have much in common as Midwestern towns modeled on recognizable originals, peopled by ordinary folk bearing names also based on recognizable originals, some slightly altered: the surnames Houghton, Kincaid, Branson, which Masters recalled from his last visit to his grandmother; Jesse Benton and Skinner Letson of Clyde becoming Jesse Bentley and Skinner Leason in Anderson's Winesburg (Duffey, p. 208). But, as books, *Winesburg, Ohio* and *Spoon River* are as different perhaps as Anderson's and Masters' epithets for Tennessee Mitchell—"princess" versus "demon."

Spoon River Anthology is a collection of free-verse "epitaphs" spoken by the dead, revealing truths which they would not have recognized or would not have spoken when alive. It is an exposé of human hypocrisy and a social criticism of thwarted village lives, containing some admiration for its subjects and much bitterness. *Winesburg* is a collection of stories or sketches of individual lives revealed from the point of view of innocent love. It is a psychological investigation of the relationships of yearning, frustrated individuals. Its effect is lyrical, poetic, undidactic.

What Anderson must have felt in *Spoon River* as he read all night was a clue to the possibilities of coming to terms with his own Midwest village background, of discovering in his own backyard, so to speak, known people to be developed into living characters, of finding in ordinary village lives truths of American life and of the human heart. There was no need for Anderson to acknowledge or to deny this debt any more than Masters needed to deny, as he did, his debts to E. A. Robinson and to Robinson's predecessor Crabbe (which Robinson acknowledged in his sonnet "George Crabbe") when reviewers noticed similarities (*Across Spoon River*, p. 372). Nor did Faulkner later need to comment on his debts to Anderson; their association in New Orleans in the mid-twenties was common enough knowledge.

From the perspective of today we can make out clear subsurface connections among these apparently distinct communities which we know as Tilbury Town, Spoon River, Winesburg, Yoknapatawpha County. This detracts not a whit from the originality or the imaginative achievement of any of their creators. Each was his own man, his own artist. And the communities which they revealed were and are authentic American microcosms. Their very connections enlarge rather than limit the significance of each. Anderson and Masters were right in denying the validity of a revolt-from-the-village school which points to nothing more noteworthy than the long process of nineteenth- and twentieth-century urbanization. We have no wish to cram them instead into a village-microcosm pigeonhole. We simply note relationships. On our literary map appears a sort of chain of geographical microcosms extending from Maine to Mississippi. The two central ones, designated Spoon River and Winesburg, lie rather close together; in fact their topographic features roughly correspond, as the west coast of Africa seems to correspond with the east coast of South America, suggesting they were once contiguous. Looking more closely, we find there are connections in fact.

Paralleling the resemblance between the towns Winesburg and Spoon River are resemblances between Anderson and Masters. They spent their childhoods in the Midwest villages of Clyde, Ohio, and Petersburg, Illinois; after reaching manhood they spent a year each at Wittenberg Academy and Knox College, respectively; at the age of 23 to 24 both had found unrewarding jobs in Chicago; at age 28 to 29 both married for the first time. At middle age, 38-40, first the frustrated Chicago lawyer Masters, then the frustrated Chicago businessman Anderson fell in love with Tennessee Mitchell for whom each was willing to leave his wife and children. Five years after meeting Tennessee, under the stimulus of William Marion Reedy and the *Greek Anthology* (which Reedy had given him), Masters published *Spoon River Anthology*; five years after meeting Tennessee, under the stimulus of Gertrude Stein and *Spoon River Anthology*, Anderson published *Winesburg, Ohio*. At age 57 each married for the last time; the bride of each was a much younger woman, born about 1900, with the initials E. C.: Ellen Coyne (Masters) and Eleanor Copenhaver (Anderson).

The one significant phenomenon which joins these parallel lives appears to be Tennessee Mitchell, the forgotten muse behind the masterworks of Anderson and Masters. Appearing first to Masters (perhaps as Calliope, muse of epic poetry) and then to Anderson (perhaps as Melpomene, muse of tragedy), she fired their emotions and their imaginations. Though she spent only three years in the life of Masters, eight years in the life of Anderson, she affected all their subsequent work. She was an artist herself. Her perfect pitch made her first a piano tuner (perhaps the first professional American woman piano tuner), then a piano teacher. During her marriage to Anderson she discovered a talent for sculpture. Anderson in a letter of 30 September 1920 reported, "Tennessee. . . has done some heads of Americans that are great."[6]

Tennessee was divorced from Anderson in 1924. In 1930 she took her own life. In *Across Spoon River* (1936) Masters memorialized her mostly

in the derogatory terms mentioned above. In his Memoirs, Anderson recalled her as "the woman Tennessee Mitchell, with whom I once lived (I
was married to her but it was a marriage that didn't take)."[7] Neither
Masters nor Anderson, nor Tennessee herself ever fully realized that she
had molded not merely "some heads of Americans," but the very literary
careers of two important American writers, Edgar Lee Masters and
Sherwood Anderson.

NOTES

[1]Ellen Coyne Masters, quoted in William A. Sutton, "Sherwood Anderson's Second Wife," *Ball State Univ. Forum,* 8 (Spring, 1966), 43; letter to John H. Wrenn, 17 Nov. 1975. All quotations from Edgar Lee Masters and Ellen Coyne Masters are with the kind permission of Mrs. Masters.

[2]"[Tennessee] " is used hereafter for Masters' "Deirdre."

[3]Cornelia Anderson, interview 10 Oct. 1946, quoted in Sutton, p. 39.

[4]Bernard Duffey, *The Chicago Renaissance in American Letters* (East Lansing: Michigan State Univ. Press, 1954), p. 206.

[5]In the Anderson collection, Newberry Library, Chicago: Sutton, p. 40, fn. 21.

[6]Letter to Lucile and Jerry Blum, quoted in Sutton, p. 44.

[7]*Sherwood Anderson's Memoirs: A Critical Edition,* ed. Ray Lewis White (Chapel Hill, N.C.: Univ. of N. Carolina Press, 1969), p. 551.

THE EDUCATION OF SHERWOOD ANDERSON

John W. Crowley

I

In a review of *A Story Teller's Story* in 1924, Robert Morss Lovett suggested that the book might well have been called "The Education of Sherwood Anderson."[1] Like Lovett, several other reviewers remarked similarities between Anderson's "autobiography" and *The Education of Henry Adams.* Lloyd Morris, for one, found the books so profoundly alike that he could not "easily read 'A Story Teller's Story' without being reminded of 'The Education.' "[2] Such statements provoked Ernest Hemingway to complain sardonically:

> The reviewers have all compared this book with the
> "Education of Henry Adams" and it was not hard for
> them to do so, for Sherwood Anderson twice refers
> to the Adams book and there is plenty in the "Story
> Teller's Story" about the cathedral at Chartres.
> Evidently the Education book made a deep impression
> on Sherwood for he quotes part of it. . . . All of my
> friends own and speak of "The Education of Henry
> Adams" with such solemnity that I have been unable
> ever to read it. "A Story Teller's Story" is a good
> book. It is such a good book that it doesn't need
> to be coupled in the reviewing with Henry Adams
> or anybody else.[3]

Hemingway was exaggerating. Not *all* the reviewers measured Anderson

185

against Adams, and even those who did praised Anderson's own achievement in *A Story Teller's Story*. Hemingway's resentment of the coupling of Adams with Anderson, and his grudging refusal to read *The Education* reflect Adams' impact on American thought and letters in the twenties. Hemingway would not have strained so hard to declare his, and Anderson's, independence from a writer who did not really matter, whose work did not threaten to overshadow their own.

Adams *did* matter because *The Education* expressed seminally many of the themes and ideas that would obsess both Anderson's and Hemingway's literary generations. After finishing the book in late 1918, Anderson wrote to Van Wyck Brooks, "I have been reading *The Education of Henry Adams* and feel tremendously its importance as a piece of American writing."[4] Ten years later, the critic T. K. Whipple described the nature of that importance when he explained why he was including Adams among his modern "Spokesmen." "It may seem strange to include in a discussion of contemporary writers a man who was seventy-six years old when the World War began," Whipple admitted; "yet Henry Adams was so remarkable a herald or forerunner of the present and formulated a philosophy so typically modern that his story clarifies and helps explain the whole trend of American literature in the last fifteen years." For Whipple, *The Education* "enables us as does no other book to watch the contemporary view of life actually in process of formation."[5] The "contemporary view" is evident not only in Adams' vision of a chaotic universe but in his vision of himself as an alienated artist. He prophetically recorded, as Whipple says, "the experience of a man endowed with the poetic temper and forced to live in a practical society."[6]

This statement applies not only to *The Education* but to *A Story Teller's Story*. As Anderson told Gertrude Stein while he was writing it, "I am trying to make a kind of picture of the artist's life in the midst of present-day American life."[7] Thus, *A Story Teller's Story* was not so much an autobiography as a parable or, as Anderson later put it, "a novel—of the mind of a man, let us say of a man who happened to be a writer."[8] Because he was writing a "novel," Anderson felt free, as Adams had, to distort or falsify the facts of his life in order "to be true to the essence of things."[9] The book, as Stein perceived, "is not a story of events or experiences it is a story of existence . . . ."[10] Anderson, like Adams, raises his own existence to the level of myth; he uses his education, the learning process through which he became a writer, as a paradigm of the life of the modern American artist.[11]

For Adams, education leads to the discovery of the multiverse, the universe of force and change, that dooms his quest for "a higher synthesis." Adams finds himself "lying in the Gallery of Machines at the Great Exposition of 1900, with his historical neck broken by the sudden irruption of forces totally new."[12] The Dynamo, the symbol of modern industrial chaos, has replaced the Virgin, the symbol of medieval religious unity. According to Adams, the Virgin's power of attraction was derived from her sexuality. Like the ancient fertility goddesses, "she was the animated dynamo; she was reproduction—the greatest and most mysterious of all energies . . . ." The Virgin, "exercising vastly more attraction over the human mind than all the steam-engines and dynamos ever dreamed of," inspired "four-fifths of [man's] noblest art." Art, Adams implies, flourishes only if nurtured by sexual energy. Conditioned by a Puritan heritage to believe that sex is sin, Americans have never felt the power of the Virgin: "An American Virgin would never dare command; an American Venus would never dare exist." As a result, "American art, like the American language and American education, [is] as far as possible sexless." Because Adams fears that Puritanism has blighted his own instincts from babyhood, he expects that he will never feel the Virgin's force, will never be an artist.

The part of "The Dynamo and the Virgin" chapter which I have just summarized is what Anderson quotes at length in A Story Teller's Story. He concludes about it: "If Mr. Adams had not spent this time as I was doing, lying on a bed and looking at his own hands, he had at least spent his time looking about. 'An American Virgin would never dare command; an American Venus would never dare exist,' he had said and it was an accusation that an American could neither love nor worship" (p. 276). Anderson wants to refute Adams' accusation. He regards Adams as an exponent of the New England cultural hegemony which, he complains, has "got such a grip on our American intellectual life." Of the "older men of New England" and their "intellectual sons" it is "perhaps true to say . . . that a Virgin would never dare command, that a Venus would never dare exist"; but, Anderson insists, it is "absurd" to say that his Midwestern people have "neither love nor reverence" (p. 276). Anderson suggests that to break the strangle hold of Adams' New England Puritanism, the American writer must reject Adams' regionally biased assumption that New England culture *is* American culture. Otherwise, the writer is condemned by Adams' pessimistic logic to despair of his artistic aspirations.

A Story Teller's Story, then, is Anderson's rebuttal to The Education of Henry Adams. Whereas Adams uses his life to exemplify a failed education, Anderson offers his life as a model of a successful education, leading not to despair but hope, leading not to idolatry of the dynamo but to worship of a modern Virgin, leading not to sterile cynicism but to Venus' fecund love, leading not to a pseudo-scientific theory of history but to art.

Of course, Adams and Anderson were vastly different in background, intelligence, and temperament; and the form and style of their books reflect these differences. I am not suggesting that Anderson consciously modeled *A Story Teller's Story* on *The Education of Henry Adams*. Rather, Anderson, like so many of his contemporaries in the twenties, was reacting to Adams' ideas, as expressed directly in *The Education* and as filtered through such social critics as Van Wyck Brooks. In particular, Anderson was struck by Adams' belief that the mediocrity of American art has resulted from the American ignorance of the Virgin (religious faith) and Venus (sex). These terms, which Anderson redefines slightly to mean "worship" and "love," provide a critical vocabulary for discussing *A Story Teller's Story*. To say that Anderson is seeking the Virgin and Venus, worship and love, does not explain every detail of this diffusive and occasionally incoherent book; but it does accurately describe the clear overall pattern of Anderson's "education."

Because Anderson is trying to counter Adams, this pattern bears little resemblance to Adams'. In Adams, education is a dizzying gyre of failures; each effort to learn results in greater and greater ignorance as Adams the manikin tries on and discards the fashionable wisdoms of his age. At the end, Adams recognizes that he must perish in the chaotic multiverse unless he imposes his own "wisdom" upon it through an act of his ordering, creative imagination. Art is the last stay against confusion—not the sacred art of the Virgin, but the profane, scientistic "art" of the dynamo. Chartres Cathedral must be supplanted by the Dynamic Theory of History. In *A Story Teller's Story*, the pattern of education is a dialectical progression; in each Book, Anderson's younger self is torn between increasingly complex antinomies. As Walter B. Rideout has observed,

> Each of the four "Books" is organized around
> contrasting themes—fact opposed to fancy in
> Book One, love turned inward on the self (Judge
> Turner) opposed to love turned outward on others
> (Alonzo Berners) in Book Two, the demands of
> business opposed to the demands of art in Book
> Three, the search for identity and community of
> the Midwest artist as opposed to the culture of
> the American East and of Europe in Book Four.[13]

By choosing the right values at each stage of his life, Anderson emerges at the end as the model of the modern Midwestern American artist. But his success is neither easy nor permanent. Anderson's sense of triumph is tempered by his awareness of the difficulty of making right choices in a culture that encourages all the wrong ones. Furthermore, as the Epilogue suggests, the artist's struggle to survive never ceases in a culture inimical to artistic integrity.

II

Anderson's education as an artist begins in childhood when he identifies himself with his story teller father. Book One opens with a sketch of Irwin Anderson, the "ruined dandy from the South" for whom "there was no such thing as a fact" (pp. 5-6). An irresponsible, childish rogue of a man, Irwin does no work that cannot be transformed into play. Although young Sherwood resents the hardship that his father's shiftlessness inflicts on the family, especially on his mother, he cannot help admiring and emulating the very qualities that make Irwin such a poor provider. Anderson sees his father as a frustrated artist, a man who "with luck . . . might have turned out to be an actor, or a writer" (p. 15), but who, unfortunately, "lived in a land and in a time when . . . the artist in man could not, by any possibility, be understood by his fellows" (pp. 22-23).

The America of Anderson's childhood is a land of facts, of bustle and enterprise, in which dreams "were to be expressed in building railroads and factories, in boring gas wells, stringing telegraph poles" (p. 23). In a land of facts there is no tolerance for fancy. Irwin Anderson is "outlaw in his community" (p. 23) because his idle fancy is subversive of a community marching to the battle cry of "Hurry!" and chanting the Franklinesque slogans of "Get on. Make money. Get to the top. A penny saved is a penny earned. Money makes the mare go" (p. 65). The bankruptcy of utilitarian, catchpenny values is dramatized for young Anderson when a cocky well-shooter comes to town, promising to usher in the Industrial Age with one blast of his magical nitro-glycerine. Like Twain's Hank Morgan, getting up one of his "effects" to dazzle the peasants of Arthurian England, the well-shooter sinks his shafts far down into the earth; meanwhile, the town elders, stuffed in their boiled shirts, dream deliriously of incalculable wealth. But when capricious Mother Earth vomits a defiling gush of mud instead of the expected gas and oil, the well-shooter is instantly deflated in young Sherwood's eyes from a hero of the New Age to just another teamster who "gets drunk and beats his wife" (p. 71).

189

Although he rejects the world of facts, Anderson does not, in retrospect, embrace the world of fancy so totally as his younger self did. If facts take no account of the forms of beauty, of man's highest ideals and aspirations, fancy takes no account of the forms of ugliness, of man's capacity for baseness. If without the buoyancy of fancy, facts are irredeemably earthbound, then without the ballast of facts, fancy is irretrievably airborne. One good use of fancy, Anderson sees in retrospect, is to relieve temporarily the harshness of facts. Thus, impoverished young Sherwood can bear the monotony of his winter diet of cabbage by imagining the cabbages, roots upturned in a backyard trench, as so many sentinels guarding his fortress-house. But an excess of fancy can be dangerous. When, for example, Anderson and his brother act out the adventures of Hawkeye and Uncas, the brother, in the intensity of his fancy, makes no distinction between Cooper's fictional realm and the real world. Not content to bloody imaginary Hurons, "Uncas" imagines a neighborhood tattletale to be "Le Renard Subtil." Oblivious to the potentially deadly consequences of his action, "Uncas" angrily hurls a hatchet at his enemy's door.

Sherwood feels awe for his brother's ability to impose his fancy so completely on facts; nevertheless, he cannot yield so far to his own imagination.

> There is something direct brutal and fine in the
> nature of Uncas. It is not quite an accident that
> in our games he is always the Indian while I am
> the despised white, the pale-face. It is permitted
> me to heal my misfortune, a little, by being, not
> a store-keeper or a fur trader, but that man nearest the Indian's nature of all the pale-faces who
> ever lived on our continent, La Longue Carabine,
> but I cannot be an Indian and least of all an Indian
> of the tribe of the Delawares. I am not persistent
> patient and determined enough. (p. 17)

Unlike his brother, Sherwood is too conscious of facts, too much a paleface, to try to live in his fancies. A century earlier, perhaps, he might have become a Hawkeye in the flesh, a pioneer of the forest. But since Cooper's frontier now exists only in fancy, Anderson can be a pioneer only of words, following "the little crooked words of men's speech through the uncharted paths of the forests of fancy" (p. 18).

The pioneer of words, the story teller, is still vulnerable to the danger of escapism. "Uncas," with the literalness of a child, substitutes fancy for facts. Irwin Anderson, the romantic story teller, does the same even though, as an adult, he should know better. In his tales of his own life, Irwin creates fancies that are so much more appealing than facts that he can scarcely tell where the reality of his life shades into his fiction of it. Despite his genius as a story teller, Irwin Anderson fails as an *artist* because his stories are too romantic, too detached from facts. His tale of the Civil War shares the faults of the bestselling historical romances of the *fin de siècle* which transfigured the brutality of the war into pageantry and melodrama. "Ah, there was moving picture stuff for your soul!" Anderson sighs about an especially overwrought touch in his father's tale (p. 50). Indeed, Irwin's story prefigures the scripts of the Hollywood dream-factory where, as Anderson later found, "Everything was fragmentary and unfinished. A kind of insanity reigned" (p. 23). Irwin and the movie people are "children, playing with dreams—dreams of an heroic kind of desperado cowboy—doing good deeds at the business end of a gun—dreams of an ever virtuous womanhood walking amid vice—American dreams—Anglo-Saxon dreams" (p. 22). Robbed of "their inheritance as artists" (p. 23) by the materialism of their culture, the romantic story tellers turn fancy upon itself. The result, as Rex Burbank says, is "grotesqueness, egocentricity, and disorder. The adult imagination comes into being when the youthful, romantic fancy is brought to bear upon the recalcitrant world of fact, when the youthful luxury of pure and innocent dreams gives way to a conscious effort to shape the world of fact and sense to its ideal of beauty."[14]

A Story Teller's Story recounts Anderson's evolution toward this theory of his art, an evolution which, by the end of Book One, his youthful self has only started. Book One ends, like the others, with an epiphany. Young Sherwood accompanies his father to do a house-painting job for a farmer who, flushed with his recent prosperity, has built a pretentious modern house to replace the humble log cabin of his youth. Sensing that the new house symbolizes the vulgar materialism of the present, Sherwood finds the old house "smiling and calling to me" (p. 97). The old house embodies the values of the frontier past that have been trampled in the stampede toward Industrialism. The boy, refusing symbolically to accept that present, turns his back on the new house; "he went not toward the future but toward the past" (p. 99). Sherwood's choosing the past coincides with the quickening of his imaginative life. Lying in the hayloft, he concocts his first tale, an absurd, childish imitation of his father's Anglo-Saxon dreams. This story, in which young Anderson improves on the facts of his own birth with a wish-fulfilled fancy of them, represents his birth as a romantic story teller, and the completion of the first stage of his education. Properly, the boy has followed his father in rejecting the present and facts in favor of the past and fancy. But he has yet to learn that to be a mature artist, the story teller must ground his fancy in facts, must rejoin the past with the present.

III

In Book Two, Anderson gradually recognizes the limitations of fancy. At first he is a young man so completely immersed in romantic visions that "the visions were sometimes stronger than the reality of the life about me" (pp. 107-08). Reality is the life of an unskilled laborer, numbed by the drudgery of his job and depressed by the squalor of his rooming house. As in his boyhood, the adolescent Anderson finds an escape through imagination. He devours romantic novels to feed his dreams. He envisions himself astride a magnificent horse, arrayed in a golden helmet and purple cloak, commanding an army in gorgeous uniforms. Later he fancies himself to be a master pugilist, only to be knocked senseless when he tests his feint and cross against a brawny fellow-worker. To Nora, his landlady's daughter, he pours out his dreams "of brave men in rich clothes walking with lovely women in a strange land . . ." (p. 150).

Young Anderson's dealings with Nora epitomize his immaturity. When, blusteringly drunk, he accosts Nora and raves "like a Napoleon or a Tamerlane" (p. 109) about the necessity of clean sheets, he manages to win her attention and sympathy with an extemporaneous tale about her sailor-fiancé. But his success in imagining the feelings of Nora's absent lover is "a purely literary trick" (p. 114). Anderson's romantic tale moves Nora, as his father's had moved Tilly (the virgin at the farmhouse), because the story teller has shrewdly tapped his listener's emotions. But, like his father, he is overly concerned with his own success in spinning the tale, in casting a spell over the woman. Whereas the romantic story teller is manipulative and egocentric, the mature artist forgets himself, empathizes with others, tells *their* stories *for* them rather than *his* story *to* them. Young Anderson, however, is still too enraptured by fancy to understand this; he is too fascinated with power to be capable of love. In order to prove his manhood, he thinks he must "conquer some woman" (p. 157); and he hopes to use story telling as a means of seduction. With Nora he fails completely; later, when he exploits a more vulnerable woman to achieve his sexual initiation, the result is "a queer silent frightened love making . . . no love making at all" (p. 174).

In retrospect, Anderson blames much of his own selfishness and egoism on the corrupting influence of Judge Turner. In his youth, Turner made his fortune as a swindling carpetbagger. After traveling several years in Europe to evade the law, Turner returned to his native Ohio, bought a large brick house, hired a Negro servant, and assumed the indolent life of a gentleman. Young Anderson is strongly attracted to Turner's learning, wit, and urbanity. He loves to lounge in the Judge's study, sipping his whiskey, smoking his cigarettes, and listening to Turner's "laughing, half cynical, half earnest kind of confession" (p. 122). Anderson learns—although he does not fully understand it at the time—that beneath his mask of gentility, Turner is a bitter and severely neurotic man. Traumatized by his father's suicide, bullied by his schoolmates, persecuted for his homosexuality, Turner has been warped psychologically. He tells Anderson how, as a youth, he lived in romantic fantasies of vengeance, how, imagining himself to be Cosimo de Medici reincarnate, he cleverly plotted to poison his enemies.

There is something of Miniver Cheevy in Judge Turner and also something of Henry Adams. Turner, the child of scorn, longs for the idyllic days of old, especially the medieval past symbolized by Chartres Cathedral. But, as his conversation with Nate Lovett the stableman suggests, Turner recognizes that the modern world prefers race horses to cathedrals; and he urges young Anderson to see "money making as the only sure method to win respect from the men of the modern world . . ." (p. 137). Thus, Turner not only sets a bad example for Anderson in his misogyny, cynicism, and egoism, but he corrupts his mind with the false doctrine of materialism. At the same time, he teaches Anderson to curse the fate that had not permitted him " to be born in the fifteenth century instead of the twentieth with its all pervading smell of burning coal, oil and gasoline, and with its noises and dirt" (pp. 186-87).

Anderson is plunged into a nightmare by Turner's Adams-like ideas. He dreams:

> I am somewhere in a huge place. Perhaps I am
> standing in that great Cathedral at Chartres, the ca-
> thedral that Judge Turner told me about when I was
> a lad and that I myself long afterward saw and that
> became for me as it has been for many other men and
> women the beauty shrine of my life. It may be that I
> am standing in that great place at midnight alone. It
> cannot be that there is any one with me for I feel
> very lonely. A feeling of being very small in the pre-
> sence of something vast has taken possession of me.

Can it be Chartres, the Virgin, the woman, God's
woman?
What am I talking about? I cannot be in the
Cathedral at Chartres . . . . I am an American and
if I am dead my spirit must now be in a large half-
ruined and empty factory, a factory with cracks
in the walls where the work of the builders was
scamped, as nearly all building was scamped in
my time.
It cannot be I am in the presence of the
Virgin. Americans do not believe in either Virgins
or Venuses. Americans believe in themselves. There
is no need of gods now but if the need arises Americans will manufacture them, many millions of
them, all alike. They will label them "Keep smiling"
or "Safety first" and go on their way and as for the
woman, the Virgin, she is the enemy of our race.
(pp. 139-40)

The triumphs of the Industrial Age, Anderson realizes, have "come to the
dull and meaningless absurdity, of say a clothespin factory" (p. 140).
Through his nightmare Anderson reaches a point of despair. Like Adams,
he feels a need to worship "some power outside himself," but the only
gods to worship are the "gods of material success" (p. 164). In a world
devoid of worship and love, Anderson must either rediscover the Virgin and
Venus or remain forever imprisoned under the great iron bell he sees des-
cending upon him at the end of his nightmare.

Fortunately, Anderson is saved by the Christlike invalid Alonzo Berners, whom he rescues from a Chicago saloon. Unlike Judge Turner, who
encourages Anderson to be "absorbed in the contemplation of my own
difficult position in life" (p. 188), Berners has the gift of empathy, the
ability to enter into another's thoughts, to give "sympathetic understanding
without sentimentality" (p. 183). He forces Anderson to ask himself, "Was
it grown up to come to the realization that oneself did not matter, that
nothing mattered but a kind of consciousness of the wonder of life outside
oneself?" (p. 185). By learning to love Berners, Anderson rediscovers Venus.
He also longs to rediscover the Virgin: "I was like one tortured by a desire
for conversion to something like the love of God . . ." (p. 197). So intense
is this desire that Anderson finally has a conversion experience. He finds
himself kneeling in silence on a moonlit road. A child cries in a nearby

house. Anderson's fancy seizes on the coincidence; he imagines himself to be a modern wise man, a witness to a new Incarnation. He rises, half committed to "devote myself to something, give my life a purpose. 'Why not to another effort at the rediscovery of man by man?' I thought rather grandly . . ." (p. 199). But Anderson has still not purged himself of Turner's cynicism. He cannot avoid perceiving a certain sentimentality, perhaps theatricality, in his conversion experience; and he points "the laughing finger of scorn" at his own earnestness (p. 199).

The ending of Book Two further qualifies Anderson's new sense of Christian brotherhood. He joins the army during the Spanish-American War, and revels in the "drunkenness of comradeship" (p. 206). But he wonders why "men should need a war to throw many of them for a time into a common mood" (p. 208). He asks himself, "Is all feeling of comradeship, of brotherhood between many men, a little absurd?" (p. 208). Are the worship and love he thinks he has discovered through Berners illusory? At this stage of his education, Anderson worships and loves only in the abstract, only in fancy. He has yet to find a concrete way of fusing fancy with facts.

IV

The way, as he learns in Book Three, is art—not the romantic story telling of his father, but a story telling based on Berners' example. Anderson focuses in this Book on his legendary repudiation of his business career. "The tale teller cannot bother with buying and selling," he warns. "To do so will destroy him" (p. 223). So, one morning, Anderson simply walks out the door of his paint factory, and wanders "along a spur of railroad track, over a bridge, out of a town and out of that phase of my life" (p. 226). He devotes himself with religious zeal to telling the "untold tales" that "looked out at me like living things" (p. 215). He sees the modern arts as "the old crafts intensified, followed with religious fervor and determination by men who love them . . ." (p. 236). Art is the new Virgin and story telling the new form of worship. The process of writing is so "purifying and fine" that he is filled with "unholy wrath" when some critics later accuse him of creating something "unclean or vile" (p. 228). As a priest of the religion of art, Anderson wants to adapt to the modern world the faith of the medieval past. Whereas the artisans of the old crafts once erected Chartres Cathedral, Anderson will build a cathedral of words.

Worship of the Virgin of art leads to a new conception of Venus, as the love expressed through and in art. Book Three climaxes with Anderson's tale of the man with a scar. For the first time Anderson becomes a mature story teller because for the first time he escapes his childish egoism and, like Berners, projects himself lovingly into the deepest feelings of others. But Anderson's education is not complete. Although this tale demonstrates how far he has evolved from the romantic story telling of his father, Anderson has not fully achieved his identity as an artist. To do so, he must define himself and his materials culturally and historically.

In Book Four, through his pilgrimages to New York and Europe, Anderson emerges as a modern Midwestern American artist. Fearful of the "culture" symbolized by New York, self-conscious of his age and his literary amateurism, Anderson comes "East to school if I could find the school" (p. 277). He expects to learn the craft of story telling from the writers he has admired from afar; but he learns, to his surprise, that "the men I had really come to New York hoping to see and know, fellows of the schools, men who knew their Europe, knew the history of the arts, who knew a thousand things I could not know . . . [were] as frankly puzzled as myself" (p. 263). The only writers in New York who are sure of themselves are not the leaders of the New Movement in the Arts, but the romancers, the literary heirs of Irwin Anderson, who live their imaginative lives "entirely in a queer pasteboard world" (p. 256). Attuned to the commercial market for fiction, the romancers mass-produce slick formula stories built around "The Poison Plot." "In the construction of these stories there was endless variation but in all of them human beings, the lives of human beings, were altogether disregarded" (p. 256). These scribblers, Anderson realizes, are the factory hands of the industrialists of literature; the disease of materialism has so infected them that they even rush "into bookstores to see what kind of books were selling well in order to know what kind of books to write. . ." (p. 266).

Anderson, feeling impregnated with tales to tell, begins to discover what kind of books *he* wants to write. His stories should have not plot but form, which grows "out of the materials of the tale and the teller's reaction to them" (p. 261). His materials must be the lives of his own people. To be an artist, "one must of necessity give oneself to the people about whom one [writes], must in a quite special way believe in the existence of these people . . ." (p. 256). The story teller also must write about them in their own language, in "the common words of our daily speech" (p. 262).

New York offers Anderson little guidance in achieving these artistic objectives. Although he yearns to join the parade of the New Movement, he recognizes that his roots and his natural literary allies are Midwestern:

> I kept thinking of middle-western men like Dreiser,
> Masters, Sandburg and the others. There was some-
> thing sincere and fine about them. Perhaps they had
> not worried, as I seemed to be doing, about the whole
> question of whether they belonged to the New Move-
> ment or not. I thought of them as somewhere out in
> the Middle West quietly at work, trying to under-
> stand the life about them, trying to express it in their
> work as best they could. (p. 287)

But before he can fully accept the life about him, before he can "quit running off in fancy to India, to England, to the South Seas" (p. 287), Anderson must first run off in fact—to Europe. Like so many of the expatriates of the twenties, Anderson discovers his true home only from a transatlantic remove. Sitting before Chartres Cathedral, worshipping the Virgin of the past, Anderson finally begins to realize that "nearly all of the reality of me was still living in the Middle West of America, in mining towns, factory towns, in sweet stretches of Ohio and Illinois countryside, in great smoke-hung cities, in the midst of that strange, still-forming muddle of peoples that is America" (p. 308). The Virgin must be wrested from the grip of "the dead past of a Europe from which we were separated by a wide ocean" (p. 315); as Europeans know better than Americans, "The future of the western world lay with America" (p. 315). Although he shares Adams' nostalgia for the Virgin of Chartres, Anderson knows he must build the Virgin a new American cathedral of words. "It was up to me to carve the stones, to make them more beautiful if I could, but often enough my hands trembled" (p. 317).

If he is to succeed in his worship of the Virgin, the artist must also reanimate Venus. In France, Anderson observes how sex is a natural part of ordinary life. Magnificent ungelded stallions prance through the streets of Paris. At a café, in plain sight, a student makes love to a girl, not hesitating to touch her body and kiss her. Such behavior, Anderson knows, would be "unnatural" in any American city. Following Van Wyck Brooks and Waldo Frank, Anderson speculates that Industrialism, "a natural outgrowth of Puritanism" (p. 273), has rendered Americans impotent. The American "passion for size," the lust for "a bigger house, a bigger factory, a faster automobile," is a pathological displacement of blocked sexual energies (p. 272). Anderson's crusade as artist must be to resist becoming impotent, to proclaim the power of Venus, even at the risk of being labelled "the Phallic Chekhov" (p. 274).

Anderson hopes it is not too late to belong "to an America alive, an America that was no longer a despised cultural foster child of Europe . . . to an America that had begun to be conscious of itself as a living home-making folk, to an America that had at last given up the notion that anything worth while could ever be got by being in a hurry, by being dollar rich, by being merely big . . ." (p. 307). If such an America can no longer exist, then Henry Adams' pessimism will have been vindicated and Anderson's education will have been worthless. Anderson often thinks of Van Wyck Brooks's theme, "that a man cannot be an artist in America" (p. 305). This theme, which Brooks borrowed in part from Adams,[15] provides Anderson's keynote in the Epilogue to *A Story Teller's Story.*

V

Far from being "superfluous," as Rex Burbank calls it,[16] the Epilogue is an integral part of the book. It is Anderson's final, sober meditation on Adams and the whole matter of education. Book Four ends optimistically. Anderson, having discovered his artistic identity, prepares to leave Europe and return to America. In his own life, he has seemingly refuted Adams' contention that "an American could neither love nor worship." But Anderson's education must be put to the test in an America where, as the disease of materialism continues to spread cancerously, Adams' prophecy of doom for American art seems closer to fulfillment.

One typical victim of the age is "Arthur Hobson," the writer of romantic football stories, who furtively confesses to Anderson that he has prostituted his talent to the bitch-goddess, Success. "Perhaps his fate is also my own," Anderson remarks ominously (p. 341). Indeed, the enormous pressure that has destroyed "Hobson" may yet crush Anderson himself. Both live in a culture "where as yet to mature in one's fanciful life is thought of as something like a crime" (p. 341), where the increasing commercialization of literature threatens to force every artist to become a man of business. Just to withstand such pressure will require extraordinary artistic courage and stamina. To do more than resist, to build a cathedral to the Virgin and a temple to Venus in the midst of industrial America, will be a heroic if not an impossible task. Unless he is willing, like "Hobson," to compromise his artistic principles, the story teller may have no readers at all.[17] In this case, Anderson's education in worship and love will benefit no one but himself; his art will exist in a cultural vacuum.

That education is ultimately self-defeating is the bitter joke of *The Education of Henry Adams.* Although he resists Adams' pessimism throughout *A Story Teller's Story,* Anderson admits in the Epilogue the possibility that an American Virgin may never dare command, that an American Venus may never dare exist, that the artist may be doomed to either annihilation by or alienation from the materialistic America he hopes so fervently to redeem.

Rex Burbank argues that Anderson's stress in *A Story Teller's Story* is on the "scarcely encouraging" condition of the artist in America. Yet, Burbank adds, "a note of hope for the future of art in America persists as a kind of undertone . . . ."[18] I would invert this interpretation: Anderson's awareness of the obstacles to artistic fulfillment in America is a strong undertone throughout the book, but his emphasis is on his personal transcendence of those obstacles. Although he acknowledges that he might become a burnt-out case like "Hobson," Anderson, even at the end, does not surrender to despair. The Epilogue is a cautionary footnote to an American success story. And if, as Burbank says, Anderson depicts "some of the tragedy that goes with being an artist in America," he also celebrates his triumph of love and reverence.

NOTES

[1]"A Story Teller's Story," *New Republic*, 40 (5 Nov. 1924), 255.

[2]"The Education of Sherwood Anderson," New York *Times Book Review* (12 Oct. 1924), p. 30.

[3]"A Lost Book Review: *A Story-Teller's Story*," *Fitzgerald/Hemingway Annual*, ed. Matthew J. Bruccoli (Washington, D. C.: NCR Microcard Eds., 1969), p. 72. Hemingway's review, along with one by Gertrude Stein, orginally appeared in *Ex Libris*, 2 (Mar. 1925).

[4]*Letters of Sherwood Anderson*, ed. Howard Mumford Jones and Walter B. Rideout (Boston: Little, Brown, 1953), p. 43. Anderson apparently read and reread *The Education*. Rex Burbank has asserted that "It was Adams . . . who had the greatest influence upon Anderson's attitudes from 1920 to 1925." See *Sherwood Anderson* (New York: Twayne, 1964), p. 110.

[5]*Spokesmen* (1928; rpt. Berkeley: Univ. of California Press, 1963), p. 23.

[6]*Ibid.*, p. 43.

[7]*Letters*, p. 95.

[8]Quoted in James Schevill, *Sherwood Anderson: His Life and Work* (Denver: Univ. of Denver Press, 1951), p. 198.

[9]*A Story Teller's Story: A Critical Text*, ed. Ray Lewis White (Cleveland: Case Western Reserve Univ. Press, 1968), p. 76. Page references for all further quotations are given in the text.

[10]*Fitzgerald/Hemingway Annual*, p. 75.

[11]On Anderson's autobiographical mythmaking, see Gerald L. Marriner, "Sherwood Anderson: The Myth of the Artist," *Texas Quarterly*, 14 (Spr. 1971), 105-16.

[12]*The Education of Henry Adams*, ed. Ernest Samuels (Boston: Houghton Mifflin, 1973), p. 382. The other quotations are from pp. 384-385.

[13]"Preface" to *A Story Teller's Story* (New York: The Viking Press, 1969).

[14]Burbank, pp. 120-121.

[15]Adams' nihilism about the future of art in America is most powerfully expressed in *The Life of George Cabot Lodge* (Boston: Houghton Mifflin, 1911), a book which Brooks quotes in his early writings and which clearly influenced him.

[16]Burbank, p. 118. In the typescript of *A Story Teller's Story* which Anderson submitted to his publisher, the Epilogue comprised the *first* thirty-two pages; but Anderson deleted it in order to publish it separately as "Caught" in *American Mercury*, 1 (Feb. 1924). At the last minute, while reading proof, he decided to reattach "Caught" to the book, this time as the *last* section. Since his publisher Ben Huebsch was pressuring him to make large cuts, Anderson had no reason to use "Caught" as an Epilogue unless he considered it essential to the book. On the publishing history of *A Story Teller's Story*, see Ray Lewis White's introduction to the critical text.

[17]In giving the pseudonym of "Hobson" to the writer of football stories, Anderson may have been punning on "Hobson's choice." That is, if "Hobson" wants material success as a writer, he has *no* choice but to prostitute himself.

[18]Burbank, p. 123.

ANDERSON AND STIEGLITZ:
A FELLOWSHIP OF SAYER AND SEER

Robert E. Ned Haines

During a visit to New York in 1919, Sherwood Anderson underwent, in his own words, a "kind of revolution." To Waldo Frank, his sponsor among the Eastern intellectuals and artists, the author of recently published *Winesburg, Ohio,* explained, "Several things happened. I saw the O'Keeffe things and the Stieglitz things. I went into a gallery and saw some paintings of Renoir. I found out again the old lesson that one cannot muddy oneself and be clean. I shall have to get out of business at once, within a month perhaps."[1]

Despite his resolve to quit business instantly, Anderson could not arrange his financial emancipation from the Long-Critchfield advertising agency in Chicago until 1922, but this fact does not diminish the importance of his epiphany. On the walls of the Manhattan galleries he had seen the good news of a mode of existence untainted by the prevailing commercialism in American life. He could never again be satisfied with the "success" he had pursued and won in the business world. This and other evidence suggests that the life and work of master photographer Alfred Stieglitz supplied a good part of the impetus which propelled Anderson into the world of art and much of the strength which sustained him once he had made his decision.

Anderson's awareness of Stieglitz reached full flower a few years later. The author told his friend that he had come "to know and really value" him by 1922. In that year the mystery of Stieglitz's invigorating presence moved Anderson to undertake an essay probing the enigma. For a time, however, he could not find a proper beginning. Then a letter arrived signed, "Your old Stieglitz." The phrase furnished the spark Anderson needed. It was only temporary weariness and ill health that caused Stieglitz to call himself "old" (at fifty-eight he was a mere twelve years older than Anderson), but for the author the word had special resonance. Remembering the village artisans he knew and admired as a boy in the pre-industrial Midwest, including of course his own father, Anderson had long regarded age as an attribute of the traditional craftsman. "Your letter did something," he told Stieglitz; "a sentence of yours awoke an old chord—just the thing I wanted to say in the beginning" (SA to AS, 9/8/22). And so Anderson began his published essay, "Old man—perpetually young—we salute you," and went on to develop one of his favorite themes, "that old male love of work well done."[2] As an incarnation of this "old chord" in the author's consciousness Stieglitz joined such figures, real and imagined, as Irwin Anderson, Sponge Martin, Joe Wainsworth, and Uncle Jim Ballard.

After becoming acquainted with Anderson, Stieglitz began reading his novels and stories as soon as they appeared in print. Since in his frequent letters to Anderson it was his habit to comment on the latest publication, Stieglitz became, in effect, an informal critic of the new author from Mid-America. In his letters from 1922 to 1938 the photographer expressly mentioned *Many Marriages* (1923), *Horses and Men* (1923), *A Story Teller's Story* (1924), *Dark Laughter* (1925), *Sherwood Anderson's Notebook* (1926), *A New Testament* (1927), "Loom Dance" (1930), *Beyond Desire* (1932), and *Puzzled America* (1935).

At first glance it might seem that a photographer would be ill-prepared to criticize the work of a major fictionist. Stieglitz's reading, in truth, was never methodical; and he was innately opposed to conventional systems of judgment. But his reading, though necessarily limited to rest periods away from his camera, was sufficiently extensive for someone who, like the later New Critics, shunned comparative evaluations. Despite the many demands on his time, Stieglitz managed to keep abreast of the latest releases—especially the new books by his friends—and he unerringly found those passages in literature and philosophy that supported the ideas he had already derived by instinct and intuition.

Stieglitz's response to his friends' writings was sometimes corrective, but the appreciative mode was more in accord with his conviction that the deepest and indeed the only absolute knowledge is intuitive rather than discursive. In keeping with this premise the ideal form of criticism is sympathetic appreciation tested against the touchstone of intuition—appreciation, that is, of an artist's motives and intentions (even if not fully realized) and intuition of his work's essence. The Stieglitz circle often referred to this essence as "spirit" or "life." They believed that artistic achievement is a function of the vital force imbuing a book or a picture or a piece of music. The distinctive quality of Stieglitz's critical approach to Anderson's fiction is best indicated by the photographer's own words. "There is Volume to all," Stieglitz declared after reading a section of *A Story Teller's Story*. "A roundness of sound—big—that of a deep baritone voice or a fine cello—or rather group of cellos.—May be that expresses it best.—In short fine music" (AS to SA, 6/26/24).[3] While professional critics were fretting over Anderson's disregard for chronological consistency in his autobiography, and brother Karl Anderson was disputing the factual accuracy of the narrative, Stieglitz's intuitive perception led him directly to the basic lyricism of Anderson's writing. Stieglitz was well equipped to recognize lyricism, for he himself, forswearing both the picturesqueness and the unintentionally deceptive realism of his early photographs, had progressed toward a purely lyric mode of expression in his prints. Just two years before *A Story Teller's Story* had begun to be serialized, Stieglitz had created his eloquently titled *Cloud Music* and *Songs of the Sky* series. He made clear the lyric motivation of this group of images when he wrote, "I wanted a series of photographs which when seen by Ernest Bloch (the great composer) he would exclaim: Music! Music! Man, why that is music! How did you ever do that? And he would point to violins, and flutes, and oboes, and brass, full of enthusiasm . . . . And when I finally had my series of ten photographs printed, and Bloch saw them—what I said I wanted to happen happened *verbatim*."[4]

Critics such as Norman Holmes Pearson eventually came to detect the lyric spirit that is the common component in virtually all of Anderson's novels, tales, and poems; and the author himself, when well past the midpoint of his career, acknowledged, "I've thought, all these years I've been writing, that if I'm any good at all, there should be music at the bottom of my prose" (*Letters*, p. 283). Stieglitz, to his credit, was among the first to recognize and applaud the underlying musicality of Anderson's prose. The sayer in turn responded to the lyricism of the seer's photographs. "Both things sing," Anderson told Paul Rosenfeld in a letter reporting that "that dear, dear Stieglitz" had made him a present of two prints (SA to PR, 7/4/23). One of these photographs, identified in Dorothy Norman's *Alfred Stieglitz: An American Seer, as Equivalent, Music No.1, Lake George, 1922*, still hangs on the wall at Anderson's Ripshin Farm near Troutdale, Virginia.

Anderson styled himself a story teller and thus invited critics to locate him in the oral narrative tradition, but Stieglitz distrusted labels and generally ignored them, and his freely orbiting sensibility observed that this writer's tone was more important than his narrative ability. Anderson's words, he recognized, are so freighted with emotion and tonal effects that his novels at times verge on opera. After reading *Dark Laughter* Stieglitz related his impressions to the author: "I told Ettie Stettheimer the other night that when I was through with it—I had forgotten the Story—the Individuals in it—even the writing—I merely felt a great relaxed feeling & heard a marvelous Baritone Voice that seemed to grow rounder & bigger—fuller—more wonderful every moment" (AS to SA, 12/9/25).

That intuition, rather than training or reasoned judgment, was the foundation of Stieglitz's esthetics is patently implied by the next sentence in this letter: "Where thinking stops Art begins." By means of this maxim—one of his favorites—Stieglitz affirmed not anti-intellectualism but meta-rationalism. Reason, he said in effect, is not the ultimate human faculty; and discursive thought is but an initial stage on the long road to truth. Since in the letter the seer did not elaborate upon the point, he may have assumed that the sayer would understand and agree that art is the supreme accomplishment of man. If this was in fact Stieglitz's assumption, it was not unfounded, for his creed harmonized with Anderson's in nearly every respect.

The depth of sympathetic understanding between Anderson and Stieglitz is plumbed in certain letters they exchanged in 1923. Anderson, when acutely aware of truth and beauty, sometimes burst into tears. It happened once in Paris as he was crossing the courtyard of the Louvre and again on a train as he was riding through the Nevada countryside during the excruciating period of his second divorce. In the latter instance, as Anderson sat in the coach, suddenly the thought of Stieglitz caused the author to "weep bitterly" and turn his face from the other passengers for shame, he said, of his apparently causeless grief. (A remarkably similar scene occurs in "The Sad Horn Blowers," a story published some four months *before* the Nevada incident.) After having described the outburst to Stieglitz, Anderson explained, "I was not unhappy. It was just that I had at last realized fully what your life had come to mean to me. In our age, you know, there is much to distract from the faithful devotion to cleanliness and health in one's attitude toward the crafts, and it takes time to realize what the quality has meant in you. I really think, man, you have registered more deeply than you know on . . . myself and others" (SA to AS, 6/30/23; *Letters*, p. 99). After gestating for a while in the author's mind, the theme of cleanliness and health in the productive life of man became a principal motif in *Dark Laughter,* the most popular of Anderson's novels.

205

Stieglitz was genuinely touched by the outpouring of emotion in Anderson's letter, and he replied in kind. He was moved, he said, by the thought that "there was a Man far away who actually knew what *feeling* meant & who could cry while just thinking of another human being" (AS to SA, 7/23/23). At this particular moment Stieglitz was undergoing a crisis of mind and body, and Anderson's letter was a positive tonic. Receiving this spiritual token from his distant friend was the cause, Stieglitz wrote, of his "regaining strength gradually—& beginning once more to feel light within." With unabashed candor two men of feeling met and saluted each other as kindred spirits in a land where tough-minded smartness had become the fashionable pose of artists and writers alike. The fellowship of sayer and seer was confirmed.

Overreaching the emotional, Stieglitz's appreciative criticism of Anderson's prose at times bordered on the visceral. Regarding *A Story Teller's Story,* Stieglitz told the author, "Every now & then I take a peep into its pages like a fellow goes to the cupboard & takes out a bottle & drinks a glass . . . . I have a copy of the book in different rooms so that I can peep as the impulse moves no matter what else I may be doing. And I always come away with an inner grin—like the fellow who has warmed up inside must grin to himself" (AS to SA, 10/27/24).

The photographer would have been less than human if *A Story Teller's Story* had not held a special place in his esteem, since Anderson had dedicated the book to "Alfred Stieglitz, who has been more than father to so many puzzled, wistful children of the arts in this big, noisy, growing and groping America." The author, moreover, had explained the dedication in advance by telling Stieglitz, "There is so much of a spirit of something—I have had clarified in me from you—in this book that I would like, if you wouldn't mind, to dedicate it to you, with a little appreciation as a foreword" (SA to AS, 6/25/23).

The spirit in *A Story Teller's Story* to which Anderson alluded is clearly the genial humaneness that glows throughout the autobiography. Stieglitz sensed this quality from the outset. "The humor is delightful," he told mutual friend Paul Rosenfeld. "But what I enjoy most is the loveable spirit running through the whole book—a generous soul" (AS to PR, 10/8/24). As he read and reread the book—some of the pages "dozens of times"—Stieglitz marveled over Anderson's magnanimity: "He's a big man—& has a real Soul. And that's what will continue to live long after Menckenese cleverness is dead and forgotten" (AS to PR, 10/27/24).

Stieglitz's comments on other writings by Anderson were characteristically terse but trenchant. "Alive" was the term he most often chose for praising the story teller's work—a word betokening the vitality he sensed in Anderson's better fiction. Such life-force infused Stieglitz's own photography, as it did, both men believed, all art worthy of the name. And so it was not empty rhetoric when Anderson devised the title *Seven Alive* for the introduction he wrote to a 1925 exhibition featuring the Stieglitz group. Somewhat earlier, Stieglitz had commented on the dynamism he held to be an attribute of the true artist. The occasion was his reading "The Man Who Became a Woman." To the author Stieglitz wrote, "I hope there'll be a few others who'll get some of what I got—the genuine beauty—the subtle something men like you & myself feel to such an extent that sometimes I wonder am I crazy" (AS to SA, 11/1/23). He went on to clarify that this elusive quality—the hallmark, he said, of the "real artist"—was nothing short of the "intensest passion for life in its every living sense." Art, for Anderson and Stieglitz, was no mere imitation of life; art encapsulated in itself the living essence. And the instrument of capture was the emotion—the "passion"—of the artist. It mattered not at all whether the medium was words or images.

The following year (1924) the author published "A Note on Realism" (reprinted in *Sherwood Anderson's Notebook*). There he distinguished between imaginative art, to which of course he himself was committed, and representational or mimetic art, which, he asserted, critics applaud simply because it has the appearance of life. But when Anderson said that art is art and life is life, he was not contradicting what Stieglitz would have called the "livingness" of true art; he was actually pointing out the deceit of the kind of realism that indiscriminately reproduces the surface details of life— the decadent *"tranche de vie"* realism that trailed the age of Zola. The true realist, both Anderson and Stieglitz believed, probed the very essence of human experience.

The fellowship between Anderson and Stieglitz extended further than matters of esthetics; the two men shared markedly reciprocal world views. This philosophical affinity emerged dramatically when the sayer and seer exchanged thoughts on the radical innocence of mankind. In the process, however, a notable difference in their respective temperaments came to the fore. Stieglitz touched off the discussion by writing to the story teller, "You see all humans represent a Great Innocence to me—And that is the wonder I see. Even those Fools who believe they run the world—the affairs of men—All Innocent when I'm alone with Each—All equally wonderful" (AS to SA, 7/30/23).

Anderson responded that human innocence was the very keynote of his work-in-progress, *A Story Teller's Story*. "In this book," he explained to

Stieglitz, "I am trying to tell, as plainly and clearly as I can, the story of a man—myself—who found out just about what you have outlined in your letter today. You see, dear man, I have been a long time finding out just that people are really innocent, and it may be that much more than you know of what I have found out has come to me because of a growing awareness of you. Since I have known you, your figure has been standing all the time a little more and more clear" (SA to AS, 8/6/23).

After admitting this affinity with and indebtedness to Stieglitz, Anderson went on to make a point which marks a crucial distinction between the two men's natural dispositions: "While a man may become aware of the innocence of people in general, he cannot quite love that innocence itself. . . . One wants comrades, grown men such as I have come to feel you—and Paul [Rosenfeld] too." Anderson, then, could intellectually accept Stieglitz's abstract proposition, but his deepest urge demanded flesh-and-blood humanity. The photographer, on the other hand, seemed more inclined to love man as a theoretical ideal than as an exasperating reality. One of the entries in the commonplace book that Stieglitz kept as a student in Germany reads, *"Die Menschheit ist gross, und die Menschen sind Klein"* (Mankind is grand, and men are petty).

Some of Stieglitz's friends thought he was reluctant to regard them as his peers. Waldo Frank, who loved Stieglitz beyond all measure, once charged him with being incapable of accepting anyone save as a disciple—though Frank's impetuosity was probably at fault here (WF to AS, 7/31/23). Anderson was more fortunate in his relations with the man Frank bowed to as *cher maître*. By virtue of their common quest for truth transcending conventional realism, Stieglitz welcomed Anderson without hesitation into his inner circle. In confirmation of their mutuality, the seer assured the sayer, "I feel you are after a similar thing & are working it out in *your* way as I work it out in *my* way" (AS to SA, 8/15/23).

Stieglitz was never more valuable to Anderson than when he rose to bolster the author against the bad press that followed the publication of *Many Marriages.* Anderson was bewildered by the attacks. To him they seemed perverse and self-contradictory. The *Dial,* after awarding him its prize for literature in 1921 and after serializing the controversial novel itself in 1922, published a retrospective review which was, as Anderson recognized, a shamefaced apology for nearly everything he had written. [5] Sensing Anderson's hurt, Stieglitz urged him to ignore both the *Dial* and the "obviously malicious" barbs of reviewer Alyse Gregory (AS to SA, 9/25/23). As a bulwark against the world's capriciousness, Stieglitz had long since evolved his own brand of self-reliance; and now, in substance, he exhorted the wounded writer to believe that what is deep is holy. Every atom of Anderson's being yearned to embrace that imperturbable code, but his faith in himself wavered whenever a critic came along and demonstrated that the deep may be obscure rather than profound.

The spirit of Emerson rose in all its mystical vigor in the letter that Stieglitz hastened to the author after the publication of *A New Testament* had inspired a certain reviewer to announce that Anderson was "sick of words" and "dying before our eyes."[6] Anderson tried hard to be stoical about adverse reviews and to believe that "body-punching criticism is a good thing," but blows as vicious as this tended to aggravate the periodic depressions he suffered *(Letters,* pp. 113, 174). And so, to this all-too-vulnerable writer Stieglitz posted a gospel of self-trust, a message climaxed with a trope worthy of the Sage of Concord himself: "Undoubtedly you are above all what's written about you—favorable as well as unfavorable—Momentarily one may be affected—more personally than otherwise. One has no choice but to march ahead for better or worse—The inner eye moves towards the Invisible Star—one's Own" (AS to SA, 8/11/27). As Emerson had put it, "Man is his own star."

The solution was not that simple for Anderson. When it came to relying on his own ego, he vacillated between bravado and gnawing doubt. In the foreword to *Tar* he gave notice that he must be himself: "It was only then [after creating the persona of Tar Moorehead] I faced myself, accepted myself. 'If you are a born liar, a man of the fancy, why not be what you are?' I said to myself, and having said it I at once began writing with a new feeling of comfort."[7] But not long afterwards he warned his son John about the dangers of excessive self-regard. A certain young man, he said, "was eaten up with contemplation of self. It had grown on him like a disease" *(Letters,* p. 182). Such ailments, the author explained, result when a sensitive person attempts to prolong those moments of acute consciousness which are his natural endowment, but which are doomed to be moments only. Here Anderson was surely speaking from his own experience. Like Hawthorne, he considered egotism to be the bosom serpent, and he alternated between embracing it and crushing it.

One realizes that a letter from Stieglitz, however inspiring, could not permanently stabilize Anderson's chronic cycle of moods. But, given the author's very human need for support, the encouragement of someone like Stieglitz—who seemed able to balance always on the crest of the wave—must have helped. Such succor, in all probability, is what Anderson had in mind when he told his photographer friend, "I hardly think, dear man, that you can know how much you have meant to all of us, how much for example your letters to me this last year or two have meant" (SA to AS, 7/26/24). The years 1923-1924 were indeed pivotal in Anderson's career. Some critics, notably Irving Howe, see these years as the beginning of a "downward curve," a slope toward personal crisis and creative disintegration.[8] Later critics, led by David Anderson, see the same period as one in which the author began to regain his equilibrium, as evidenced by the rays of optimism and affirmation that began to brighten the inner landscape of his work.[9] If the latter interpretation is correct—and I am convinced it is—then we should all remember Stieglitz in our orisons, for he was a fountainhead of Sherwood Anderson's faith in all that is clean and honest.

NOTES

[1]SA to WF, 12/?/19, in *Letters of Sherwood Anderson,* ed. Howard Mumford Jones and Walter B. Rideout (Boston: Little, Brown, 1953), p. 51. Quotations from the letters and other writings of Sherwood Anderson appear herein with the permission of Mrs. Eleanor Anderson. Letters hereafter will be cited parenthetically in the text, and the short title *Letters* will be used in citations of Anderson's published correspondence.

[2]*New Republic,* Oct. 25, 1922, p. 215.

[3]Quotations from the letters of Alfred Stieglitz appear herein with the permission of Miss Georgia O'Keeffe.

[4]From a 1923 article by Stieglitz entitled "How I Came to Photograph Clouds," reprinted in *Photographers on Photography: A Critical Anthology,* ed. Nathan Lyons (Englewood Cliffs, N. J.: Prentice-Hall, 1966), p. 112.

[5]Alyse Gregory, "Sherwood Anderson," *Dial,* 75 (Sept. 1923), 242-46. See also *Letters,* p. 109, for the author's reaction.

[6]Lawrence S. Morris, "Sherwood Anderson: Sick of Words," *New Republic,* Aug. 3, 1927, pp. 277-79.

[7]Sherwood Anderson, *Tar: A Midwest Childhood* (1926; rpt. Cleveland and London: The Press of Case Western Reserve University, 1969), p. 10.

[8]Irving Howe, *Sherwood Anderson* (New York: Sloane, 1951), pp. 197-213.

[9]David Anderson, *Sherwood Anderson: An Introduction and Interpretation* (New York: Barnes and Noble, 1967), p. 92.

THE SEARCH FOR A LIVING PAST

David D. Anderson

One of the most persistent and most misleading attempts at interpreting Midwestern literature is the so-called "Revolt from the Village" myth, first articulated by Carl Van Doren in the *Nation* in 1921. Essentially Van Doren insisted that many Midwestern writers—the most frequently mentioned then and since have been Edgar Lee Masters, Sherwood Anderson, and Sinclair Lewis, although virtually every other Midwestern writer has been mentioned at one time or another—were rejecting the Midwestern American villages of their youth, insisting as they did so that the innocence and virtue of the village were in reality moral and psychological enslavement. At the same time they sought their personal fulfillment through denunciation, exposure, and flight, the latter both literary and personal, as they and their creations moved from country to city, to Chicago, New York, and beyond.

The conviction with which Van Doren stated his case has made that interpretation of Midwestern literature a fixture of modern American criticism, so much so that forty years later, in the decade we have just concluded, several important attempts have been made to use Van Doren's generalization as the basis of conclusive interpretations. Among them are Frederick J. Hoffman's *The 20's* (1955; revised edition 1962) and Anthony Channell Hilfer's *The Revolt from the Village 1915-1930* (1969).

In *The 20's* Hoffman revamps Van Doren's image as "the Midwest as Metaphor," what he calls a metaphor of abuse compounded of rural settings and middle-class values, a metaphor in which the traditional American movement westward in search of social or economic fulfillment (clearly the

212

Jeffersonian concept of the pursuit of happiness, although Hoffman fails to mention it) had become a movement eastward, in search of literary or psychological fulfillment (this time a more sophisticated twentieth century version of nineteenth century Jeffersonianism).

More recently, Hilfer's concept of "the Revolt from the Village" sees two points of attack by Midwestern writers, that defined in emphasis on the "buried life," in which its people are unable to articulate their dreams, and the "attack on conformity," a conformity which many of the people of the village, including the writers, are unable to accept. Rather than a metaphor of a more limited time, however, Hilfer sees the revolt in three stages, from 1871 to 1899, and from 1915 to 1930, the two stages when the rejection of the village took place, and then the continuation of the concern of some of its participants into the 1930's when, he insists, several of them rejected their own rejection and began an idealization of a village only remotely like that of their origins.

Both critics make persuasive cases and each marshals impressive evidence in support. Unfortunately, however, each has his foundation planted in the sandy interpretation originally constructed by Van Doren on the basis of a few isolated works. Moreover, neither Hoffman nor Hilfer—Hoffman because of the time limitation on his work and Hilfer because his acceptance of limited views of work in the twenties and after, ignoring or dismissing important evidence and unnecessarily complicating his thesis as a result—looks clearly at either the works they claim are documents of revolution or the Midwestern myths that the works perpetuate.

In essence, these revolutionaries are not condemning the village, its people, its mores, or its conventions; they are decrying instead the weaknesses imposed upon man by nature and the values introduced with the money and the factories of the East—the very elements that had been decried by Thomas Jefferson in the years in which the Midwest began. Corruption, the corruption defined by these Midwestern writers, is an alien corruption introduced into the village from the outside. Even in Mark Twain's "The Man That Corrupted Hadleyburg," corruption—money—comes from without, brought by a stranger. And Twain was certainly no celebrator of the idyllic. For many of the writers, corruption, whether of values or people, is New England in origin.

There is, however, a valid and inclusive means by which a comprehensive interpretation of Midwestern literature may be made. This approach is through the myth that Midwestern writers combine to create, a myth that grows out of the fundamental myth of the Midwest, the myth of movement. In the works of Midwestern writers, particularly but not entirely of those who dealt with the small town, it becomes the myth of the search, compounded of the conviction that the time and place for an honest, uncomplicated life have passed, that the people of the writer's youth had been corrupted, and that the only remaining hope lies in a search for understanding and for a new, uncorrupted fulfillment. The search becomes evident in the act of literary creation itself and then, ultimately, tentatively, and with a good deal of doubt, in an attempt to create not a new myth, but a new reality, in effect, to recreate a reality of a living past in a meaningful present.

This myth of the search, based on the recognition of the passage of a time and place, the corruption of its peoples, and the search for a new reality rooted in the values of the past, is the substance of the works of two of the Midwest's most perceptive interpreters and ablest writers: Sherwood Anderson and Louis Bromfield. Each of them came out of small-town Ohio to write a substantial body of work rooted in his Ohio experience, and each went on to a significant measure of success, convinced that the past out of which he wrote and the myths to which he had given his allegiance in his youth had been lost in the refuse heap of an industrial civilization. Finally, only after much introspection and examination, did each writer complete the myth as each of them, Anderson in rural Virginia and Bromfield in rural Ohio, sought and became convinced he had found the recreation in fact of what he had so long described in fiction. For each it was a rediscovery of reality, with all its imperfections, rather than a pastoral perfection and idealization.

There are many similarities, some obvious and others of varying degrees of subtlety, in the lives, the experiences, and the works of the two men. Anderson was the older, by some twenty years, the less-educated, and the more sensitive writer, but Bromfield was perhaps more closely attuned to the nature of the Midwestern countryside and the eighteenth century vision of a perfect agrarian society that had been largely responsible for its peopling and development in the years before the Civil War. However, both of them were witnesses to, even, perhaps, unwilling or unthinking participants in the corruption of their state, their region, and their people, and both of them attempted, in their early fiction, to define what had happened and to try to understand it. Significantly, each of them was convinced that he had escaped personal contamination or more accurately, having been corrupted, Anderson by business and Bromfield by the war, each had undergone an almost ritualistic purification.

Both Anderson and Bromfield indulge, in their early works, in a headlong assault on industrialism as the source of the frustration, bewilderment, and dehumanization that had corrupted a Midwest with the potential for social perfection. Anderson's *Windy McPherson's Son* (1916) recounts the rise of Sam McPherson from humble origins in Caxton, Iowa, to business and commerical success in Chicago, and it makes clear the cost of success in human values as Sam finds himself cut off from meaningful relationships with others. He realizes that material values are meaningless, and he begins a search that is only vaguely successful for a meaningful way of life to re-place materialism. Sam's search for meaning is far less vivid than his rise to power, as Anderson realized, and his dissatisfaction with the indecisive end-ing is emphasized by his rewriting it no less unsatisfactorily for the second edition of 1922. In his second novel, *Marching Men* (1917), Anderson launched another assault on the system, only to find that that, too, was un-successful; his conclusion at this point is implied but clear: man can revolt against the materialism of industrialism, but after the act of rebellion there is nothing else. He can neither make peace with the system, destroy it, nor find peace outside of it. At that point, Anderson found little hope for the individual or for his fulfillment in a dehumanized system. He learned that rebellion was not fulfillment, that the end had been lost in the means, and he changed direction drastically.

Bromfield, too, reached essentially the same conclusions in his first four novels, *The Green Bay Tree* (1924), *Possession* (1925), *Early Autumn* (1926), and *A Good Woman* (1927), conceived of as what he called "panel" novels, that is a series of novels in which he explored the anti-materialist revolt of a Midwestern town's young people. The theme of revolt was for Bromfield as for Anderson intensely personal, highly autobiographical, and ultimately unsatisfactory.

Essentially the attempt to redefine the Jeffersonian ideal in a society that denies it and to reassert the nature of Jefferson's natural aristocracy in an age dominated by material standards and a pseudo-aristocracy, the panel novels trace, in succession, the attempt of Lily Shane to escape the material values of the town, only to find industrialism triumphant in the War; the attempt of Ellen Tolliver to escape through music, only to find herself still isolated from life; and then the attempt of Olivia Pentland to escape, only to find herself trapped by a dead tradition. Finally, in *A Good Woman*, Bromfield's first male protagonist, Philip Downes, finds, like Anderson's Beaut McGregor in *Marching Men,* that there is no freedom, even in physical revolt. For Philip , however, the only ultimate escape is in death.

Having experienced the ultimate frustration in their inability to resolve the predicament of the individual in a mass industrial society through rejection and rebellion, both Anderson and Bromfield sought new directions and new dimensions in their work. Anderson moved in a direction that had decidedly mixed results but that was ultimately rewarding, and Bromfield turned in a direction that took him far from his serious purpose with results equally ambiguous but with less ultimate satisfaction.

Anderson's new direction had important literary results: the unsuccessful collection of free verse and verse-prose, *Mid-American Chants* (1918), and what is still his most significant achievement, *Winesburg, Ohio* (1919). Bromfield's new direction resulted in *The Strange Case of Miss Annie Spragg* (1928), his first critical failure. But the effects of the new directions on their writing careers and critical reputations were less important than the effects on the future course of their lives and work.

Significantly both of them turned away from the present, from industrialism and its concomitant effects, and into the half-remembered, half-imagined past out of which they had come. Anderson's introspection resulted in a new style and a new search for insight, not in terms of social movements but in the sometimes fulfilling but often inhibiting or destructive relations among people; Bromfield, on the other hand, turned to the myth of fertility, of people and of land, a fertility ambiguous in its effects, but no longer attainable or realizable in the modern world.

Anderson's success in *Winesburg, Ohio* permitted him to approach, with decisive results, the problems of human isolation and frustration. Increasingly it became evident to him that human closeness had once been a reality—in childhood, in small towns, in uncomplicated moments—but in adulthood, in cities, in the resulting increasingly complicated human relations of the modern world it had become impossible. The mark of a time, a place, and a way of life beyond recall or re-creation, human closeness had vanished, except in fiction, in the twentieth century.

The 1920's were for Anderson a period of personal and literary frustrations, of sustained introspection, and finally of remarkable discovery. The first effects of that turmoil are evident in *Poor White* (1920), his major attempt to combine the substance of *Windy McPherson's Son* with the moments of understanding he had found in *Winesburg, Ohio*. The ambiguity of that novel, of Hugh McVey's attempt to find fulfillment with his wife even as the factory whistles shriek in mockery at the end, is intensified by the descent into murky emptiness in the next, *Many Marriages* (1923), and the adolescent conflicts and confusions of the two collections of short stories, *The Triumph of the Egg* (1921) and *Horses and Men* (1923). At this point, with the failure of the present, with the search for personal fulfillment more frustratingly unsatisfactory than it had been for Anderson at any

216

time since he left the paint factory in Elyria in 1912 to begin his own personal odyssey, he turned to his own past in a disjointed search for the substance if not the reality of the subject matter of fulfillment, and he began aimlessly to wander across America—to New York, to Reno, to California, to New Orleans, and finally to the hill country of western Virginia.

These years produced *Dark Laughter* (1925), his rejection of bohemia, and the two important volumes of autobiography, *A Story Teller's Story* (1924) and *Sherwood Anderson's Notebook* (1926), the works in which he re-examined his values, his work, his life, and his search and found the early years, those of his youth, to be the most meaningful. This discovery he celebrated in *Tar: A Midwest Childhood* (1926). But, although his discovery of the significance of his youth was clear in these volumes, equally clear was his conclusion that the past, that of innocence, however brutal, and of human closeness, however imperfect, the past of the post-Civil War Midwest before the impact of industrialism, was gone forever, and the note of regret, of loss, of adult aimlessness is evident as Tar becomes "Jobby," an ambitious early adolescent dominated by the drive for material success.

Even while *Tar* was in press Anderson discovered the hill country of western Virginia, a section of the country not yet contaminated by industrialism or by the values of a materialistic society. Here he built a house and edited the weekly papers of the town of Marion, convinced that he had found a refuge, a place in the twentieth century but not of it. For the rest of the decade of the twenties he belonged to the town, once more himself a townsman, like the town itself, in but not of his century. Between 1927 and 1929 he continued to edit the town's two weekly papers, a role as nearly like that played by the editor of the nineteenth-century Clyde, Ohio, *Enterprise* as it was possible to find in the second quarter of the twentieth century.

While Anderson was editing his papers, enmeshing himself in the life of the town, Bromfield had begun to write fiction that was not only less convincing but far less deeply felt than any of his earlier works: *Awake and Rehearse* (1929), a collection of weak or mediocre stories written for popular magazines, *Twenty-Four Hours* (1930), a structural *tour-de-force* suffering from contrivance and irresolution, and *A Modern Hero* (1934), another story of the despoilation of the Midwestern countryside, a study of exploitation that begs the question and a study of virtue that confuses ignorance with innocence.

These lapses, each, however, a commercial success, are perhaps most explainable in terms of a project that Bromfield had been considering for several years and that resulted in what is unquestionably his best work.

217

This is *The Farm,* published in 1934. Bromfield's most deeply-felt work, it is also his most autobiographical; in fact, in many respects, it is Bromfield's *Tar: A Midwest Childhood.*

Like *Tar, The Farm* is the story of a boy's life in rural Ohio in the late nineteenth century; it is the story of that boy's growing ambition and his growing awareness of the demands made by an increasingly impersonal world. But while Tar went eagerly into the world mesmerized by the image of success in the new world of business, young Johnny leaves the farm of his grandfather reluctantly and uncertainly, knowing only that the farm, which was to be the center of a self-sufficient family enjoying the freedom and fulfillment of a Jeffersonian agrarian paradise, could no longer be maintained in the face of industrialism triumphant and materialism rampant. In spite of this difference in attitude, however, *Tar* and *The Farm* are curiously alike in their conclusions. In the last lines of *Tar,* Anderson writes:

> . . .What he had to do was to bring into the
> family all the money he could. Heaven knows,
> they would need it all. He had to tend up to his
> job.
>
> These [were] the thoughts in Tar Moorehead's
> head as he grabbed his bundle of newspapers and,
> wiping his eyes on the back of his hand, raced away
> up the street.
>
> Although he did not know it Tar was, at that very
> moment, perhaps, racing away out of his childhood.[1]

The last paragraphs of *The Farm* are equally conclusive:

> The Farm was sold to a man who bought it as
> a speculation because now it was within the sound
> of the mills. The Town would come nearer and
> nearer until presently the great barn and perhaps
> the rambling house itself would be pulled down.
> Streets would be cut through it and hard ribbons
> of cement sidewalks laid down. The long double
> avenue of ancient locusts would disappear, and
> presently the Farm would cease to be.
>
> It was over and Johnny went away, not into
> the Far West like his uncles and his cousins, but
> to Europe and to the war. . . .[2]

218

In both cases the note of finality is evident. Not only has time passed and the child become a man, but for both Anderson and Bromfield an era was at an end, innocence lost, and the alter ego thrust through circumstance into the world beyond, that of commerce, of conflict, of acquisition, of competition and destruction. In neither case does the protagonist "escape" as those who see a revolt from the village would have it; there is no suggestion of a "metaphor of abuse" nor of spiritual poverty, but more properly a metaphor of fulfillment snatched away, of innocence corrupted, of a life to be filled with competition, with combat, with an inevitable dehumanization.

The meaningful world had passed, for Bromfield as for Anderson, and only accidentally, as the result of another war, did he discover the possibility that it might be recaptured. Two years after Bromfield published *The Farm*, Hitler marched into the Rhineland; by 1938, it was evident that another war was imminent, and he sent his family home to rural Ohio, to the country out of which he came.

Bromfield followed a few months later, determined to attempt to recreate that which he had commemorated in *The Farm:* a way of life that had disappeared from the modern world. He began to buy up run-down farms in rural Richland County, Ohio, and to build a house.

In many respects, the farm, named Malabar Farm after his Indian experience in the mid-1930's, became for Bromfield what the papers in Marion, Virginia, had become for Anderson. Just as Anderson had become a country editor in fact and in practice, Bromfield became a practical dirt farmer. As Anderson spent the years of his editorship renewing his acquaintanceship with small-town Americans and the values that gave substance and direction to their lives, Bromfield determined to restore soil worn out by poor farming practices through learning to work the land in accordance with the laws established by nature for the development of natural fertility, natural water movement, and a natural relationship among animate and inanimate things.

Bromfield's goal at Malabar Farm was to recreate in the middle of the twentieth century what had been impossible in its early years: a farm so nearly self-sufficient for those who worked it that all the food for its people, with the exception of salt, coffee, and sugar, would be raised there. Such a goal was far more ambitious than Anderson's simple determination to become a townsman, and in time Bromfield was to learn that such a dream was no more realizable in the middle of the century than it had been at the beginning, just as Anderson had already learned in the early 1930's that he could never become as completely a townsman as his father had been a half-century before. But both men had, in the process, discovered a great deal about the past, about the present, and about their own roles as writers and as interpreters of America, its people, and its values. Much of what they learned manifested itself almost immediately in the house that each built, primarily to provide an articulation and an affirmation of his new identity. A bit later, the new experience provided for each of them the substance of the significant work that he was to complete in the years he had remaining.

Anderson built his house at Ripshin Farm near Marion in the summer of 1926. A massive building with its main section of fieldstone walls eighteen inches thick, it had two squared log wings, all of which contained four bedrooms, three baths, four large and one small fireplace, a large tile-floored kitchen, a living room, and a dining room. In front, Anderson had built a stone terrace; in the rear a screened-in porch. The house from the beginning looked ancient, as though it had sprung fully-built from the stony hillside, very much in keeping with its surroundings but very much larger than any other establishment in the area. This fact Anderson was later to regret keenly when he realized that the size and substance of the house helped make it impossible for him to become completely one with his neighbors, and he realized that he had inadvertently disturbed an ancient value system.

Bromfield's house was no less pretentious or traditional. Built in 1940 on the watershed between the Ohio River and the Great Lakes, Bromfield used as the basis a nondescript old frame farmhouse, but he expanded it in two directions, incorporating two architectural traditions representing the two cultural traditions, those of New England and of the South, that had come together to form the unique value system of the Ohio country.

Like Anderson, Bromfield built to last, and he too built too well too soon because for much the same reason he found it impossible to become the simple farmer that he insisted he was. Just as Anderson found after two years that his editorship was simply not fulfilling enough to challenge his imagination and interest permanently, Bromfield had a similar experience with farming. Both of them found, perhaps, that complete fulfillment was impossible, at least for them in their attempts to recreate and to relive ways of life of the past. But each man found that the way of life he had found, almost literally by accident, had a new, unique value for each. For Anderson, the town, and for Bromfield, the farm had become a refuge, a source of renewed strength, and a source of constant wonder and stimulation. For each the result was renewed creative energy and new insights into man, his society, and his universe.

In the last twelve years of his life Anderson produced some of the best work of his career, much of it drawing its substance from his new experiences in the town and in his excursions out of it. *Hello Towns!* (1929) is drawn from his newspaper writings, a volume as full of life and meaning as the hill country out of which it came; *Perhaps Women* (1931) examines the inroads of industrialism in the hills as textile mills sap the energy and destroy the dignity of the hillmen; *Death in the Woods* (1933) contains some of his best short fiction; *Beyond Desire* (1932) and *Kit Brandon* (1936) are well-conceived, timely novels that further examine the impact of industrialism on the South. *Puzzled America* (1935) is perhaps the most vivid description of the effects of the Depression on rural America that it is possible to find. But of most importance in terms of what Anderson found are his last two published works, *Home Town* (1940) and the posthumously-published *Memoirs* (1942). Both are tributes, tributes to the nature of life itself, particularly in uncomplicated moments and places, and both are celebrations of the durability of the human spirit. In both an Anderson becomes evident who would be a complete stranger not only to the Anderson who had been the salesman, the advertising writer, the company president, but also to the conscious literary artist determined to find fulfillment and expression in the act of protest or the definition of despair. In his last works Anderson celebrates the timelessness of values he had thought long gone: of uncomplicated human closeness and love; of kindliness and neighborliness; of reaching out across the barriers of social status, money, prestige, sex, and all the other things that separate, mislead, and ultimately confuse and corrupt human beings. In these last works Anderson had indeed sought the past and found it alive.

Bromfield's last fifteen years were equally productive and equally revealing: he published seventeen volumes, ten of them fiction and seven nonfiction of a kind for Bromfield significantly new. The fiction, Bromfield admitted, was largely written out of habit during these years, and his convictions, creative energies, and insights were largely reserved for the nonfiction that began with *Pleasant Valley* in 1945 and ended with *From My Experience* and *Animals and Other People* ten years later.

In these works Bromfield insists that there is meaning in human life in the middle of the twentieth century, that direction and fulfillment can be found, not by pursuing the dream of material success, but in learning, in eighteenth century fashion, to understand the laws of nature, to live in accordance with them, and to emulate them. A new wisdom, a new insight, a new richness results, and life itself, whether that of man himself or the old pike in the farm pond, becomes the supreme value and the great adventure.

At their deaths, Anderson in 1941 and Bromfield in 1956, both men were reasonably content. Neither, of course, had found it possible to return in fact to the past or create a present that was pristine and uncomplicated; both men were themselves too complicated and certainly too honest to think that they might. But they did find that the old values were not the product of a time or a place but of an attitude, a way of life, a determination to transcend the immediate, the world of conflict, competition, and accumulation, and to seek in meaningful work and in a new but timeless closeness to nature and to men whatever it is that gives meaning and depth and purpose to human life. This for Anderson and for Bromfield was both metaphor and reality, a metaphor of meaning, a way of life, and ultimately a recognition that time and value were, are, and will be a continuum, if one can learn to live in accordance with values that exist, somewhere and somehow, in every age. They had, in effect, discovered a principle defined by another Midwestern writer at the end of his best, most Midwestern work: "So we beat on, boats against the current, borne back ceaselessly into the past."[3]

The values of the past, distorted or disguised, remain; we are their creatures; and the search beyond materialism is a search for life, for meaning, for a living fulfillment if we are capable of knowing and accepting it. Both Sherwood Anderson and Louis Bromfield make clear that this is the nature of the myth and the reality that lies beyond: that there can be only meaningful work and a life that taps the wellsprings of a natural eternity.

NOTES

[1]Sherwood Anderson, *Tar: A Midwest Childhood* (New York: Boni & Liveright, Inc., 1926), p. 346. Used by permission of Harold Ober Associates, Inc.

[2]Louis Bromfield, *The Farm* (New York: Harper & Brothers Publishers, 1933), p. 344. Used by permission of Harper & Row Publishers, Inc.

[3]F. Scott Fitzgerald, *The Great Gatsby* (New York: Charles Scribner's Sons, 1925), p. 182.

TWO DISMOUNTED MEN:
SHERWOOD ANDERSON AND J. J. LANKES

Welford Dunaway Taylor

The name of J. J. Lankes (1884-1960) has traditionally been linked with that of Sherwood Anderson in two prominent ways: first in Anderson's *No Swank* essay "Mr. J. J. Lankes and his Woodcuts"[1] and, second, in connection with the woodcut appearing on the dust jacket and frontispiece of *Perhaps Women*. Aside from these associations, and two letters included in the Jones-Rideout edition of *Letters of Sherwood Anderson*,[2] there is virtually nothing published to indicate the nature and extent of a friendship at once loyal, enduring, and mutually beneficial. Doubtless the reason for this condition is that Lankes, though widely acclaimed in his prime by connoisseurs as an artist and decorator of books, has attracted little scholarly attention. Also, during the last two decades of his life, his production fell off markedly from what it had been in the 1920's and '30's.

The fact that Lankes is known to so few moderns is indeed lamentable, for in many ways his work stands alone, in both the genres of the woodcut and of American book decoration. Born in Buffalo, New York, on August 31, 1884,[3] Julius J. Lankes was educated as an engineer. Drawing and penmanship had been his favorite subjects, however, so in 1907 he decided that art was to be his vocation, and he embarked on a study that was to last through 1913. Between 1908 and 1917, he recorded having completed more than eight hundred designs in oil. More importantly, he had come to recognize the woodcut as his true metier. In the 1920's he quickly made his mark as a woodcut artist by executing dozens of bookplate designs[4] and by decorating the volumes of such period writers as Robert Frost, Genevieve Taggard, Charles Malam, Lizette Woodworth Reese, Julian Green, and Ellen Glasgow.[5] In the next decade, his designs would grace the work of Roark Bradford, H. W. Freeman, Robert P. Tristram Coffin, W. R. Burnett, and Anderson.[6] In addition, during this period he published two of his own titles, *Virginia Woodcuts* (1930) and *A Woodcut Manual* (1932).[7]

With many of these artists Lankes became friends; several recorded their praise of his work. In an early issue of *Print*, a graphic arts journal, Ray Nash related an account of how Lankes and Robert Frost became known to each other.[8] He said that Frost was struck by the Lankes woodcut "Winter," which appeared in the January, 1922 issue of *The Liberator*, and that shortly thereafter, when asked by Carl Van Doren to do a long poem for *The Century*[9] and to choose his own illustrator, Frost immediately chose Lankes. The two thereupon became friends. Nash described them with a statement made by Frost himself, which defined mastery in art as "When a man's right up on his high horse and ridin' easy. . . And you know the horse's name—Pegasus." Nash considered Lankes and Frost "two mounted men."

Lankes' relationship with Anderson, which proved to be no less meaningful than that with Frost, began with no such apocalyptic encounter. It rather started with a mundane note, requesting a sample copy of one of Anderson's Marion newspapers and offering some examples of his own woodcuts in exchange. The first item to have survived is Anderson's response, which admits, "Your own things seem to me beautiful. I will just send you a copy of the paper."[10] It was not long, however, before a friendship began forming, as Anderson, grateful for the woodcuts, placed the artist on the free subscription list and began discussing with him the possibility of designing new mastheads for both newspapers. Regrettably, this was one of numerous projects that Lankes, uncomfortable with prescription work and deadlines, never implemented.

It is, however, significant that Anderson should have made such a request so early in their friendship. For there exists in the work of both men numerous common denominators that each was quick to recognize. Both dealt with authentic American subjects that often tended to be rustic and to reflect the life of the common man. Both appreciated the rural as opposed to the urban; the humble as opposed to the pretentious; the natural as opposed to the fabricated. There is in each a vivid—at times almost jolting—realism. Yet both had a strongly pronounced sense of nostalgia for the simplicity of the rural and village American past. Thus it was that a middle aged Anderson spent half a career writing of rural American boys trying to make their way in an America become increasingly complicated. And Lankes executed woodcuts of gnarled apple trees, barn yards silent in the winter snow, and several portraits of Abraham Lincoln. There has probably never been a master of the woodcut genre more able in the difficult matter of creating an emotional response by means of light and shadow, and perhaps none who states so profoundly the overwhelming natural force upon Man and his edifices.

In his search for a semblance of a lost past, Sherwood Anderson had discovered Marion, Virginia at almost the very time J. J. Lankes had discovered the coastal town of Hilton Village.[11] Anderson found the hills, the mountain folk, and much of the old simplicity. Lankes discovered Tidewater tobacco fields, Negro shacks, coastal watermen, and an unreconstructed Williamsburg, before the advent of the Rockefellers. From his new ambience, Anderson wrote sketches of country life, fashioned characters from native fabric, and in so doing recaptured at least a part of time past. Lankes made woodcuts of dilapidated cottages, country stores complete with philosophers, and mouldering church yards.[12] This quality was perhaps best summarized by Anderson himself in a laudatory essay on Lankes: "He is a man deeply concerned with life, but it is his way to get at life through things. He feels always the reflected life in things, in barns, sheds back of barns, in little houses in which poor people live. He is always asserting something. 'Look,' he says. 'Look again. Don't you see it?' He is telling you about something. 'It is human life,' he says. 'Life is here in these inanimate things people have touched.' "[13]

The idea of "life reflected in things" seems to have been to Anderson the characteristic in Lankes' work most like his own. For, in the same essay,[14] Anderson cites a particular Lankes woodcut that shows a single tree in a barnyard encircled by a crude wooden fence, and immediately, in the fashion so ingrained in his creative method, he proceeds to weave a background story of the woman who had planted the tree.

The fact that each was the other's kind of artist made itself obvious in numerous ways as correspondence between the two progressed. Early in 1929, Lankes sent Anderson the proof of a bookplate he had designed for him. This design, featuring a nude female in a forthright, yet unassuming pose—her hands resting on Anderson's initials—is one of Lankes' most distinctive. Later in the year, Anderson delighted Lankes with a copy of the just published *Hello Towns!*

In 1930, Anderson expressed his first and most famous public opinion of Lankes' work in the essay, "J. J. Lankes and His Woodcuts,"[15] which was published in *The Virginia Quarterly Review*, along with three examples of the artist's work. A few months later, he ran reviews of Lankes' new *Virginia Woodcuts* in both Marion papers, saying that "this delightful book," by "one of the most vigorous and talented American artists," would bring the reader closer to Virginia "than any story, novel or history."[16] Lankes, in turn, mentioned *Winesburg, Ohio* (in the same sentence with Voltaire!) in a story published in the October, 1930, *American Mercury.*[17] Earlier in the same issue Anderson once again mentions *Virginia Woodcuts* in an article of his own.[18]

Throughout the 1930's the exchange of letters continued, at much the same pace as in the late 1920's. At times, when an important matter was under discussion, letters would be sent every few days for perhaps several weeks. However, sometimes months would separate such outpourings. It was primarily through letters that the friendship flourished, as meetings were few and widely spaced. As a matter of fact, judging from the unpublished letter file, which is lacking but a few pieces of known correspondence, the two did not meet for the first time until 1930, the year of mutual compliments. This meeting took the form of a train trip across the state for Lankes and a pleasant several days spent with Anderson and his sons at Ripshin Farm. Evidently the two artists got on as famously in person as on paper, and Lankes made numerous drawings in Marion and Troutdale, several of which were eventually executed as woodcuts.[19]

As the Depression deepened, the sale of woodcuts, which was never to provide a lucrative livelihood for Lankes, fell off to virtually nothing. However, in the spring of 1931 came an important commission from Anderson to illustrate the forthcoming *Perhaps Women*. This woodcut, which reflected the book's theme of woman's having retained selfhood while man has relinquished his to the machine, shows a strong female figure astride a handsome horse; she is leading a lowly nag, on which an insignificant man is riding.

By the end of 1931,[20] Lankes announced to Anderson a project that he hoped would bolster his ailing fortunes. During his visit to Ripshin, he had discussed the possibility of doing a woodcut manual, and he was pleased that Henry Holt would be publishing it sometime in 1932 and hopeful that it would sell. In May, his hopes were once again raised by his appointment as a visiting lecturer at Wells College in Aurora, New York. But the *Woodcut Manual* sold badly,[21] and for the free spirit who had at best a distrust of educational institutions, the teaching at Wells got off to a predictably uneven start.

Letters trailed off as Professor Lankes went into his second year of "teaching the gals to make simple linoleum cuts of bookplates and greeting cards, posters for college activities and all the rest of that damned crap." However, he admitted that "It's a job and a regular salary so I ought to be properly thankful" (Oct. 24, 1934). Also, the man to whom privacy and freedom meant everything was occasionally tempted to lecture for additional badly needed funds.

Anderson, always sympathetic with the dedicated artist struggling for a livelihood, made what proved to be a heartening gesture by reprinting in *No Swank* (1934) the essay he had published four years before in *The Virginia Quarterly Review*. This time he mildly embarrassed his friend by titling the piece *"Mr. J. J. Lankes and His Woodcuts,"* but the artist's spirits were raised considerably.

While Lankes toiled at teaching the undergraduates how to make linoleum blocks, Anderson travelled about America a good deal. Lankes would often keep in touch by sending copies of new woodcuts, and Anderson was always high in praise and gratitude. But it was apparently not until the spring of 1937 that the two met again. The occasion was what Lankes termed "May Day flippancies" (March 7/8, 1937) at Wells, but the finale of the occasion was a production of *Oedipus,* for which Lankes had designed the sets. The Andersons attended, bringing with them Mary Emmett, with whom they had been staying in New York. The friendship was rekindled, and all enjoyed the reunion. The Wells girls were impressed by having a famous author on their campus, and Lankes asked Anderson back to lecture in the autumn.[22]

In the summer of 1938, when Anderson was collecting photographs of his friends to hang in Ripshin, he included Lankes, who sent one taken in his Hilton Village studio that delighted Anderson. "It connects you with your work," Anderson responded, "which, as you know I feel, is very beautiful" (July 24, 1938). The two missed seeing each other again in February, 1939, though on May 10th Anderson made a belated visit to Wells to lecture to a student group on the problem of the mill girls, which he had treated in *Perhaps Women.*[23] It was to be the last personal meeting. Plans fell through for Lankes to visit Ripshin a second time in the summer of 1939. Lankes found himself out of a job at the end of the academic year, and was soon expressing fears for survival not only in the fact of the usual difficulties, but in an America that he feared was about to be attacked by the Nazis.[24]

In the last year of Anderson's life the letters increased once more, as the two talked about the coming of war and the state of the country and the world. Anderson sent Lankes a copy of *Home Town* (1940), and Lankes responded with a copy of Gray's *Elegy,* which he had decorated with woodcuts that had required fourteen years to complete.[25] Anderson talked of the memoirs he was working on during the summer, and at the end of the year announced a forthcoming trip to South America (Dec. 5, 1940), and the death of his mother-in-law (Dec. 20, 1940).

Lankes' last letter is dated March 7, 1941, the day before Anderson died. He has read of his illness and calls it "rotten luck." It ends thus: "I wish you could join me this moment; am having tea fortified with a suitable quantity of Old Grand-Dad—a remnant of a Christmas present. I am taking the treatment only because the weather is so disagreeable—cold rain and a howling wind."

Lankes' expression of devotion did not end there, however. After reading the special Sherwood Anderson number of *Story,* he wrote Eleanor Anderson to comment upon the various articles and to assert that "to me [Sherwood] was the great writer of our time [,] the man who caught the essence of America and preserved it" (Sept. 1, 1941). When Paul Rosenfeld's edition of *Sherwood Anderson's Memoirs* appeared the next year, Lankes once again wrote Eleanor, this time to say that he saw himself reflected in the book. "So much of it is like me," he said. "The details are different but the essence is the same. The lonely walks, dissatisfactions, uncertainties, soul searchings, hungers, heartaches. It may be that all sensitive people go through the same mill" (April 13, 1942).

The 1940's saw Lankes divorced, elected to the National Academy of Design, and once again employed—this time as head of the Technical Illustrating Section at the Langley Memorial Aeronautical Laboratory in Virginia. After leaving this post, he spent his final years free-lancing once again. He died on April 22, 1960.

Between Anderson's and his own death, Lankes had continued to encounter many of the disappointments and frustrations that he had often discussed with his friend. Several of these he mentioned in the final extant letter to Eleanor Anderson. This letter bemoans the crafts being killed off by the war, the "people from the backwoods. . .making more money in a week than they saw in a year," and having to use "strong language with Civil Service sewer sleuths" (Mar. 24, 1944). At the same time he tells of returning to the *Memoirs,* and of longing for "at least a look-see in New York." Once again, the American artist was entrapped, as Anderson had so frequently felt.

Although Lankes weakly acknowledged his gratitude for a regular job, it was clear that he chafed more than ever under the new yoke. Both men had selected the life of the artist knowing of the inherent difficulties, yet each had much to say about America's insensitivity toward the artist, as well as about the garishness of much of American civilization. In their expressions concerning these topics, both frequently sounded like typical icono-clasts of the period. Lankes berated "the damned radio noise" as being "one of the trials of living in . . . America" (Feb. 13, 1939), and he viewed with ironic humor the fact that "the alleged artist" (June 19, 1931) of the comic strip "Andy Gump" could have been robbed of $51,000 in jewels.

Not surprisingly, both men probed at the roots of a political system that exalted garishness while failing to reward serious art and artists. Again, their questionings and resulting attitudes ran along lines followed by num-erous intellectuals of the 1920's and '30's. The new government in Russia was considered an experiment of vital interest by the American intelligent-sia, especially since Capitalist America seemed to have uttered a loud final gasp with the stock market crash of 1929. Lankes and Anderson were by no means immune to the beckonings of the new order. But by the time that each began revealing his political leanings to the other, Lankes had retreated from the extreme left to a somewhat more moderate position. On Janu-ary 8, 1929, he confessed, " . . . I was all for the worker—I mean the Work-er. One day it dawned on me that the worker does not care a stale damn for the artist. I imagined Max Eastman reading a poem to a street car full of R. R. men on which I was riding . . . I could not conceive of Max getting anything but an obscene reception. The thought of it almost made me sick to my stomach. No, Democracy is fatal enough to art; Socialism would be sure death." He could, nevertheless, refer with cynicism to " 'is Ludship 'erb 'oover" (May 21, 1932) and express unabashed glee over the essay "In Washington" in *Hello Towns!* (1929),[26] which contrasts seeing Chinese paintings in the Freer Gallery to a visit with the President (May 27, 1929).

Anderson, on the other hand, confided as late as mid-1931 that he was "getting nearer Communism all the time" (June 26, 1931). In February, 1932, he wrote Lankes of a plan (which never materialized) to visit Russia (Feb 2, 1932). In late summer he did attend the Marxist "World's Congress against War" in Amsterdam.

By the late 1930's, however, as the threat of Nazism grew in Europe, and as the New Deal began to bring various forms of relief at home, America became more attractive to the two men. Hitler's voice on the radio "makes me ill," Anderson reported to Lankes. "I get it in the pit of my stomach, want to vomit" (Jan. 30, 1939). And Lankes responded that he found a book on the Nazi philosophy, while "quite a profound work," a "perversion of reason" (Feb. 7, 1939). As the war clouds thickened, Lankes became fearful that America would be attacked by the Germans, so he bought a plot of land and actually began a one-room cabin near the water where he could live, work, and produce enough food to carry on a Spartan existence.[27]

Among the last letters exchanged are several statements supporting the American system, despite its imperfections. "Democracy at least gives a man something of a chance to control his own life," wrote Lankes, "and it gives him the chance to hear the other sides of the story—and he can pick his own choice and act on it. He is in a great measure the master of his own destiny. And that is worth fighting for" (Oct. 29, 1940). Anderson too expressed support of democracy, when faced with fascism as an alternative. "Our one hope is to stick to democracy no matter what its evils . . . For us the only job worth a damn has something to do with the creation of understanding, not new hatreds" (Feb. 11, 1939).

Just a few months before his death, Anderson had speculated that "we are probably going into a new kind of civilization and God only knows what it will be like" (June 4, 1940). A little later he had predicted an end to "the horror of power [,] politics [,] war and killing [,] but when [?] Will we live to see it?" (Nov. 3, 1940). Had Anderson lived through the war he would have found himself thereafter in a situation all too familiar. At least Lankes did. Even though Nazism was eradicated and fascism was retarded by the war, the life of the artist in the American system showed little change. As he continued to produce high quality woodcuts and to free lance in the greeting card, bookplate and illustration markets, he found the world no more inclined to pay good money for his creations than before the war. In one of his last letters to Eleanor Anderson, he lamented the fact that he and Sherwood had been all too much alike in being "Unsuccessful" artists (April 13, 1942). To the end, however, he remembered with fondness the pleasure he had had from commiserating with a kindred spirit about the so called lack of success.

To view this friendship from the standpoint of the correspondence is not to view two men astride Pegasus, but rather in the dismounted state. The depths, far more than the heights, of the artist's existence are revealed, as are the candid, rather than the formal, aspects of their personal lives. And, like many of the contributors to the memorial issue of *Story* (September-October, 1941), Lankes was left with a warm memory of Anderson the man. ". . .Regardless of his position as an artist I had great affection for him as a man. I used to tell my students at Wells—as part of their education—that Sherwood was the only man I could confess my sins to, and feel he would understand, and forgive them. He could have been a father confessor . . . . His friendship I count as one of my rich rewards in my not too well rewarded life" (Sept. 1, 1941).

NOTES

[1]"J. J. Lankes and his Woodcuts," *Virginia Quarterly Review,* 7 (Jan., 1931), 18-27, was reprinted as "Mr. J. J. Lankes and his Woodcuts" in *No Swank* (Philadelphia: Centaur Press, 1934), pp. 21-29.

[2]Howard Mumford Jones and Walter B. Rideout, eds., *Letters of Sherwood Anderson* (Boston: Little, Brown and Company, 1953), pp. 243-44; 276-77.

[3]For biographical information used in this essay I am primarily indebted to Mr. J. B. Lankes, of Richmond and Hampton, son of the artist.

[4]See Wilbur Macey Stone, *Lankes, His Woodcut Bookplates* (Gardenville, N. Y.: Frank J. Lankes, 1922) and Burl J. Osburn, *A Descriptive Checklist of the Woodcut Bookplates of J. J. Lankes* (Millersville, Pennsylvania: Serif Press, 1937).

[5]A sampling of the titles from the 1920's which had some form of decoration (e.g. cover or dust jacket design, frontispiece, full-page illustration, headpiece or tailpiece) are: Robert Frost, *New Hampshire* (1923) and *West-Running Brook* (1928); Genevieve Taggard, ed., *May Days* (1925); Charles Malam, *Spring Plowing* (1928); Lizette Woodworth Reese, *A Victorian Village* (1929); Julian Green, *Avarice House* (1929); and Ellen Glasgow, *Barren Ground* (1925).

[6]A similar sampling from the 1930's includes: Roark Bradford, *John Henry* (1931); H. W. Freeman, *Hester and Her Children* (1935); Robert P. Tristram Coffin, *Saltwater Farm* (1939); W. R. Burnett, *The Goodhues of Sinking Creek* (1934); and Sherwood Anderson, *Perhaps Women* (1931).

[7]*Virginia Woodcuts* (Newport News, Virginia: The Virginia Press, 1930); *A Woodcut Manual* (New York: Henry Holt and Company, 1932).

[8]Ray Nash, "Two Mounted Men," *Print,* III, 1 (Spring, 1942), 63-64;

the frontispiece of this number was Lankes' "Twilight Bringing Home the Sheep."

[9]Robert Frost, "The Star-Splitter," *The Century,* 106 (Sept., 1923), 681-685.

[10]Sherwood Anderson (hereafter S. A.) to J. J. Lankes (hereafter J. J. L.), Dec. 2, 1927. All letters referred to are unpublished and are owned either by Mr. J. B. Lankes or the University of Texas. Thanks are extended Mr. Lankes, Mrs. Sherwood Anderson and the University of Texas for permission to quote.

[11]The Lankes family moved to Hilton Village in the autumn of 1925; the summer of 1925 was the first Anderson spent in Virginia.

[12]Many such scenes appear in Lankes' *Virginia Woodcuts* (See n. 7).

[13]Anderson, *No Swank,* p. 28.

[14]*No Swank,* pp. 27-28.

[15]See above, n. 1.

[16]Sherwood Anderson, "Virginia Woodcuts," *Marion Democrat,* May 6, 1930, p. 4; *Smyth County News,* May 8, 1930, p. 2.

[17]J. J. Lankes, "Afternoon and Evening," *American Mercury,* 21 (Oct., 1930), 238-243.

[18]Sherwood Anderson, "They Come Bearing Gifts," *American Mercury,* 21 (Oct., 1930), 129-37.

[19]Mr. J. B. Lankes' catalogue of his father's work lists "In Grayson County, Virginia (Sherwood Anderson's Farm)" (Oct. 20, 1930); "Mt. Town—Troutdale, Virginia" (Oct. 24, 1930); "Troutdale, Virginia (Toward Ripshin Farm)" (Oct. 30, 1930); "Hill Town, S. W.—Virginia" (Sept. 30, 1932); and "Main Street, Troutdale, Virginia" (Oct. 28, 1932) as products of his father's visit.

[20]J. J. L. to S. A., Dec. 11, 1931.

[21]In J. J. L. to S. A., April 30, 1933, Lankes tells of the book's having thus far failed to produce sufficient royalties to offset the $300 advance.

[22]Apparently Anderson did not go; there is no extant correspondence from June 10, 1937 to June 12, 1938.

[23]S. A. to J. J. L., May 12, 1939.

[24]See especially J. J. L. to S. A., May 29, 1940.

[25]J. J. L. to S. A., Sept. 1, 1940.

[26]"In Washington," *Hello Towns!* (New York: Horace Liveright, 1929), pp. 118-26.

[27]See J. J. L. to S. A., May 29, 1940.

HORSES OR MEN:
PRIMITIVE AND PASTORAL ELEMENTS IN SHERWOOD ANDERSON

Glen A. Love

Perhaps no alternative to the shrill disorder of industrial civilization had so seductive an appeal to Sherwood Anderson as a return to the primitive. Both as subject-matter—especially in his celebrated race-track stories, in *Tar, Dark Laughter* and *Many Marriages*—and as a touchstone of Anderson's own sense of himself as an artist, primitivism would seem to be an essential characteristic. "It may sound childish, but men will have to go back to nature more. They will have to go to the fields and the rivers. There will have to be a new religion, more pagan. . . ."[1] The reader and student of Anderson encounters such statements frequently. One recalls his description of how the theme of *Marching Men* appealed to " 'my rather primitive nature,' "[2] and his letter to a friend claiming that "horses and Negroes seem to be the two things in America that give me the most ascetic [sic] pleasure . . . . We pay something . . . for our silly minds, don't we . . .?"[3] Anderson as self-proclaimed primitive and primitivist has been echoed by some of his most influential critics. Oscar Cargill, for example, in his *Intellectual America,* includes Anderson under the heading of "The Primitivists," Maxwell Geismar calls him "an Ohio primitive," and Irving Howe concludes of Anderson's middle period that "the call to primitivism was tinged with a feckless irresponsibility."[4] While recent readings of Anderson have gone far in separating the author from the apparently guileless and groping, "primitive" voice behind much of his best work, Anderson's use of primitivistic

235

materials in his writing deserves further examination.

What I would claim here is that much of what is called primitivism—and left at that—in Anderson is more meaningfully seen as pastoralism, and that the primitivist label as it has been so casually applied to Anderson fails to encompass the author's larger motives and methods, and distorts his most significant treatment of primitivistic materials. These materials—including the life of the senses, nature, childhood, the subconscious, and, for Anderson and his age, the Negro—are, of course, seen frequently in Anderson's work. But his use of these themes and subjects is, for the most part, uncharacteristic of doctrinaire primitivism, in which the key element is a total rejection of or escape from civilization. Rather, Anderson's representative note is one of a struggle toward resolution between the character and a threatening society. If there is rejection or escape, it is typically undertaken so that the individual can somehow bring himself to cope with an inescapable and complex urban present. The essential tone in Anderson is reconciliatory, and in this sense his work may be seen as a contemporary version of pastoral.

The traditional literary genre of pastoral, as we all know, treats simple country people and manners. But it is concerned not so much with a celebration of rural life as it is with the contrast between rural simplicity and urban complexity, and with the need for those participants in this complexity, that is, the writer and his audience, to measure their world against the radical vision of country life. As John F. Lynen writes,

> Though urban life is obviously superior in wealth
> and formalized knowlege, the country has its own
> special values. Pastoral plays the two against each
> other, exploiting the tension between their re-
> spective values, elaborating the ambiguity of feel-
> ing which results, and drawing attention to the
> resemblances beneath the obvious differences. [5]

The essential element, then, in pastoral is this contrast which underlies its best examples whereby the relationship (as seen by the urban writer and his sophisticated audience) between complexity and simplicity, present and past, urban and rural, becomes the center of attention.

Pastoral has, through the ages since Theocritus and Virgil, undergone an expansion in its traditional subjects to a point where William Empson forty years ago in his influential study, *Some Versions of Pastoral,* extended the limits of pastoral even beyond the rural world. Nature, according to

Empson, need not be an element in pastoral, but rather only nature's gift, simplicity of manners, the traditional quality of the shepherds of the old pastorals. Hence he classifies such diverse and apparently unlikely works as Gay's *Beggar's Opera* and *Alice in Wonderland* as pastoral because of the critical vision of simplicity which they embody. As Empson writes, "you can say everything about complex people by a complete consideration of simple people."[6] More recently, Leo Marx, in *The Machine in the Garden* (1964), has characterized nineteenth-century American literature and culture as another assertion of pastoral, with the dialectic formed around the contrarieties of America as nature and as machine civilization. Although Marx does not pursue his study beyond the end of the nineteenth century, it is clear that Sherwood Anderson, as perhaps no other writer of the twentieth century, embodies and reflects the main fact of American cultural history behind this pastoral tension: a comparatively simple agrarian life overtaken by an industrialized, urban civilization of bewildering magnitude and complexity. In Anderson may be seen both pastoral's thematic concerns for the countrified, the uncouth, the poor, and the naive, and its impulse for harmony and reconciliation between the opposing worlds out of which it draws its unique meanings.

The main body of Anderson's work, I would then claim, may be delineated in terms of pastoral. His first two novels, *Windy McPherson's Son* (1916) and *Marching Men* (1917), both define and explore what was always for Anderson the critical question: what are the possibilities for meaningful individual life in an urbanized industrialized America. Both concern young men from the hinterlands who come to the city and win success but find themselves still unfulfilled. Their search for meaning continues, along ever-widening lines of divergence. Sam McPherson denies the aspiration to money and power, forcing himself back into the "little" life of family and town. Beaut McGregor of *Marching Men* rejects such a solution and dissolves into a proletarian mist as the leader of a shadowy body of marchers, an example of "thinking big" which Anderson later repudiated, both in his own analysis of *Marching Men* and in the direction of his later work.[7] Along with his other pre-*Winesburg* book, *Mid-American Chants* (1918), these early novels express the pastoral tensions between country and city, quietude and shrillness, natural strength, simplicity and health, and the diseases of complexity and artificiality.

Winesburg, Ohio (1919) distills these tensions into a "moment" in which the small town and its inhabitants are poised in an uneasy equilibrium between an agrarian past and the threatening industrial age ahead. The keynote of *Winesburg* is the balancing of these two worlds in innumerable ways.

The old world, the source of the book's evocation of a lost innocence and goodness, is the world of the setting, the fields and farms around Winesburg, as well as the simple round of daily life in the town itself. Set against this is the implicit presence of the city, which stands on the horizon of the book's scenes and events, an analogue of irresistible change. The "grotesques," the figures which move through the stories, are curiously isolated not only from one another and from the great world in the distance, but also from the natural self-sufficiency of the setting. George Willard, the artist as a young man, seems finally both to express and to unify the attributes of village, grotesque, and great world. Standing Janus-like between the states of innocence and experience, youth and maturity, agrarian past and city future, he is a synecdoche for Winesburg itself. And the lesson of silence which he learns, the difficulty of meaningful human contact, leads, ironically, to the artist's understanding which may allow him one day to break down the walls of frustrated communication which surround the grotesques.[8]

If *Winesburg, Ohio* portrays the village and its attendant spirit, George Willard, in a state of arrested pre-experience, *Poor White* (1920) pushes them over the verge, "sweep[s]Winesburg into the modern industrial life . . . "[9] Although Anderson's motive of reconciliation led him to treat his new hero, the industrialist-inventor, Hugh McVey, as sympathetically as he could, nevertheless his ambivalent feelings toward "the machine" are reflected in the split between intention and feeling at the book's conclusion, and in the attitude of the other characters toward McVey. The creation of an uncomprehending mechanist-hero who destroyed the pastoral world which nourished him was the beginning point of a long search by Anderson for the means to reconcile the attributes of machine civilization with his characteristic association of the worthwhile life to natural and organic—rather than mechanistic and artificial—phenomena. Despite his heroic efforts to will himself toward its acceptance, the machine remains eternally hostile to the cornfield, and Anderson's sympathies remain firmly rooted in the natural world.

It is at this mid-point in Anderson's career that the primitivist themes become most insistent in his works. On such race-track stories as "I Want to Know Why" in *The Triumph of the Egg* (1921), "I'm a Fool" and "The Man Who Became a Woman" in *Horses and Men* (1923), and in his novels *Many Marriages* (1923), *Dark Laughter* (1925), and *Tar: A Midwest Childhood* (1926), Anderson's reputation as a primitivist rests. Yet despite his very real desire to present alternatives to the frustrations and pressures of machine-America and to re-enter what he saw as the restorative realms of sensation and simplicity—the world of the child, the race-track "swipe," and the Negro—Anderson's characteristic treatment of these themes exemplifies not the escapism of the primitivist, but the drive toward reconciliation of the pastoralist.

A close examination of one of these works, his well-known "I Want to Know Why," reveals how Anderson converts primitivistic material into pastoral expression. The story is narrated by a boy who loves race-horses and the track life, and who has discovered to his disgust and bewilderment that one of the horse-trainers whom he greatly admires can feel the same toward a hard-mouthed prostitute as toward a clean-limbed and magnificent thoroughbred race-horse. The boy, nearly sixteen now, looks back almost a year to the occurrence about which he has been puzzling ever since. "I'm getting to be a man and want to think straight and be O.K., and there's something I saw at the race meeting at the eastern track I can't figure out."[10] The boy's wish to "think straight and be O.K." contrasts sharply with his earlier behavior, which is an innocent celebration of the sub-rational life of his senses.[11] He is, at the time of the earlier incident, child enough to belong quite wholly to the primitive realm of the race-track, the horses and the "swipes," the trainers, the sights and sounds, the feelings and smells of the racing world, his keen enjoyment of it recalling Huck's adoration of the Mississippi.

> Well, out of the stables they come and the boys
> are on their backs and it's lovely to be there.
> You hunch down on top of the fence and itch
> inside you. Over in the sheds the niggers giggle
> and sing. Bacon is being fried and coffee made.
> Everything smells lovely. Nothing smells better
> than coffee and manure and horses and niggers
> and bacon frying and pipes being smoked out of
> doors on a morning like that. It just gets you,
> that's what it does. (pp. 11-12)

In this primitive milieu of sensory impressions, of trainers and "niggers," of "aching" admiration for the hard and lovely thoroughbreds, the boy moves as naturally as a fish in a stream.[12]

In contrast to these primitive elements are the obligations of adult responsibility represented by the boy's parents, particularly his father. He seems a rather unsuccessful country lawyer who cannot afford to buy the boy things, as Henry Rieback's father, a gambler, does for his son. But the narrator's father does not disapprove of his associating with Rieback and Henry, as do the fathers of the other boys. The narrator's father emerges as a reserved but not uncompassionate figure, above all as a steadying influence upon his son. When the boy swallows a cigar to try to stunt his growth so that he may become a jockey, a course urged upon him by the town practical joker, and becomes ill, he says that most fathers would have whipped him for such behavior, but his didn't. The father understands the boy's love for horses and the track life and does not attempt to discourage it. "More than a thousand times I've got out of bed before daylight and walked two or three miles to the tracks. Mother wouldn't of let me go but father always says, 'Let him alone' " (p. 10). At the same time, the father will not allow his son to become a stable-boy.

Another father-figure is involved in the moral dilemma with which the boy has been struggling. He and three other young boys from the town had run away to see the big race meeting at Saratoga. Just before an important race, the narrator senses that Jerry Tillford, the white trainer of Sunstreak, shares his awareness of the "raging torrent" inside the horse. Sunstreak

> wasn't bragging or letting on much or prancing or
> making a fuss, but just waiting. I knew it and
> Jerry Tillford his trainer knew. I looked up and
> then that man and I looked into each other's
> eyes. Something happened to me. I guess I loved
> the man as much as I did the horse because he
> knew what I knew. (p. 15)

The boy feels himself, the horse, and the trainer drawn together into a bond of primal awareness. "Seemed to me there wasn't anything in the world but that man and the horse and me. I cried and Jerry Tillford had a shine in his eyes" (p. 15). "I liked him that afternoon even more than I ever liked my own father" (p. 16). Later, after Sunstreak has won the race with a record-breaking performance, the boy sets out to find Jerry Tillford, "like wanting to see your father at night when you are a young kid" (p. 17). He follows Tillford and some other men to an old farmhouse, presented as a perversion of the clean and attractive sensory world of the track. The "lovely" race-track, the shiny, sweaty horses, the smooth, green lawns, and the riders in their colorful silks are here contrasted with the "rummy looking house" and the drunken men and women inside. "The place smelled rotten and there was rotten talk . . ." (p. 18). Unlike Sunstreak, who "wasn't bragging or letting on much, or prancing or making a fuss," Jerry Tillford "lied and bragged like a fool. I never heard such silly talk" (p. 18). Finally the boy sees Tillford looking at one of the prostitutes, his eyes shining as they had when he looked at Sunstreak. The boy becomes so angry that he wants to kill Tillford, but, instead, creeps away, gathers together the other boys, and starts for home, where, nearly a year later, he is still wondering why "... a man like Jerry Tillford, who knows what he does, could see a horse like Sunstreak run, and kiss a woman like that the same day" (p. 19).[13]

What the young narrator is struggling with is, above all else, his own incipient maturity, forced upon him after seeing the primitive confraternity of horse, child, and man shattered by the trainer's actions in the rummy farmhouse. Previous to the race, the boy has felt himself at one with the horses and the track Negroes in a ring of primitive understanding. Then, in the moment with Sunstreak before the race when he and Jerry Tillford "come alive" to each other, the realization suddenly comes to him that the trainer, a white adult who, unlike his own father, seems to share his devotion to the horses and the rarefied track life, also "belongs" within this primitive ring. The boy is ecstatic, having found an idealized, "spiritual" father. "I liked him that afternoon even more than I ever liked my own father . . . It was the first time I ever felt for a man like that" (p. 16). But after seeing Tillford's actions in the farmhouse, the boy realizes that the trainer, who values a prostitute (who "was tall and looked a little like the gelding Middlestride, but not clean like him, but with a hard ugly mouth"), has betrayed the boy's vision (p. 18). Revealed as neither innocent nor noble, the trainer must be excluded from the boy's idealized world. "It was rotten. A nigger wouldn't go into such a place" (p. 18).

But anger at Jerry Tillford, alone, can hardly account for the boy's violent and protracted reaction to the incident. What is finally involved is his still-unacknowledged awareness that he himself must also follow Jerry Tillford out of the primitive circle. His first reaction to the scene in the rummy farmhouse, before the anger arises toward the trainer, is a wish that he had not seen what he did see: "I stood there by the window—gee!— but I wished I hadn't gone away from the tracks, but had stayed with the boys and the niggers and the horses" (p. 19). His anger at Tillford, which follows, only masks his primary realization of the beginning of his own loss of innocence. Similarly, as Arthur Sherbo points out, the act of following Jerry Tillford to the farmhouse ("... I went along that road because I had seen Jerry and some other men go that way . . . . " [p. 17]) suggests that the boy's life must henceforth lead him away from the clean, amoral world of the track.[14] Thus his continuing anger and bewilderment have less to do with Tillford than with his violent and painful initiation into a flawed world. That the boy's entry into maturity is nearly completed is suggested

241

by the end of the story. No longer is he a creature of sensations. "At the tracks the air don't taste as good or smell as good . . . . I keep thinking about it and it spoils looking at horses and smelling things and hearing niggers laugh and everything" (pp. 19-20). But if the boy loses his sensory keenness, he has gained something in understanding and awareness of adult responsibility, the attributes of his father. Unlike Jerry Tillford, the father never crosses over into the boy's world. Although the father does not, therefore, share any blinding moment of awareness with his son, neither does he betray him through disillusionment. The father remains blessedly predictable, someone the boy can count on.[15] And we sense that the father's presence and his settled values are helping the boy through his crisis. Centainly he has assimilated some of his father's calm stability: "I'm getting to be a man and want to think straight and be O. K." This attitude must be set against the boy's childish and impulsive actions at the beginning of the story which he is relating: running away from home, wanting to be a Negro so that he can be near horses ("It's a foolish thing to say, but that's the way I am about being around horses, just crazy"), and wanting to be a stable-boy (p. 6). His persistent questioning as he narrates the story—"I'm puzzled," "I can't figure it out," "I can't make it out," "What did he do it for?" "I want to know why" —suggest not merely bewilderment but also the beginning of a rational approach toward dealing with his dilemma and a responsible attitude toward himself. (The bewildered narrator is, of course, a concealment for the rhetorical stance of the author, who has carefully calculated his methods and effects. Anderson himself is not bewildered, as some of his critics seem to forget.) The emerging awareness of the narrator suggests that he will ultimately accept the fact that, because of his whiteness, his ties of family and responsibility, and time which reaps all innocence, he cannot return to the tracks "with the boys and the niggers and the horses" (p. 19).

Besides its internal integrity as a work of art, "I Want to Know Why" reveals important differences from doctrinaire primitivism. First of all, the primitive elements of the story, the innocence and purity of the horses, the boys, the swipes, and, for a moment, the trainer, are not simply celebrated, nor are we asked to reject society for their world. Rather, the story establishes clearly that this is a world closed to the audience, as it becomes closed to the narrator; "escape" is not even to be considered. The story's primitive elements are framed by the non-natural world through the comprehension of a narrator who is now beyond innocence. Although he is still close enough to the world of feeling to portray vividly the richness of its sensual life, he looks back upon it as the story closes from across a deep gulf. He speaks no longer for the primitive's world of sights and smells and tastes, but for the adult world of obligations and responsibilities, of complex moral problems. Thus, the primitive elements are viewed within the context of the real world—finally, the world of the reader. The juxtaposition of the two worlds suggests not primitivism so much as pastoralism, in its creation and exploration of a middle ground between the natural world and society. Primitivism leaps over this middle ground to a glorification of the natural world in terms which preclude any continuing alliance with the complex and the civilized state of man. Pastoral, in playing the natural world against the actual world, calls upon us to measure critically our own lives and surroundings by drawing attention to the simple and the innocent, as the young boy in the story is forced to measure his emerging awareness of himself against the innocent he had been before.

The central meaning of both "I Want to Know Why" and "The Man Who Became a Woman" is an awareness of a certain disillusionment, not with the natural life of the track, but with the narrator's *place* in such a life. The adult narrator of the latter story, especially, expresses clearly both regret at passing out of the primitive world and the understanding that one cannot call it back. And although he does not realize it, the actions of the narrator of "I'm a Fool" clearly reveal that he, too, has outgrown the track, even though he has, to his sorrow, not grown away from it. Hence, Anderson's three famous race-track stories resist the primitivist or escapist classification. They present the racing world as caught up in its own sensual music and finally lost to all but those from whom the narrator and his audience are inevitably separated. The direction of all of these stories is toward a letting-go of the dream of escape. As Anderson wrote to Alfred Stieglitz at the time of the publication of *Horses and Men,* "We have together the love of horses. In my own boyhood I went to them, lived with them, was groom to running and trotting horses . . . they were the most beautiful things about me. But it did not suffice. Will not suffice. The horse is the horse, and we are men."[16]

Anderson's autobiographical *Tar: A Midwest Childhood,* also concerned with the gulf between childhood innocence and maturity, similarly recreates the sensations and feelings of an earlier world while at the same time dramatizing the impossibility of remaining within it. But if the race-track stories and *Tar* correct the notion that one can hope to escape the demands of maturity and complexity by lingering forever in fields of clover, *Many Marriages* and *Dark Laughter* reject the opposite view that one must deny the sensual life entirely while upholding respectable appearances. Unfortunately, both novels lack the authorial control, the firm sense of presence, which one feels behind Anderson's best work. With *Dark Laughter* Anderson seems to have believed that the book's primitivist currency would carry it ("It is the kind of book that just now ought to arouse a lot of interest," he wrote to his publisher).[17] And the gestures of revolt in both works seem unexamined and sentimentalized, a sitting duck for the sharpshooting satire of Hemingway's *The Torrents of Spring.* Anderson's penetration into the primitive, as the failure of these two novels suggests, is, like Thoreau's, most successfully undertaken not as an end in itself, but as a way of coming to terms with society's nagging responsibilities.

In 1927, Anderson moved to Marion, Virginia, where he spent most of his later years. His return to the village is a remarkable metaphor of self-expression as well as an appropriate interpretation of his American experience. If the skeptical side of his nature warned him that he could not go home again, the artist-dreamer could envision the Marion venture as a return to the actual counterpart of the mythical town he never really left, to the lost boyhood villages in which his first four books of fiction are steeped, especially to the pastoral world of Winesburg where he knew by now that he had touched his highest mark as a writer. In those days of the late twenties when his reputation had begun to slide and he began hearing the whispers that "Anderson is finished," he sought in the town some new source of inspiration, a means of re-establishing himself. "I wanted to bury myself in the field and come up green," he wrote to Paul Rosenfeld after arriving in Virginia; "I'm done with cities."[18] While he was not, of course, done with cities, his statement affirms the spirit in which he moved to the South, the belief that the country offered possibilities for the renewal of communal life and hence for the rejuvenation of his own creative powers. In his later years it was the South which still provided, as both Anderson and the Southern Agrarians believed, the possibilities for the integration of the public and private self in modern America. Not nature, free and primitive, nor the machine-God of the city were to receive Anderson's final allegiance, but rather the emblem of their meeting, the town. Thus his last works center upon the small town and upon a renewed interest in individual lives during a period of social collectivism. His last two novels, *Beyond Desire* (1932) and *Kit Brandon* (1936), differ significantly from the proletarian modes of the time principally in their appeal for understanding and reconciliation. *Home Town* (1940) looks ahead with hope for the town as *Winesburg* had looked back with reverence. These last works are characteristic of Anderson's struggle to encompass the divisive oppositions of the old America and the new.

In his own personal involvement in both the simple life which he celebrates and the great world to which he finally belongs, Sherwood Anderson, it must be acknowledged, differs from the traditional pastoral artist. Distance was the hallmark of the old pastoral poet; he stood outside the mythical world and his call to return to it was not wholly serious. Both the artist and his audience knew too well that they could not take to the woods or the countryside. Yet Anderson's literary works as well as the record of his personal life suggest that he actually believed that there is the possibility, if not of reclaiming the idealized pastoral myth, of at least making a new start based upon some of its enduring values. He arrives at his pastoral stance, thus, not from a conscious awareness of the tradition, but from his adoption of the pastoral motive of reconciliation and new harmony: "I, myself a writer," he wrote, "have wanted more than anything else to make Americans in the civilization in which I am compelled to live, better known to each other."19 His version of pastoral, like the traditional pastoral, was first of all a serious criticism of life. But more than that, the synthesis at which pastoral ultimately aims was the promise of a new life for himself, for that idealized artist-self whose importance we come increasingly to recognize, and for the America about which he cared so deeply.

NOTES

[1] Sherwood Anderson, *Perhaps Women* (New York: Horace Liveright, Inc., 1931), p. 57.

[2] *Letters of Sherwood Anderson,* ed. Howard Mumford Jones and Walter B. Rideout (Boston: Little, Brown and Company, 1953), p. xv. Hereinafter abbreviated as *Letters.*

[3] *Letters,* p. 101. Anderson's attitude toward the Negro is discussed in n. 12, below.

[4] Geismar's judgment is found in his edition of *Sherwood Anderson: Short Stories* (New York: Hill and Wang Company, 1962), p. xviii; Howe's remark is found in his *Sherwood Anderson* (New York: William Sloane Associates, 1951), p. 193. Paul Rosenfeld also describes Anderson's primitivistic impulses in his preface to the section entitled "Pastoral" in his *Sherwood Anderson Reader* (Boston: Houghton Mifflin Company, 1947), p. xx, but, I would argue, errs in calling these escapist tendencies pastoral.

[5] *The Pastoral Art of Robert Frost* (New Haven: Yale University Press, 1960), p. 10. The subject of my essay here and throughout is treated at length in my unpublished doctoral dissertation, "Sherwood Anderson's American Pastoral" (University of Washington, 1964).

[6] *Some Versions of Pastoral* (London: Chatto and Windus, 1935), p. 137.

[7] Of *Marching Men,* Anderson recalled later that "it was not a success. I had been thinking too big. My imagination had betrayed me. When I later returned, in my work, to life on a smaller scale, in the individuals about me, I was on solider ground" ("Man and His Imagination," in *The Intent of the Artist,* ed. Augusto Centeno [Princeton: Princeton University Press, 1941], p. 62).

[8]This interpretation of *Winesburg, Ohio* is developed in my *"Winesburg, Ohio* and the Rhetoric of Silence," *American Literature,* 40 (March, 1968), 38-57.

[9]*Letters,* p. 58.

[10]*The Triumph of the Egg* (New York: B. W. Huebsch, Inc. 1921), pp. 8-9. Further page references will be incorporated into the text.

[11]While I find myself in agreement with some of the individual points made by Donald A. Ringe in his "Point of View and Theme in 'I Want to Know Why,' " *Critique,* 3 (Spring-Fall, 1959), 24-29, I would place more emphasis upon the intimations of growing maturity in the narrator than does Ringe, who calls him "quite clearly a prisoner of his own five senses."

[12]Anderson's portrayal of the Negro here is, of course, unacceptable to most of today's readers, nor can it be dismissed as merely attributable to the limited understanding of the boy-narrator, since it is quite consistent with Anderson's own conception of the Negro as "rather noble, but . . . physical, like the running horse or dog" *(Letters,* p. 101). Rather, Anderson's attitude in these race-track stories and in *Dark Laughter* reflects a popularly-held primitivistic stereotype of the Negro during the 1920's. (See, *e.g.,* Malcolm Cowley's *Exile's Return* [New York: The Viking Press, 1956], pp. 237-238.) By the early 1930's Anderson's attitude had changed, as had the times. He satirized the writers of "nigger stories" in his "A Meeting South" in *Death in the Woods* (New York: Liveright, Inc., 1933), p. 225, and in a book review in *The Nation* of July 11, 1934, p. 49. In his own work, the picturesque "niggers" of the race-tracks and the New Orleans docks had become "Negroes," or "brown men," and Anderson was writing, "I can't see this sharp difference between the impulses of Negroes and myself. I think that decent Negro men and women have the same feelings I have" ("Look Out, Brown Man!" *The Nation,* Nov. 26, 1930, p. 579). The presence of the qualifiers "sharp" and "decent" suggest that Anderson may not have been wholly regenerate on the matter.

[13]Arthur Sherbo, in his "Sherwood Anderson's 'I Want to Know Why' and Messrs. Brooks and Warren," *College English,* 15 (March, 1954), 350-351, corrects the misreading in Brooks and Warren's *Understanding Fiction* (New York: F. S. Crofts Company, 1948, pp. 348-349, of ". . . a man who knows what he *does"* to ". . . a man who knows what *he* does." Brooks

and Warren's interpretation, it should be noted, is the first to treat the initiation theme in the story.

14Sherbo, p. 351.

15The most thorough and, in my opinion, judicious treatment of the father in the story is in John E. Parish's "The Silent Father in Anderson's 'I Want to Know Why,' " *Rice Unversity Studies,* 51 (Winter, 1965), 49-57.

16*Letters,* p. 106.

17*Letters,* p. 143.

18*Letters,* p. 171.

19"The Sherwood Anderson Papers," *Newberry Library Bulletin,* ser. II (December, 1948), p. 65.

THE AMBIGUOUS ENDINGS OF SHERWOOD ANDERSON'S NOVELS

Nancy L. Bunge

The characters, plots and conclusions of most Anderson novels fall into a clear pattern: the major character, frequently a businessman, struggles to free himself from the crippling codes of his society, eventually concluding that a healthy relationship with a woman will liberate him. The novel stops with his decision; not only does Anderson shun the difficulties of portraying its realization, but evidence from the rest of the novel, as well as Anderson's other works, also challenges the viability of the character's solution. The ending ignores the problems hovering in the background, embracing instead a fog of illusory optimism. Examination of Anderson's non-fiction helps explain both his almost obsessive repetition of plots and characters as well as his recurrent inability to bring his novels to a neat and consistent resolution.

Anderson's novels grow from and reveal his general dissatisfaction with contemporary American life. He believes modern Americans, although born healthy like all human beings, become progressively alienated from the land, themselves and each other through the combined impact of the repressive social norms inherited from the Puritans and the inhuman patterns incorporated into society with the machine. Factories stunt the growth of the rich individuality which comes from extending the self, not isolating it: "As you lose yourself in others, life immediately becomes more interesting. A new world seems to open out before you. Your imagination becomes constantly more and more alive."[1] Although Anderson also acknowledges the more obvious offenses of industrialization to individuality, like mass production, he worries more about the elimination of the established vehicles of transcendence, and thus, of those intoxicating experiences which make life and people valuable.

One traditional way of escaping selfishness is identity with nature, but industrialism pulls people from the land, shutting them up in buildings where their actions must be accommodated to the movements of a machine. This artificially structured world necessarily vitiates the bond of its inhabitants with the land and the natural order it manifests. The environment cannot be eroded or ignored without maiming those who live on it: "If we are to live on the American land as a great people, we will have to preserve it, feed it, manage it."2

Another means of transcendence the machine disturbs is craftsmanship which ties its practitioners to nature while allowing them to express their individuality through the act of shaping things drawn from the natural order. A craft calls on all capacities and revitalizes them: "In the crafts only one may exercise all one's functions. The body comes in, the mind comes in, all the sensual faculties become alive."3 The machine operator passively satisfies the needs of a physical object; he too becomes mechanical and cannot easily shake the mental death his work demands, for that requires a confidence most surely produced by the craft taken from him. Anderson believes that as mechanization spreads, workmen and, consequently, American society grow progressively more impotent: "The outward signs of that impotence that is the natural result of long illness are all about us in America. It is to be seen in our architecture, in the cowboy plays in our moving picture theaters and in our childish liking of the type of statesman who boasts of walking softly and carrying a big stick. True maleness does not boast of its maleness."4 Vicarious power acquired by using enslaving machines substitutes for the authentic molding of nature; glossing over discontentment with frenzied motion replaces self-control; offensive and defensive bragging hides the decay of relationships with women. Anderson fears it may all lead to fascism which he sees as "the attempt to get back feeling of manhood by identification with the state."5

The fact of motherhood binds women indissolubly to nature, making them relatively immune to the destructive impact of the machine. But women still suffer irreparably, for they need men; and the man who has lost his craft and self-esteem cannot return love, and Anderson believes women cannot function or be beautiful without love. Some adapt by becoming less womanly. Anderson notes that among the spiritually exhausted "modern factory hands, street-car conductors, and all such fellows" lovemaking "almost always . . . was preceded by a quarrel, often blows were struck, there were tears, repentance and then embraces. Did the tired nerves of the men and women need the stimulation of the fights and quarrels?"6 The relations between men and women which should console only further implement the woes of contemporary society.

The corruption of individual integrity necessarily corrodes the entire political and social order which in turn perpetuates the sickness from which it grew. Courtroom dramas epitomize the absurd, sad conflict between the large irrational forces controlling society and particular human problems. Anderson notes a kind judge struggling with the decisions his position demands and the law enforcers drinking the liquor appropriated from the still operator and concludes it makes no sense: "In spite of all the bodies of lawmakers the real crimes of life are not reached by the law."7 Formation of labor unions offers some hope, not because they have power, for society sides with the machine, but because they revitalize the workers: "There is this sense of brotherhood come back, shoulder touching shoulder, at last in these lives a period of aliveness and of hope, of warmth, of brotherhood in struggle."8 It should not surprise that political institutions share the indifference and brutality of the machines since the same hands shape them: "The machines are cruel as men are cruel. The little flesh and blood fingers of men's hands drive, direct, control the machines."9

Anderson's craft, writing, has yet to be mechanized and satisfies his need to shape things and thus lift himself into relation with the world as well as with others. The act of writing evokes that transcendence, that impersonal identity with nature he enjoyed as a boy:

> I became . . . just one of a long, long pro-
> cession of men . . . any one other figure in the
> procession certainly as important as myself . . .
> a kind of new gladness inside. I even think there
> was a kind of nice inner honesty sometimes. I
> found it pretty swell.
>   And so naturally I think of writing as a
> kind of giving out, a going out.10

Although he repeatedly disavows the role of reformer, Anderson must hope his writing evokes in others their latent capacity to perceive life keenly; and imaginative awakening must produce social change. Anderson concludes that any good writer makes a social comment, but it emerges naturally from his materials rather than dominating them; and if he has the penetrating grasp of the ambiguities of experience necessary for good story-telling, he lacks the simple convictions which direct the reformer. Although the artist's theme gives his work a coherence real life lacks, it should reflect the complexity of reality. Consequently, Anderson's novels end in confusion. He repeatedly follows characters through their attempts to work out a happy life in the muddle of modern society and stops as they decide love for another will solve their problems. Their optimism casts a hopeful aura over the novel's end, but the pessimism implied by Anderson's refusal to follow the relationship through becomes explicit in his non-fiction where he explains that healthy relationships grow from full individuality which in turn depends on the contact with nature and practice of a craft denied most of Anderson's contemporaries and characters. Although the conclusions of Anderson's novels fail aesthetically, they satisfy his view that form reflects belief: " 'In this matter of form, it is largely a matter of depth of feeling.' " [11] The incongruous synthesis of overt sentimentality and unarticulated cynicism with which his novels close reflects Anderson's ambivalent feelings on the topics he turns to so compulsively; although he sees little reason to hope, he does.

Unhappy businessmen who support his view that adjustment to contemporary society is personally costly stand in the background of Anderson's novels. Fred Grey in *Dark Laughter* and Judge Long in *Beyond Desire* descend from successful families, and adopt their lifestyles with little conflict. Still, both hide from reality. Judge Long gets hysterical at the suggestion that Christ may not have risen because he counts on an afterlife so heavily; this life apparently disappoints him. Fred Grey eagerly retreats from the unpleasantness he confronts in Europe during the war into the boundaries of his father's factory where he can manage all problems: "There he moved about, a little king in a world of smaller officials, clerks and workers. The factory and his position meant even more to him because of his experience as a private in the army during the war. At the factory something within him seemed to expand. It was, after all, a huge plaything, a world set apart from the town—a walled town within the confines of a town—in which he was ruler." [12] Both men consider themselves aristocrats, and worry about respectability. Too repressed to content their more vital wives, they not only fail to acquire the sons they desire, but Judge Long's wife openly abuses him while Fred Grey's wife leaves. They are both children who avert their eyes from reality, particularly those base desires they share with the rest of humanity, concentrating instead on community codes which they satisfy so well that their personal lives collapse.

The self-made businessmen like Tom Halsey of *Kit Brandon* and Tom Riddle of *Beyond Desire* concern themselves less with respectability than with money and power, but still evade contentment. Tom Halsey has imagination, and the narrator wonders if all self-made man are thwarted dreamers: "The acquisitive instinct, that enables a man to grow rich and powerful, may be, after all, but a perversion, a twist of some finer instinct."[13] Both men pour all their passions into making money, and use anyone available to satisfy their greed, including their wives. Both believe that "the law was a game. All of life was a game,"[14] and their apparent serenity derives not from the fullness of their lives, but the depth of their cynicism. Thus, whether self-made or inherited, business success invariably brings personal failure in Anderson's novels. These frozen individuals stand in the background while the central characters of the novels recognize and attempt to escape from the trap spun by social norms.

Sam McPherson of *Windy McPherson's Son* and Hugh McVey of *Poor White* are achievers who finally reject their unsatisfying lives. Healthy youthful influences lay the groundwork for their revolt. Sam McPherson learns love of life and beauty from John Telfer, receives motherly love from Mary Underwood and "felt that he had been shriven" when "he thought that he had got hold of the idea of brotherhood that John Telfer talked of so often and so eloquently."[15] Sam forgets these lessons as he grows up, remembering only the social humiliation of his family's poverty, and uses everyone he encounters to make all the money he can.

Hugh McVey dreams as a child, but Sarah Sheperd disciplines this "weakness" out of him and makes him determined to overcome the idleness bred into him as a descendant of poor white trash. He especially resists prophetic visions of the destructive relationship between nature, man and machine: "The clouds of which he felt himself a part flew across the face of the sky. They blotted out the sun from the earth, and darkness descended on the land, on the troubled towns, on the hills that were torn open, on the forests that were destroyed, on the peace and quiet of all places. In the country stretching away from the river where all had been peace and quiet, all was now agitation and unrest. Houses were destroyed and instantly rebuilt. People gathered in whirling crowds."[16] Hugh uses work both to channel his imagination into projects acceptable to his age, and shut out his loneliness.

Women force both men to face the limitations of their lives. Sam meets Janet Eberley, "the first woman who ever got hold of and stirred his manhood" (*WMS*, p. 150), and she makes him see life in broader terms. After Janet's death, he marries Sue Rainey who exposes him to the pleasure of relaxing in nature: "For six weeks they led a wandering, nomadic life in that half wild land, for Sue six weeks of tender love making, and of the expression of every thought and impulse of her fine nature, for Sam six weeks of readjustment and freedom, during which he learned to sail a boat, to shoot, and to get the fine taste of that life into his being" (*WMS*, p. 187). The marriage first deteriorates, then collapses as Sam reinvolves himself in obsessive money-making. Eventually Sam repents the shallowness of his life, sets out to find truth, and finally returns to Sue hoping he can keep from running away. At the novel's end, Sam acknowledges his need to involve himself, but whether he can fulfill it is ambiguous. Despite Sam's recognition that he needs to care for people more than he needs to use them, an act of will cannot solve his problem; the ability to love rests on a capacity to abandon self-absorption sorely stunted in contemporary American society. Sam looks in the right direction for the strength he needs; he likes nature, hopes to involve himself in meaningful work and re-establishes contact with the child society stifled out of him: "The boy of Caxton was still alive within him. With a boyish lift of the head he went boldly to her. 'Nothing but boldness will answer now,' he kept saying to himself" (*WMS*, p. 328). These general goals appropriately match Anderson's philosophy, but their specific realization in Sam McPherson's world remains highly problematic. Anderson posits the hopeful aims, but cannot honestly portray Sam fulfilling them, so the novel stops with what little optimism can be gleaned from Sam's situation.

Hugh's work grows from healthier impulses than does Sam's, but he too must be "saved" by a woman. He initially interests himself in a corn planting machine because the grotesque movements of a family of planters appall him. He sees a chance to simultaneously make their lives more comfortable and give his imagination a definite project. Hugh is a craftsman. His townspeople worship his gift because it makes money, while Clara Butterworth recognizes that Hugh's greatness derives not from his material achievement, but from his ability to use imagination: "There was but one man of them all who was not a schemer. Hugh was what she wanted to be. He was a creative force. In his hands dead inanimate things became creative forces" (*PW*, p. 247). She also understands that Hugh's pursuit of a craft restores him to the unity with nature lost in others and that through him she can re-establish contact: "There was something in his eyes that was like the things most grateful to her own nature, the sky seen across an open stretch of country or over a river that ran straight away into the distance" (*PW*, p. 248). Although she has companionship, Clara, like Hugh, has been lonely. She wants a man who is neither childish nor vain, who wants neither to dominate nor be dominated, because she believes she needs a man to be complete: "There was a creative impulse in her that could not function until

she had been made love to by a man. The man she wanted was but an instrument she sought in order that she might fulfill herself" *(PW,* p. 244),
and she believes Hugh might be the man. Despite Hugh's greater creative
ability, Clara's awareness is finer. She accepts the realities Hugh fights to
shove out of his mind. She too has a frightening vision, but unlike Hugh she
embraces hers believing it makes love possible for her:

> An obsession, that the whole world was aboard
> the moving train and that, as it ran swiftly along, it
> was carrying the people of the world into some
> strange maze of misunderstanding, took possession
> of her. . . . It seemed to her that the walls of the
> sleeping-car berth were like the walls of a prison
> that had shut her away from the beauty of life. . . .
> The walls, like life itself, were shutting in upon her
> youth and her youthful desire to reach a hand out
> of the beauty in herself to the buried beauty in
> others. . . . It was . . . the most beautiful night she
> had ever lived through, and it remained in her mem-
> mory throughout her life. She in fact came to think
> later of that night as the time when, most of all, it
> would have been beautiful and right for her to have
> been able to give herself to a lover. *(PW,* pp. 177-
> 178)

Although the narrator knows that an enormous fund of sympathy
exists between Clara and Hugh, they approach each other uncertainly.
They rush into marriage to save Clara's pride, and a wall of embarrassment
delays the consummation of their marriage and impedes communication
between them during the first three years. Only when Clara, although intellectually opposed to industrialization, defends Hugh from a harness maker
crazed by the death of his craft, does a strong emotional bond develop: "At
that moment the woman who had been a thinker stopped thinking. Within
her arose the mother, fierce, indomitable, strong with the strength of the
roots of a tree. To her then and forever after Hugh was no hero, remaking
the world, but a perplexed boy hurt by life. He never again escaped out of
boyhood in her consciousness of him" *(PW,* p. 360). The same incident
ignites Hugh's doubts about the value of machines. Unable to conclude
that working in a factory does less harm than farming, he begins to dream
again. The novel closes hopefully with Hugh and Clara anticipating the

birth of their child. Despite the strong implication that they will transcend the warping influence of their age and establish a fulfilling relationship with each other, many unarticulated problems remain. Clara appropriately detests child-men before she marries Hugh, yet she now welcomes his dependence and confusion. As long as Hugh fails to commit himself to any activity, he will remain a child; and Hugh's craft gave him both the courage to approach Clara and the manhood which drew her to him. What more productive craft will he find in an industrial age than the one he considers renouncing at the end of the novel? Their problematic history and their hopeful reliance on their child raise questions as to whether Clara and Hugh have found or ever will find the happy relationship which has eluded their contemporaries.

The title character in *Kit Brandon* is a female version of Hugh and Sam, for she also escapes from a poor childhood into the business world, finds it unsatisfying and vows to find a man who will love her as the novel ends. Kit runs away from home at sixteen, works in stores and mills until she discovers she can rise faster if she marries well. She frustrates Gordon Halsey, the son of a wealthy rum-runner, into marriage, settles into her own hotel room with a closet full of clothes and discovers she is unhappy. She turns to rum-running herself, taking pleasure in the adventure and power; but loneliness pursues her. When the law interrupts her business, she decides to work out some other kind of life for herself. She tries to contact Agnes, a revolutionary, to suggest that they work together on the land, but later encounters a happy farm couple and then a young man who is both cynical and kind. These experiences convince Kit that she wants a healthy relationship with a man: "There was in her mind an almost definite notion of a new kind of adventure she might begin. She felt warm and alive. Young Hanaford had done that for her. She had been carried out of herself and her own problem and into the life of another puzzled human. There were people to be found. She would get into some sort of work that did not so separate her from others. There might be some one other puzzled and baffled young one with whom she could make a real partnership in living" (*KB*, p. 373). Considering Anderson's other works and views of society expressed in the rest of *Kit Brandon,* her search will be extensive; there are few men capable of love, but once more, this troublesome fact remains unacknowledged, and the novel ends hopefully.

Many Marriages and *Dark Laughter* begin as the businessmen break out of their comfortable cells and enter into a relationship. Their new liaisons receive fuller treatment than in the other works and correspondingly, some serious problems surface. Still, the books end on a positive note. In *Many*

Marriages, John Webster's breakthrough satisfies a number of Anderson's criteria. He becomes intensely aware of the life about him: he sits in the park and notices nature; he takes an aesthetic look at his room and clothing; he undresses and stares at his body and he responds to the people around him. All these activities signal a movement outside himself to lose himself in a new, vague identity: "One could not be just a manufacturer of washing machines in a Wisconsin town. In spite of oneself one became, at odd moments, something else too. One became a part of something as broad as the land in which one lived. . . . He himself was a man standing, clad in ordinary clothes, but within his clothes, and within his body too there was something, well perhaps not vast in itself, but vaguely indefinitely connected with some vast thing. It was odd he had never thought of that before."[17] He connects these "new" feelings with childhood when he was more aware of the country and less inclined to crush his dreams out of himself. He accepts the love of his secretary Natalie, tries to share his new awareness with his wife and daughter, and leaves his house. His wife kills herself, but his daughter, although shattered, seems to have acquired a new knowledge of life and love from her father:

> Now she was quite alone. Her father had gone away and her mother had killed herself. There was no one. One walked alone in darkness. One's body struck with a soft thump against soft gray unyielding walls.
>
> The little stone held so firmly in the palm of the hand hurt and hurt.
>
> Before her father had given it to her he had gone to hold it up before the candle flame. In certain lights its color changed. . . . The yellowish green lights were of the color of young growing things pushing their way up out of the damp and cold of frozen grounds, in the spring. (*MM*, pp. 239-240)

Although his behavior includes a lot of activities Anderson approves, even John Webster pauses to consider that he may be just an old man having an affair with his secretary who has given himself an elaborate set of self-justifications. While fleeing with his mistress, it occurs to him that he has hardly spoken to her; what he thought pregnant silences may have simply been silences. Nor has he shed his concern with respectability; he asks her to walk on the grass so no one will hear them and laugh at him. And he also lacks the craft needed to give him enough self-esteem to love anyone. The question raised in the "Foreword" constitutes the book's theme: "If one seek love and go towards it directly, or as directly as one may in the midst of the perplexities of modern life, one is perhaps insane"; but the extensive attention paid to John's philosophy and the scant discussion of the problems it ignores, obscures his doubts, making them seem like the last feeble pangs of decadent values as John Webster moves into a life directed by undistorted impulses. Although pushed to the side, the problems remain.

Bruce Dudley of *Dark Laughter* walks away from his wife and his job as a newspaper reporter in a vague search for something better. He relaxes for a time, watching the world with a new acuteness: "The strangeness and the wonder of things—in nature—he had known as a boy and that he had somehow later lost—the sense lost living in a city and being married to Bernice—could he get it back again? There was the strangeness and wonder of trees, skies, city streets, black men, white men—of buildings, words, sound, thoughts, fancies" *(DL,* p. 108). He returns to youth literally as well as imaginatively by taking a factory job under an assumed name in his home town. He works next to Sponge Martin, a man who survives the machine age as a craftsman and as a result is sure of himself and his wife; "Sponge in relation to the town, the Ohio River Valley, sleeping on an old sawdust pile—his relation to the ground beneath him, the stars overhead, the brush in his hand as he painted automobile wheels, the caress in the hand that held the brush, profanity, crudeness—love of an old woman—alive like a fox terrier" *(DL,* p. 60). Bruce is attracted to Aline, the factory owner's wife, and takes a gardening job at her home. Aline is deeply frustrated with her life and wants to fall in love. She consoles herself by going into the garden, pretending she is a statue, and achieving the unity with nature she longs for, but cannot reach through her husband:

> It was a dramatization, childish, meaningless, and full of a kind of comforting satisfaction to one who in the actuality of life remains unfulfilled. Sometimes when she stood thus in the garden, her husband within the house reading his paper or asleep in his chair, minutes passed when she did no thinking, felt nothing. She had become a part of the sky, of the ground, of passing winds. When it rained, she was the rain. When thunder rolled down the Ohio River Valley, her body trembled

slightly. As a small, lovely stone figure, she
had achieved Nirvana. Now was the time for
her lover to come—to spring out of the ground
—to drop from the branches of a tree—to take
her, laughing at the very notion of asking con-
sent. (DL, pp. 207-208)

Aline and Bruce make love; Bruce leaves and returns to get her. Once more
Anderson brings together two people who have rejected social norms in
favor of passion and sends them off into the sunset, and once more there
are many silent difficulties. Aline likes expensive clothes, Bruce likes to see
her in them, but he has no job, nor has he a craft; he vaguely tries to write
poetry, but his efforts dissatisfy him. Before their liaison, Bruce argues that
beauty exists only in moments, that it is best he and Aline never marry:
"If she belonged to him he would have to go into the house with her, sit
down with her at table, see too much of her. The worst was that she would
see too much of him. She would find out about him. That was hardly the
point of his adventure" (DL, p. 234). Furthermore, sexuality revolts him:
"For Bruce, to try to think of Sponge and his wife in their hour of pleasure
in each other, such pleasure as youth knew, was like that. It left a faint un-
pleasant smell in his nostrils—like decayed eggs—dumped in a wood—across
the river—far off" (DL, p. 120). Although critical of society, Bruce is a
romantic rather than a hero in Anderson's terms. Sponge Martin is the
strong man here, and Bruce condescends to him while silently assuring himself he is finer, less crude than Sponge. Aline moves towards Bruce through
a fantasy built upon his resemblance to a man at a party in Paris who rejected her for a woman who told of wanting to experience ugly lust. Bruce
would have been as repelled by the woman as Fred Grey. In Dark Laughter
the operation of fantasy on the relationship comes through more clearly
than in Many Marriages, although on the face of it, both novels end happily.
In both the couples set off to begin a new life and the novel shifts back to
the desolation of those too frightened to consider abandoning their deadly,
conventional life. The endings draw attention to the desperately sick characters, while the ambiguous ones creep out the back door.

In Beyond Desire Anderson finally follows through the relationships
established between modern men and women searching for love, and the
denouement is not pretty. Red Oliver is a young man who wants to achieve
a relationship like that recounted in letters from a friend: "Neil even tried
to describe the feeling in his fingers when he touched her body, the warmth
of her flesh, the sweetness of it to him. Red himself hungered with all his

being to find such a woman for himself but never did. Neil's letters made him also hungry for some relationship with life that was sensual and fleshly but beyond just flesh" *(BD,* p. 6). Red becomes interested in Ethel Long who also yearns for a relationship. They make love and she rejects him. Her shame makes her marry someone who tells her she will be nice ornamentation. Red tries to restore his pride by losing himself in political action; he is killed. Red and Ethel come together in search of love and mutilate each other.

Both Ethel and Red have been misshaped by their environment. Ethel appropriately regards her respectable father as a child, but this does not prevent his incapacity for love from infecting her. She uses her sexual drives to simultaneously get the material things she wants and sabotage her father: he wants her to have an education, so she gets a pathetic graduate student to do the work for her; Red Oliver attracts her because he records radical ideas which would shock her father; her marriage to the ruthless Tom Riddle humiliates her father. Red Oliver's mother gets little attention from his frequently drunken father, and so she prays to Jesus while her son lies in his bedroom wishing he could go to her. Had his mother turned to Red instead of Christ, he might have had enough self-esteem to seek love instead of destruction.

The social forces distorting these two characters operate on everyone, and all the relationships in the novel are bad. Ethel's father marries a woman looking for a provider who later decides she has been robbed and takes out her hurt and frustration on him; recognizing that Ethel has an instinctual vitality her husband lacks, she makes an unsuccessful attack on Ethel. The relations between those who work in the mill are no less destructive. Doris wanders into a boring marriage and fantasizes that if she were a man she would pursue Nell, a woman who hates the men around her. These frustrated women contrast with the lifeless Grace who has simply given up. Since impotent men surround these women, it is not surprising that they turn to each other for emotional life or wither. Men and women have drives which push them towards each other, but somehow their instincts have become so twisted that once they find each other all they can do is destroy each other: "People were perpetually doing it to each other. It wasn't just this one thing . . .two bodies clasp together trying that" *(BD,* p. 208).

The only healthy relationship is a secret one between Neil and his schoolteacher, two incipient revolutionaries who believe that before one can reframe society, one must learn to love. The philosophy articulated in Neil's letter to Red states the germ of Anderson's beliefs:

> People needed warmth, Neil thought, they needed
> romance and, most of all, the romance of feeling, of
> thinking they were trying to go somewhere.
>   People, he said, needed to hear voices coming
> from outside themselves.
>   Science also had raised hell and the cheap sort
> of popular knowledge . . . or what was called know-
> ledge . . . spread about everywhere now had raised
> even more hell.
>   There was, he said in one of his letters, too
> much emptiness in affairs, in the churches, in
> government. *(BD,* pp. 3-4)

Even this relationship cannot escape the destructive forces pervading the world of the novel. When Red dies, Neil's letters are found on his body: "It was a letter about Neil and his school-teaching love—an immoral letter" *(BD,* p. 357). Presumably their relationship will be exposed and routed.

Beyond Desire fully complements the despair at the modern American's capacity to get outside himself that Anderson articulates in his nonfiction and suggests that had Anderson started his novels at the point where most end, chaos would pervade the entire book, not merely the ending. Ultimately, Anderson sees little to be positive about. Even the feeble attempts of Americans to free themselves must be contaminated. Yet, Anderson feels that hope is very important. He thinks it is healthy that when Americans fall they curse themselves, not the social order; Americans have not been totally devoured by cynicism: " 'I failed. I failed. It's my own fault.' You get it on all sides. There may be stupidity in it, but there is also humility. It gives you occasionally at night a dream of what we Americans, properly led by men who can be at least partially disinterested, may some day do."[18] Anderson would rather write novels with indeterminate endings than reinforce the despair he sees around him. The generous wish that Americans can be cured rather than a faulty aesthetic sense makes him stop in mid-air rather than follow the lives of his characters through to their logical conclusion.

NOTES

[1]*A Writer's Conception of Realism* (Olivet, Michigan: Olivet College, 1939), p. 12.

[2]"Give Rex Tugwell a Chance," *Today,* 4 (June 1935), 21.

[3]*A Story Teller's Story* (New York: The Viking Press, 1969), p. 327.

[4]*Sherwood Anderson's Notebook* (New York: Boni and Liveright, 1926), p. 153.

[5]*Sherwood Anderson's Memoirs* (Chapel Hill, North Carolina: University of North Carolina Press, 1969), p. 390.

[6]*A Story Teller's Story,* p. 226.

[7]*Hello Towns!* (New York: Horace Liveright, 1929), p. 285.

[8]"Let's Have More Criminal Syndicalism," *New Masses,* 7 (February 1932), 4.

[9]*Perhaps Women* (New York: Horace Liveright, 1931), p. 10.

[10]"Why Men Write," *Story,* 8 (January 1936), 105.

[11]Quoted in Norman Holmes Pearson, "Anderson and the New Puritanism," *Newberry Library Bulletin,* Series II, No. 2 (December 1948), 57.

[12]*Dark Laughter* (New York: Liveright, 1970), p. 189. All future references appear in the text preceded by the abbreviation *DL.* Quotations from *Dark Laughter* and other Anderson books are with the permission of Mrs. Eleanor Anderson and Harold Ober Associates.

[13]*Kit Brandon* (New York: Scribner's, 1936), p. 122. All future re-

ferences appear in the text preceded by the abbreviation *KB.*

14*Beyond Desire* (New York: Liveright, 1970), p. 198. All future references appear in the text preceded by the abbreviation *BD.*

15*Windy McPherson's Son* (Chicago: The University of Chicago Press, 1965), p. 45. All future references appear in the text preceded by the abbreviation *WMS.*

16*Poor White* (New York: Viking Press, 1966), p. 29. All future references appear in the text preceded by the abbreviation *PW.*

17*Many Marriages* (New York: B. W. Huebsch, Inc., 1923), p. 12. All future references appear in the text preceded by the abbreviation *MM.*

18*Puzzled America* (New York: Scribner's, 1935), p. 46.

NOTES ON CONTRIBUTORS

DAVID D. ANDERSON is Professor of American Thought and Language at Michigan State University and the Founder and Executive Secretary of the Society for the Study of Midwestern Literature. He has published several books, including *Sherwood Anderson* and *Louis Bromfield.*

NANCY L. BUNGE is Assistant Professor of American Thought and Language at Michigan State University. Her studies of American writers have been accepted for publication by *Studies in Short Fiction, North Dakota Quarterly,* and *Walt Whitman Review.*

HILBERT H. CAMPBELL is Associate Professor of English at Virginia Polytechnic Institute and State University. He is the author of *James Thomson (1700-1748): An Annotated Bibliography,* and his articles on eighteenth-century British literature have appeared in several journals, including *Philological Quarterly, Modern Philology,* and *Studies in English Literature, 1500-1900.*

JOHN W. CROWLEY is Associate Professor of English at Syracuse University. He is the author of the forthcoming book *George Cabot Lodge* and has published widely on American writers in such journals as *New England Quarterly, American Literature, Nineteenth-Century Fiction,* and *Journal of American Studies.*

ROBERT E. NED HAINES is presently engaged in an independent book project. A Stanford Ph.D. who is also a distinguished photographer, he has travelled more than 40,000 miles since 1973, involved in writing and photographing a book on literary America tentatively entitled *World of American Writers: A Photographic Evocation of the Literary Landscape.*

DIANA HASKELL is Curator of Modern Manuscripts at the Newberry Library. Her report on the Newberry Library's manuscript holdings appeared in *Illinois Libraries* in 1975.

THADDEUS B. HURD is a retired Clyde, Ohio, architect, ex-president of the Sandusky County Historical Society. An authority on local history, genealogy, and architecture, his researches on Anderson and other topics have appeared in *Northwest Ohio Quarterly* and in reports of the Ohio Historical Society and the Ohio Genealogical Society.

GLEN A. LOVE is Professor of English at the University of Oregon. His article *"Winesburg, Ohio* and the Rhetoric of Silence" appeared in *American Literature* in 1968. The author of a number of books on rhetoric and composition, he has also published studies of American authors in *American Quarterly, Western American Literature,* and *Negro American Literature Forum.*

CHARLES E. MODLIN is Assistant Professor of English at Virginia Polytechnic Institute and State University. His articles, mostly on American literature, have appeared in *Early American Literature, Proceedings of the American Antiquarian Society, Markham Review,* and *Medium Aevum.*

AMY WOOD NYHOLM was for more than twenty years curator of the Anderson manuscripts at the Newberry Library. Mrs. Nyholm, who now resides in Santa Barbara, California, was responsible for arranging the extensive Anderson collection.

WILLIAM L. PHILLIPS is Associate Dean, College of Arts and Sciences, at the University of Washington. His important study "How Sherwood Anderson wrote *Winesburg, Ohio,"* appeared in *American Literature* in 1951. His other studies of Anderson, Faulkner, Hemingway, and Dreiser have been published in *Studies in Bibliography, University of Chicago Magazine,* and *PMLA.*

WALTER B. RIDEOUT is Harry Hayden Clark Professor of English at the University of Wisconsin. He is associate editor of *Letters of Sherwood Anderson,* editor of *Sherwood Anderson: A Collection of Critical Essays,* and author of the forthcoming *Sherwood Anderson: A Critical Biography.* He is also the author of *The Radical Novel in the United States, 1900-1954.*

G. THOMAS TANSELLE is Professor of English at the University of Wisconsin and co-editor of the Northwestern-Newberry edition of *The Writings of Herman Melville.* His articles on Anderson have appeared in *Papers of the Bibliographical Society of America, Modern Language Review,* and

Notes and Queries. He is also the author of *Royall Tyler; Guide to the Study of United States Imprints;* and articles on descriptive bibliography and editing in *Studies in Bibliography, PBSA, The Library,* and *The Book Collector.*

WELFORD DUNAWAY TAYLOR is Professor of English at the University of Richmond. His work on Anderson includes an edition of *The Buck Fever Papers* and articles in *Virginia Cavalcade* and *Newberry Library Bulletin.* Also the author of *Virginia Authors: Past and Present* and *Amélie Rives,* he is currently editor of *The Winesburg Eagle,* the official publication of the Sherwood Anderson Society.

JOHN H. WRENN is Professor of English at the University of Colorado and was formerly editor of *Abstracts of English Studies* and Director of the University of Colorado Writers' Conference. He is the author of *John Dos Passos* and of a forthcoming study of Edgar Lee Masters, on which he is collaborating with his daughter Margaret M. Wrenn.

MARGARET M. WRENN is currently employed in building her own house in the mountains west of Boulder, Colorado, and in writing, with John H. Wrenn, a book on Edgar Lee Masters.

INDEX

Editors' note: This list does not include the already alphabetized entries in "A Catalog of Sherwood Anderson's Library" (pp. 83-144).

Burchfield, Charles   41

Burnett, Whit   36

Caples, Don   52

Chambrun, Jacques   54-55

Chase, Cleveland B.   14

Chase, Stuart   86

Chekhov, Anton   73, 84, 197

Church, Ralph   130

Claflin, Tennessee   177

Clemens, Samuel L.   162, 189, 213

Colwell, Laverne W.   118

Connick, Charles J. and Mabel   45-46

Cooper, James Fenimore   190-191

Copenhaver, Bascom E.   28, 29, 30, 32, 34, 38, 69, 70, 73

Copenhaver, Laura   26, 27-40, 41, 69, 70-71, 76, 229

Copenhaver, Randolph   31, 48

Cournos, John   73

Cox, Charles   51, 59

Crabbe, George   181

Crandall, Harry J.   146

Cronk, John   32

Cronk, Katharine Scherer   32

Darrow, Clarence   175-76

Dean, Austin F.   138

Defoe, Daniel   162

Dell, Floyd   81

Derleth, August   176

De Vries, Carrow   53-54

Dostoevsky, Fyodor   12, 73, 84

Dreiser, Theodore   34, 73, 74, 75, 81, 86, 197

Eastman, Max   230